D0103871

MONEY and SOCCER
A *SOCCERNOMICS* GUIDE

ALSO BY STEFAN SZYMANSKI

Soccernomics: Why England Loses, Why Spain, Germany, and Brazil Win and Why the US, Japan, Australia–and Even Iraq– Are Destined to Become the Kings of the World's Most Popular Sport
(with Simon Kuper; Nation Books, 2009)

Fans of the World, Unite! A Capitalist Manifesto for Sports Consumers
(with Stephen F. Ross; Stanford University Press, 2008)

Il business del calcio
(with Umberto Lago and Alessandro Baroncelli; Egea, 2004)

National Pastime: How Americans Play Baseball and the Rest of the World Plays Soccer
(with Andrew Zimbalist; Brookings Institution, 2005)

Playbooks and Checkbooks: An Introduction to the Economics of Modern Sports (Princeton University Press, 2009)

Winners and Losers: The Business Strategy of Football
(with Tim Kuypers; Viking Books, 1999; Penguin Books, 2000)

Football Economics and Policy
(Palgrave Macmillan, 2010)

The Comparative Economics of Sport
(Palgrave Macmillan, 2010)

MONEY and SOCCER

A *SOCCERNOMICS* GUIDE

Why Chievo Verona, Unterhaching, and Scunthorpe United Will Never Win the Champions League, Why Manchester City, Roma, and Paris St. Germain Can, and Why Real Madrid, Bayern Munich, and Manchester United Cannot Be Stopped

Stefan Szymanski

Introduction by Simon Kuper

NATION
BOOKS

New York

Published by
Nation Books, A Member of the Perseus Books Group
116 East 16th Street, 8th Floor
New York, NY 10003

Nation Books is a copublishing venture of the Nation Institute and the
Perseus Books Group.

Books published by Nation Books are available at special discounts for
bulk purchases in the United States by corporations, institutions, and
other organizations. For more information, please contact the Special
Markets Department at the Perseus Books Group, 2300 Chestnut
Street, Suite 200, Philadelphia, PA 19103, or call (800) 255-1514,
or e-mail special.markets@perseusbooks.com.

A catalog record for this book is available from the Library of Congress.
Library of Congress Control Number: 2015936760

ISBN: 978-1-56858-476-8 (paperback original)
ISBN: 978-1-56858-477-5 (e-book)

10 9 8 7 6 5 4 3 2 1

For the fans of Scunthorpe United and
all the other clubs who prove that winning
is not the *only* thing

CONTENTS

FOREWORD

Simon Kuper

IN 2007 I MET STEFAN SZYMANSKI AT A CONFERENCE IN ISTANBUL, and almost immediately we were having conversations about soccer that I'd never had before. Everyone in soccer has opinions. Stefan, very unusually, had data too. He had been assembling it since the 1980s, a time when almost no serious economist on earth was thinking about soccer. He was even willing to let the data change his opinions. And he could explain his opinions clearly to people who weren't economists. "So here's one way of thinking about it . . . " was a formulation that I've become familiar with in the years since.

Further, Stefan is more than an economist. He's a historian of sports who understands how the origins of professional soccer in nineteenth-century Britain have shaped the game's path. By 2009 we had written a whole book together, *Soccernomics*, and remained friends and interlocutors. Whenever I'm wrestling with a question about the soccer business, Stefan is the first person I call.

He also has a distinctive view. Back in 2007, I must admit I shared the conventional wisdom about the soccer business: that it was riding for a fall. At the time I imagined that big banks were entirely safe, but that many big football clubs, with their unpayable debts, risked disappearing. The rich kept getting richer and spending more, and everyone else was overspending in an effort to keep up. When the global financial crisis struck in September 2008, many of us imagined it was the beginning of the end for big soccer. Michel Platini, president of the Union of European Football Associations (UEFA), said that half of Europe's professional clubs had financial troubles of some kind. "If this situation goes on," he added, "it will not be long before even some major clubs face going out of business." I rang Stefan to ask what he thought. Patiently and politely he explained why Platini and I and almost all the other pundits were wrong. Soccer clubs almost never die, said Stefan. This book—Stefan's mature thinking on soccer—explains why.

As I write, six years into Europe's worst economic crisis since World War Two, Stefan has been proven right. No "major club" anywhere on the continent has gone out of business. If you search hard, you can find about a dozen smaller ones that have collapsed since 2008: UD Salamanca, Lorca Deportiva, and CD Badajoz in Spain; HFC Haarlem, SC Veendam, AGOVV, and RBC Roosendaal in the Netherlands; Beerschot in Belgium; Gretna in Scotland; FC Arsenal Kyiv in Ukraine; and Unirea Urziceni in Romania. Admittedly, Unirea played in the Champions League in 2009/10, but historically it was a tiny club from a small town. It owed its brief rise to a passing sugar daddy. When he lost interest, Unirea expired.

Anyway, several of the defunct clubs were immediately refounded in a slightly different form. Gretna 2008 now plays amateur soccer in Scotland, as do RBC and AGOVV in the Netherlands. Salamanca actually has three successor clubs, each claiming the mantle. In other words, Stefan was prescient to argue that the top end of soccer didn't need the unprecedented, draconian regulation represented by UEFA's misnamed "Financial Fair Play" rules. That is because he understands the soccer business and its history like no one else.

In this book, Stefan explains that two basic facts have always been part of the soccer business: dominance and distress. Always, there were a few big clubs that dominated, both nationally and in European competitions. Always, most clubs made losses. Unlike American sports, European soccer has never been a profitable industry.

The book shows why dominance and distress persist, and why the industry thrives regardless. Big clubs like Real Madrid and Manchester United built their brands over the decades by winning prizes. They still have to spend heavily each year to maintain their brands because otherwise they will start losing and be rejected by fans. But as long as they are willing to spend, they can dominate the soccer market. It's simply too expensive for their rivals to build comparable brands. Distress, too, is as old as professional soccer. That's chiefly because very few soccer clubs are out to make profits. Most put every penny they have into trying to win matches.

In this sense, clubs are not like normal businesses—and Stefan has always rejected the facile "Soccer is a business" mantra. Because there are some rival clubs willing to spend even more than their last penny, the inexorable logic is debt. And yet soccer clubs almost never fold, because hardly any creditor wants to pull the plug on a beloved and ancient local institution. Even when a creditor does, it's easy enough simply to refound the club at once. In fact, this often happens.

It's true that the recent tendency has been for clubs' debt to keep growing. But then clubs' revenues keep growing too. Manchester United's debt is in the hundreds of millions, but the club's estimated market value is nearly $3 billion. In any case, as Stefan points out, very few clubs owe debt to banks. Rather, most owe it to owners—the modern sugar daddies who have poured $4 billion into English clubs alone since about 2000. Most of these owners are pursuing glory rather than profits. Buying a soccer club is rather like buying a Picasso. It won't make you an annual return, but it will impress your friends, and if one day you want to sell it again, you'll probably find you've made a capital gain along the way.

The club owners' funds are therefore better understood as philanthropic donations rather than loans. Roman Abramovich, the Russian oligarch who owns Chelsea Football Club, as Stefan points out here, formally converted the "debt" that Chelsea notionally owed him into an equity stake in the club. He will never get that billion quid back. But it bought him glory.

Neither Chelsea nor Manchester United is going to succumb beneath its debt. The tendency of Stefan's work is to deflate the hysteria peddled by many critics of the soccer industry. Reading his book, you come to see that the Platiniesque critique of the sport is at bottom a moral critique. We all grew up with a simpler, poorer, more local soccer. Many fans yearn for it still. To them, the sight of Russians or Arabs throwing millions at Latin Americans to play for English clubs seems loathsome. So they conclude that it is unsustainable. Stefan, by contrast, tends to steer clear of moral critiques and makes a cool-headed economic argument.

Taking his point of view, you start to question the prevailing narrative—pushed by UEFA and many pundits—that soccer is in economic crisis. Instead, in Stefan's telling, these are probably the best of times. Back in the 1970s, the soccer industry was tiny compared with any of the American major league sports. (Stefan's vantage point at the University of Michigan equips him perfectly for transatlantic comparisons.) Then, from 1978 to about 1989, the game sank into what Stefan terms the dark ages: decaying stadiums, hooligans, shrinking crowds, and contempt from the media. Since the 1990s, attendances have soared in the big European countries. Today's rising ticket prices and spoiled overpaid soccer players are problems of success.

It's quite likely that times will get even better. The four biggest countries on earth, India, China, the United States, and Indonesia—with about 45 percent of the world's population between them—are just starting to switch on to soccer. Further, the growth of social media will help. For decades, clubs had no idea how many fans they had, let alone have any way of reaching them. But now clubs can talk to their supporters (or perhaps consumers) every day, offering them all manner of stuff to buy.

In September 2014, Real Madrid announced annual revenues of over $600 million—the highest of any club in any sport in history. When Stefan first began studying the game, such numbers were unthinkable. A few years from now, they may seem rather modest.

The same month, a fresh wave of scandals was breaking in the most popular American sport, gridiron football. A player had been filmed beating his fiancée unconscious in an elevator; another player had given his four-year-old son a "whooping" with a tree branch that left the boy cut and bruised; some sponsors were pulling out; and hanging over the game was the recent revelation that a third of all players will end up with brain damage. Gridiron has barely any fans outside North America. No US sport comes close to soccer's global popularity. Which sport would you bet your money on in the next few decades of globalization? Amid the prevailing anguish over the soccer business, this book offers a cool and optimistic corrective.

AUTHOR'S NOTE

I STARTED WRITING ABOUT THE FINANCES OF SOCCER CLUBS A quarter of a century ago, soon after joining London Business School as a post-doctoral fellow. Back then I worked in a research center that was trying to use economic analysis to understand what it is that makes some businesses successful in a competitive environment (monopolies are not so interesting—they don't have to work for their success). Soccer clubs were perfect because they operate in very competitive markets, there is not much argument about who is successful (we know who won the game), and financial accounts for dozens of clubs stretching over decades were available. This made it possible to establish the connection between investment in players, success on the field, and financial results. There are very few competitive industries in the world where one can do that.

Over the last twenty-five years my views have evolved, but my fundamental assessment has not changed: this is a highly competitive business where money buys success and profits are negligible. Moreover, despite the constant financial problems of individual clubs, the business has been on an extended boom that, coincidentally, began about twenty-five years ago and shows no sign of ending any time soon. A lot of my own work over the years has been about collating the data (I now have financial accounts for most English clubs stretching back to 1958 and intend to push back at least to the 1920s) and testing different theories using the data. In due course, I will publish all of the data so anyone can look it up for themselves.

The English accounting data is audited data: it has been signed off by the club's accountants and can therefore be considered reliable in the sense that it is derived directly from the financial records of the clubs themselves. For various reasons, it is not easy to obtain similar data for other countries, although gradually some is becoming available. For this reason English soccer is the most commonly used example in the book. England's Premier League also happens to be the wealthiest soccer league in the world today. That was not true twenty-five years ago, and it may not be true in twenty-five years' time. Although I lived all my life in England until joining the University of Michigan in 2011, the focus on England is not about nationalism or parochialism—it just happens to be the soccer nation with the longest and most complete financial records. That said, part of the point of this book is to show that the organizational model of soccer, which England shares with almost every other nation, generates similar results around the world; so this book also relies on newly emerging data sources from other countries. The two most-cited sources in the book are the Deloitte *Annual Review of Football Finance* and the UEFA *Club Licensing Benchmarking Report*, both of which provide invaluable financial information on data for countries outside England. The UEFA data is especially useful because it summarizes the financial accounting information that clubs from fifty-four national leagues are required to supply to the governing body of European soccer. I also use *Wikipedia*—mainly for league tables, numbers of championships won, when games were played, and other factual information over which there can be little dispute. I am a big fan of crowdsourcing, which is particularly good for gathering detailed information on sports statistics that are non-controversial.

There are many other data sources that offer financial information, and while they can be useful (and I do use them), they need to be treated with caution. One of the best examples is the website transfermarkt.de. This provides individual valuations for players generated by groups of fans that subscribe to the website. These are therefore *estimated*, not actual valuations. They may be highly *correlated* with actual transaction values, but they are not the same thing. The problem is that there is no number of opinions that can ensure we get to the true figure in such cases— if player wages or transfer fees are not released publicly, no amount of guessing will get us there. Again, such figures may be useful in some contexts, but they are of limited value if we are trying to understand the decision making of clubs or players, which will be based on the actual values, not guesses.

Likewise, figures published in the newspapers about transfer fees and wages are only indicative. Usually these figures are leaked by the club or the player's agent, and are not necessarily reliable or complete—they are certainly not audited numbers. Unlike the accountant, the reporter did not see the contract, the invoice, or the bank statement related to the transaction. Finally, video games, such as Football Manager, and fantasy soccer games often publish data on player wages and transfer values for the purposes of playing the game, but again these figures are only estimates. They do not have access to audited data because in public both clubs and players observe confidentiality (unlike players in the North American major leagues whose salaries are made public by the player unions). As in many fields, it's important to be clear about the quality of the data source if one is to rely on it for making statements about what is going on.

There are many people I need to thank for their help and support. Over the years, I have worked with many coauthors whose insights have helped me to understand the operation of sports markets in general: Kevin Alavy, Wladimir Andreff, Giles Atkinson, Tunde Buraimo, Luigi Buzzacchi, Bastien Drut, Filippo dell'Osso, David Forrest, Pedro Garcia-del-Barrio, Steve Hall, David Harbord, Takeo Hirata, Tom Hoehn, Todd Jewell, Georgios Kavetsos, Stefan Késenne, Simon Kuper, Tim Kuypers, Umberto Lago, Stephanie Leach, Victor Matheson, Susana Mourato, Susanne Parlasca, Thomas Peeters, Ian Preston, Steve Ross, Rob Simmons, Ron Smith, Tommaso Valletti, Jason Winfree, and Andy Zimbalist. I have also benefited from the advice of colleagues at work (especially Rod Fort and Mark Rosentraub), conferences, and seminars (I hope you know who you are).

An army of students has assisted me by copying accounting data into spreadsheets, including Jobin Abraham, Jean-Paul Bewers, Blake Bogdanovich, Jake Kaufman, Tom Lambert, Ben Manko, Karan Mirpuri, Akeeb Patel, Thomas Peeters, Patrick Spicer, Cedrick Song, Robert Snyder, Robert Vanderpluijm, Valeriya Vitkova, Naglis Vysniauskas, Zach Winston, and Kelly Xu. This would have taken so much longer without you!

I owe a special debt to Simon Kuper for our collaboration on *Soccernomics* (he is without doubt the perfect coauthor) and his generous foreword to this book. He also put in some hard yards reading through an early draft of the book. I am grateful to Marni Mortensen for explaining Faroe Islands soccer to me. Several other people provided detailed comments on some or all of the contents, including John Foot, Simon Gleave, John Holme, David Lampitt, Ben Lyttleton, Stephen F. Ross, Leon Sunstein, and Silke Weineck. Chapter 10 of the book, on Financial Fair Play, is a reworking of my article "Fair is Foul" published in the *International Journal of Sports Finance* in 2014; I am grateful to the publisher for allowing me to reuse much of the text. I'm grateful to Alessandra Bastagli and everyone at Nation Books for their support and enthusiasm for this project, and John Wilcockson for his thorough copyediting. Above all, I thank Silke: I owe you a summer.

1

DOMINANCE AND DISTRESS

DOMINANCE

In 2014 Real Madrid achieved the unprecedented feat of winning *La Décima*—its tenth Champions League title—three more than its nearest rival (AC Milan) and twice as many as the next nearest (Bayern Munich and Liverpool). Appropriately enough given its name—"real" means "royal" in Spanish—Real Madrid is the closest thing in the world to soccer royalty. According to Deloitte's *Annual Review of Football Finance*, the Spanish club generates more revenue annually than any other soccer club in the world, and according to *Forbes* it is the most valuable soccer "franchise" in the world. If Real Madrid were for sale (and in 2014 there were rumors of a partial stock flotation) *Forbes* reckons it would be worth $3.4 billion, making it the most valuable team in any sport anywhere.

The basis of Real Madrid's strength is its dominance of La Liga. It has played continuously in the Spanish league since its foundation in 1929. It has won the league thirty-two times altogether and twenty-two times in the last fifty years alone, well ahead of archrival FC Barcelona (fourteen times) and way ahead of anyone else (in fact, only five other teams have won the league in the last half-century).

Real Madrid has a lot in common with HB. Havnar Bóltfelag, to give the club its full name, is the largest team in Tórshavn, a town of 18,000 souls that also happens to be the capital and largest town of the Faroe Islands. Founded in 1904 (two years after Real Madrid), HB was a founder member of its national league in 1942 and has won the league twenty-two times, well ahead of nearest rival Kí Klaksvík (eight times). Only nine other clubs have won the league in the last fifty years.

To take another example of dominance, Jeunesse Esch of Luxembourg (founded in 1907) has won twenty titles in the last fifty years, nine more than its closest rival, F91 Dudelange. Jeunesse also once held Liverpool to a 1-1 tie at Anfield, the best international result in the club's history. Compared to HB, Jeunesse is a giant. According to the popular website transfermarkt.de, the total squad value of HB in 2014 was half a million euros ($625,000), compared to nearly one and a half million ($1.8 million) for Jeunesse. The revenue of the Luxembourg league is 50 percent larger than that of the Faroese clubs according to the Union of European Football Associations (UEFA). Yet in both countries we see the same pattern. Real Madrid is larger still, with a squad valued in 2014 at more than 600 million euros ($750 million). But large or small, the relationship of these clubs to the other teams in their domestic leagues is the same—they are dominant.

BOX 1.1: FAROE ISLANDS SOCCER

Tórshavn, the capital of the Faroe Islands, translates as "Harbor of Thor," the hammer-wielding Norse god of thunder and strength. Since 2005, a hammer has been on the crest of HB Tórshavn (usually shortened to HB) in recognition of the team's power. As the team of the capital, the most populous city, and the nation's most successful team, HB is the Real Madrid of the Faroe Islands, beloved by its fans and hated by everyone else.

The Faroes is a group of eighteen islands located between Iceland, Scotland, and Norway. It is a self-governing nation within the Kingdom of Denmark. The population is just under 50,000 and the local economy relies primarily on fishing; it is also a soccer-crazy nation. Almost everyone on the islands plays, and everyone follows an English Premier League team. The oldest surviving team of the Faroes is Tvøroyrar Bóltfelag (TB) founded in 1892, which still plays in the (Faroese) Premier League.

There are four tiers in the system, with a First and Second Division below the Premier League, and each of these three contains ten teams. The fourth tier varies in composition depending on the number of teams that want to enter. The bigger clubs have second and third teams that play in the lower divisions (but cannot be promoted to play alongside the first team). Soccer clubs are mostly member associations that run women's, youth, and senior sections.

The league was founded in 1942, during the wartime occupation by British troops. The large-scale presence of British soldiers seems to have reignited interest in the game—although the competition remained low-key, consisting of only five teams as late as 1970. Traveling between the islands was difficult and playing an away match could mean up to three days away from home. This began to change in the 1970s with the development of a better road system and the construction of tunnels between islands.

It was during the 1970s, under the forward-looking coach Johan Nielsen, that HB started to dominate competition on the islands. When it entered UEFA in 1990, the extra money the Faroe Islands Football Association received for participation in UEFA competition also helped it secure the services of the best players. Although almost all players remain amateurs to the present day, the best players can now make some money from the game, and the richer clubs gather the best talent from across the country, compared to the old days when players always stayed with their local clubs.

Not that this has been without problems—as Marni Mortensen, chief annalist of Faroe Islands soccer, HB fan, and designer of the club crest, explained to me. Clubs are community enterprises and are run by local people who are voted into office; ticket prices are low (80 DKr, about $15, for an adult, with children free) but crowds are small—maybe 400 for a typical game and 1,500 for a big game. Financial controls are often weak and the financial accounts are not always well kept, leading to a good deal of insolvency. HB itself got into financial troubles in 1990 and was bailed out by the municipality, which owns the stadium. The club turned the organization of the first team into a limited liability company in 1990 in order to separate the "business" element of the association from its leisure activities, but this was not entirely a success and the association took over control again in 2012.

CONTINUES

In recent years, there has been an influx of foreign players into Faroe Islands soccer, mostly from Eastern European—countries such as Poland and Russia—but even from Brazil. Mortensen reckons about 20 percent of current players in the Premier League are foreign. A few Faroese have gone abroad to play over the years, including Todi Jónsson, from the rival team Klaksvík, who had an illustrious career with FC Copenhagen. And Gunnar Nielsen, currently goalkeeper for the Scottish team Motherwell, is something of a national hero for being the only Faroese player to appear for an English Premier League team, having played several games for Manchester City.

Dominance is a feature of almost every soccer league in the world. Table 1 shows a selection of leagues from across Europe ranging from the plutocratic (England, Germany, Spain, Italy) to the impoverished (Faroe Islands and Luxembourg). Regardless of size, most leagues tell a very similar story: a small number of big clubs dominate. The most dominated league in the half-century was Scotland, where Celtic won twenty-four titles—almost half. Not far behind were Germany (dominated by Bayern Munich), the Netherlands (AFC Ajax), Spain (Real Madrid), Portugal (FC Porto), and Norway (Rosenborg Ballklub). Only in the Republic of Ireland, France, and Poland did the dominant club not get into double figures. On average, the dominant team in the leagues of each of these countries won one third of all the titles.

One of the most important features of the soccer league system as it operates in most of the world is the promotion-and-relegation system. National leagues are arranged in a hierarchy, and the best-performing teams in a given division are promoted at the end of each season to play in the immediately superior division, swapping places with the worst-performing teams from the higher division. The process is determined by sporting merit rather than financial capability. Over time, this means that even if there are only twenty teams in a league at any given moment, there are potentially many more league champions. If every team in the league hierarchy were of equal strength, and each game played was equally likely to end in a win or loss for the home team, then over a fifty-year period you would expect to see about forty different teams win the league championship.[1] Yet

TABLE 1.1 Dominance in 20 European leagues over the last 50 years

Country	Average club revenue 2012 $m	Most league championship wins in last 50 years	Number of league championship winners in last 50 years
England	173.8	15	11
Germany	135.0	23	12
Spain	116.3	22	7
Italy	107.5	18	11
France	72.5	8	14
Russia	70.0	13	14
Turkey	38.8	17	5
Netherlands	30.0	23	5
Switzerland	23.8	16	11
Portugal	22.5	22	4
Norway	13.8	22	12
Scotland	12.5	24	5
Poland	7.5	9	12
Romania	7.5	19	11
Hungary	2.9	11	11
Finland	2.0	16	14
Republic of Ireland	1.1	7	15
Luxembourg	0.8	20	11
Faroe Islands	0.5	19	11
Champions League		12	11

Note: Champions League refers to nations, not clubs. Figures cover seasons 1964/65–2013/14 except Faroe Islands, Hungary, Iceland, and Norway refer to the period 1963/64–2012/13, Finland to 1962/63–2011/12

Source: UEFA and Wikipedia

in Portugal only four different teams have won the league in the last fifty years, and in the Netherlands, Scotland, and Turkey there have been only five winners over the half-century. The greatest number of teams winning a national championship over this period is fifteen, in the Republic of Ireland, and across the twenty leagues in our sample the average is ten, a long way below what you would expect to see if there were balance in the league.

Looking at Table 1.1, there seems to be no relationship between the size of the league and the extent of domination. Small leagues are as likely to be dominated by a small number of teams as are big leagues. Germany, the country with the largest population and the greatest wealth in our sample, looks rather like tiny Luxembourg or the Faroe Islands.

The UEFA Champions League, the pan-European club competition for the fifty-four national associations that belong to UEFA, tells a similar story.[2] Until 1997 the competition involved only the national champion, but since then the larger nations have been permitted more than one entry, and currently up to four teams. Over fifty years, teams from England have won the competition twelve times, and teams from only eleven nations have ever won it. This resembles the averages for the twenty leagues. In this way, at least, the Champions League looks like just another European league.

Many people believe that dominance is a relatively recent phenomenon in soccer, or that dominance has increased significantly over the last two decades. Commercialization, according to this sentiment, has dumped large amounts of money into the game that has corrupted the system, and created a world of "haves" and "have-nots." There is no question that the amount of money in the game has increased, but in fact there is little evidence to suggest that dominance has intensified dramatically. When we compare the last quarter of a century to the preceding one, the pattern of dominance appears almost indistinguishable. In the last twenty-five years of the Champions League, the highest number of wins for one nation is eight (Spain), and clubs from eight different nations have won the Champions League trophy. Lo and behold, the quarter of a century before that the numbers are identical. Table 1.2 illustrates the difference between the two periods for twenty leagues.

To be sure, the story does play out with some variations, and some countries have indeed seen an increase in dominance in their domestic leagues. For example, Germany stands out: not only did the most successful team win more frequently in the last twenty-five years than during the previous twenty-five (Bayern Munich in both cases), but the number of different teams winning the championship fell from nine to six in the same period. In Scotland, always dominated by Rangers and Celtic, at least some other teams won the league in the earlier period; no one else made it past those two in the last twenty-five years. In total, however, there were only nine leagues where the highest number

TABLE 1.2 Dominance in each of the last two quarter-centuries

Country	Most wins by one club 1964/65 –1988/89	Most wins by one club 1989/90– 2013/14	Number of winners 1964/65– 1988/89	Number of winners 1989/90– 2013/14
England	11	13	9	7
Germany	10	13	9	6
Spain	14	12	6	5
Italy	10	8	10	7
France	7	7	8	11
Russia	11	10	11	7
Turkey	9	11	4	4
Netherlands	12	11	4	5
Switzerland	7	9	8	7
Portugal	15	17	3	4
Norway	6	17	9	8
Scotland	15	16	5	2
Poland	9	8	9	8
Romania	8	11	8	7
Hungary	9	6	6	10
Finland	6	10	9	8
Republic of Ireland	6	6	11	9
Luxembourg	13	11	8	6
Faroe Islands	10	9	6	9

SOURCE: Wikipedia

of wins increased, compared to eleven where it stayed the same or fell. There were twelve cases where the number of different champions fell—suggesting increased dominance—but eight where the number stayed the same or increased. Across the nineteen national leagues, the total number of championships won by the most successful team increased from 188 to 205—an increase of 9 percent—while the total number of different winners fell by 9 percent from 143 to 130. If dominance increased, then surely not by that much.

Of course, a small shift is not no shift at all, and to some fans, even a modest increase in dominance will matter. I am not arguing with that point of view—I do maintain, however, that dominance has always been a part of the/ soccer system, regardless of time, and regardless of the size of the league. Another way to crunch the numbers is this: 79 percent of national championships in our sample have been won by the top three teams in each country in the past quarter-century. In the previous twenty-five years it was 73 percent. In other words, a pattern of dominance was already well established twenty-five years ago.

BOX 1.2: MEASURING CONCENTRATION

There is no unique way to measure dominance. The two measures used here—the highest number of championships won by any one team and the number of different teams winning a championship—are correlated but not identical (the correlation coefficient for Table 1 is –0.64; the minus sign means that the more championships won by one team, the fewer the total number of champions is likely to be). There has been a lot of research on measuring concentration for soccer and for North American league sports (the term "competitive balance" is often used). These studies tend to look at three types of concentration—(1) within each game (how close individual matches tend to be), (2) within the season (how close the championship is), and (3) dominance over time, which is the type of dominance analyzed here. Each type of dominance can be measured differently, although different measures tend to be correlated.

In a recent paper, John Curran, Ian Jennings, and John Sedgwick[1] looked at teams finishing in the top four places in the top division in England and showed that there had been a gentle increase in the dominance of the four most successful teams until the end of the 1990s—since when the top four have been increasingly dominant, which is almost certainly a consequence of the growing financial importance of the Champions League.

Using an approach that focuses on the dispersion of results within a given season, Arne Feddersen and Wolfgang Maennig[2] show that there is very little evidence of any trend in concentration of results—so even if the big clubs are more dominant, they do not seem to win championships by a wider margin than in the past.

Back in 2003, I did some research with Luigi Buzzacchi and Tommaso Valletti[3] in which we compared the number of teams that in theory have the potential to reach the top five positions over a period of time compared to those that actually do. Because of promotion and relegation, the number of clubs that could in theory reach a top-five place if they got the right results becomes very large once you consider a long period of time. Suppose, for example, that every team in every division had an exactly equal probability of winning each game it played. Then, over the fifty seasons from 1950 to 1999, we would have expected 105 different teams to finish in the top five places of Serie A in Italy. In reality, through this half-century, there were only nineteen teams that finished the season in the top five.

1. Curran, John, Ian Jennings, and John Sedgwick (2009). "'Competitive Balance' in the Top Level of English Football, 1948–2008: An Absent Principle and a Forgotten Ideal," *The International Journal of the History of Sport*, 26:11, 1735–1747.

2. Feddersen, A., and W. Maennig (2005). "Trends in Competitive Balance: Is there Evidence for Growing Imbalance in Professional Sport Leagues?" *Hamburg Contemporary Economic Discussions*. 01/2005.

3. Buzzacchi, L., S. Szymanski, and T. M. Valletti (2003). "Equality of opportunity and equality of outcome: open leagues, closed leagues and competitive balance," *Journal of Industry Competition and Trade*, Vol: 3, ISSN: 1566–1679, pp. 167–186.

If dominance has characterized the leagues for so long, what accounts for it? It is, I suggest, the natural consequence of the competitive structure of soccer, which is almost identical everywhere on the planet. The patterns of dominance can be explained by some relatively straightforward relationships, which then account for the success or failure of individual teams. The object of this book is to explain how competition in soccer works, both at the sporting level—who wins on the field—and from the perspective of a commercial enterprise—how does soccer operate as a business.

If dominance emerges from a common competitive framework, clubs still become dominant in different ways. Take Real Madrid, Manchester United, and Bayern Munich.

THE ROYAL TEAM

Real Madrid was founded in 1902, but it was only in 1920 that King Alfonso XIII granted the club his royal patronage. Before the Spanish Civil War and the victory of the fascist General Francisco Franco, the club was by no means the most successful club in Spain. Its fortunes rose under Franco—but how was this possible? During Franco's rule as dictator (from 1939 to 1975), the country was a political outcast because of the Generalisimo's barely concealed support for Hitler and brutal repression at home. So how did Real Madrid establish itself in the 1950s, not only as the dominant team in Spain but also as the first dominant team of Europe?

The memory of the Franco years still generates strong emotions, and Spaniards in general find it hard to talk of the rise of Real Madrid dispassionately. It's not as if Franco issued large sums of cash to bankroll the team, or even that he took a direct interest in the management of the club. But surely there was never a political environment more favorable to a team that embodied the pride of Castile and the capital of the nation. Santiago Bernabéu, a player, club captain, and then manager before World War Two, became club president in 1943. His ambition to create a great club was symbolized by almost his first act—the decision to construct a new stadium, which would ultimately bear his name, adjacent to the old one but three times as large. Far larger than many people at the time thought a "small club" needed, and right in the heart of the swankiest part of Madrid, the new stadium made a statement. Bernabéu surrounded himself with financially savvy administrators who managed the club as a proper business, not in the amateur way that most clubs were run in those days. The right contacts with the regime were essential—and Bernabéu was able to ensure that Real got the best of everything. Barça fans in particular will point to the peculiar tale of the legendary Argentine player Alfredo di Stéfano's signing: he had first agreed to terms with and even played for Barcelona, only to be spirited away by Real Madrid. Even more sinister, many detractors will say that the core of the club's strategy was fixing the referees.

Once he had his stadium, Bernabéu set about hiring the greatest players of the era from all over the world—not only di Stéfano, but also the Hungarian Ferenc Puskás and Frenchman Raymond Kopa. While most clubs firmly focused on domestic competition, Bernabéu set out to prove that Real was the best club in Europe. Between 1956 and 1960 it won five European Cups (forerunner to the Champions League) in a row. And from that point the club became an aristocrat of soccer.

Like the Habsburg dynasty of old Spain, the club's decadence opened the door to northern Europeans. By the 1970s, Dutch, German, and English marauders had singed the King of Spain's beard. The death of Franco in 1975, the transition to democracy, the devolution of power to Catalonia and the Basque Country all sapped the strength of Real. But the Madridistas never forgot, and as the economy of Spain emerged into the light of a Europe without borders in the late-1980s, the city of Madrid now represented a golden opportunity. Hot money flowed in from all over Europe in a frenzy of construction and modernization, and the construction magnate and Real Madrid president Florentino Pérez promised to bring a share of this wealth to the club.

Nothing sells better than royalty, and so Pérez launched a global marketing campaign to make the image of Real the image of soccer. To do this he needed to show that the club was really the heir to di Stéfano's throne, so in one of the most important deals in soccer history he sold the club's training facility to the city and bought players so out of this world they could only be called the *galácticos*—Zinedine Zidane, Luis Figo, Ronaldo (the Brazilian, not the Portuguese Cristiano Ronaldo, who came later), and David Beckham added to homegrown talent such as Raúl and Iker Casillas.[3] It was proof positive that the royal blood line had survived—as was the team's victory in the 2002 Champions League final, which produced one of the greatest goals in the history of European soccer: Zidane's left-foot volley from the edge of the penalty box.

There is a Marie Antoinette quality about Real. All around it, Spanish soccer clubs (all except Barça) are in financial meltdown, unable to afford the perquisites necessary to shine in the royal presence, but the club has no intention of sharing what it has with the peasants.[4] Unlike the major clubs in every other league, Real does not have to share its sparkly broadcast rights revenue. Its courtiers struggle to muster 20,000 fans per game, while Real glistens in the Bernabéu with 70,000 subjects on average and 80,000 on state occasions. The club demands in tribute some of the highest ticket prices in the world—an average of €90 ($112) per fan per game. But with its international outlook and global presence, Real does not need to notice the poverty on its doorstep. The club is royalty; it's above all that.

BOX 1.3: FIRST MOVERS AND
THE DOMINANT DESIGN

Preston North End won the inaugural Football League Championship in 1888/89 and won the trophy again in the following season. The club has never won it since, and in the last fifty years it has drifted between the three lower tiers. VfB Leipzig is recognized as the first German national champion in 1903, but the club was reorganized in East Germany after World War Two. Since reunification, it has struggled and currently plays in a fourth tier regional league. Genoa CFC (for Cricket and Football Club) was the first champion of Italy and won that title nine times between 1897 and 1924. However, while it has had several seasons in Serie A over the last fifty years, Genoa has spent more seasons in Serie B and has even played in the third tier—it has not been a title contender in this period. All of these clubs had a first-mover advantage, but while they have survived as soccer clubs they have not managed to become part of the dominant group in their countries. In the four big leagues, only Barcelona, which won the first Spanish championship in 1929, has managed to convert that first-mover advantage into long-term dominance.

This might seem surprising, but it is a common phenomenon in many businesses—early innovators often fall by the wayside. That said, dominant firms are dominant because they have been there a long time. Two business school professors, James Utterback and William Abernathy, suggested an explanation of this using the concept of the "dominant design."[1] First movers are creative, but it often takes several years to perfect an innovation—and this is often done not by the innovator, being justly proud of its creation, but by followers who make small but important changes to make the product more consumer friendly. Eventually, a dominant design emerges—and the firms that first exploit this do become dominant.

In soccer, "dominant design" should be taken to refer to an established structure of competition that commands national attention. While the Football League was established in 1888 it did not reach is current structure until 1923, and it was only after this that teams like Arsenal and Manchester United emerged as dominant clubs. In Germany, the Bundesliga was not founded until 1963, and it was almost at once dominated by Bayern Munich, while Serie A was not established until 1930—its first champion was Inter Milan and the second was Juventus.

1. Abernathy, William J., and James M. Utterback. "Patterns of industrial innovation." *Technology Review. Ariel* 64 (1978): 228–254.

RED DEVILS AND RED MEAT

Louis Edwards was a successful Manchester butcher in austerity Britain—that's 1950s austerity, not the version that Britain is going through sixty years later. Butchers do well in hard times. People like red meat and will pay to get it even when they have to economize elsewhere. But people do not want to know too much about how the meat got to their table—butchers, like undertakers, do not get the recognition their services deserve. Edwards wanted status, and so he decided to buy it by acquiring the second most popular soccer club in Manchester. In those days, not as fancy as their City rivals, the Red Devils were perfectly suited to an unapologetic butcher.

Manchester United was then a limited liability company, like almost every English soccer club. Its shares had been sold to investors back in the mists of time, held by middle-class fans who owned them as a badge of loyalty rather than a financial investment. By the 1950s and 1960s, those investors had mostly passed away, and their shares in many cases were owned by their widows, this at a time when women were not encouraged to take an interest in the beautiful game. To gain control, Edwards needed to buy these shares. In 1962, he obtained a copy of the club's share register, handwritten on heavy paper in black ink, and he copied out in long hand the shareholders' names and addresses—no photocopiers then, nor faxes or Internet searches.

Then he paid a city councilor with a history of corruption to go around the suburbs of Manchester knocking on doors, offering to pay for the shares in the currency that had made him rich—a few quid plus a pound of sausages! The widows didn't seem to care, and many of them probably didn't even know about the share certificates buried in the attic. But they dug them out for him, and in this way the butcher got the recognition that goes with representing, rather than merely feeding, a community.[5]

When Edwards secured control of the club in 1964, Matt Busby had already been the manager for twenty years. Busby had agreed to take on that role in 1945, when the club was ailing, on condition that he be given complete control. Before him, the "manager" in English soccer was little more than a fitness trainer; it was the board of directors that bought and sold the players and picked the team on Saturday. Busby knew he was better than that, and he proved it, winning the FA Cup and two First Division titles (predecessor of the Premier League) by 1956.

It was an era when a smarter manager could make a difference on his own. At the time, player wages were still fixed at a maximum, and because that maximum was fixed at a level little better than those of a manual laborer, any player could be afforded by more or less any club. Moreover, players were tied to their clubs by the transfer system, which not only allowed clubs to sell players to each other during their contracts, but also to dictate which club they could move to after their contracts expired. If you could pick better players and train them to play better, then you could also be confident of holding onto your players for most of their careers, bringing long-term success and even turning a profit for the club.

Now, in passing, it must be said that the system was manifestly unfair. The players did the work but could not materially share in the rewards of their efforts. Not only were wages fixed at a low maximum, but also players had no right to move to a different club—even if the club no longer wanted their services. Rightly, in the swinging sixties, this feudal system started to crumble. A player strike eliminated the maximum wage in 1961 and a few years later a judge ruled the transfer system in breach of basic law; almost overnight, English soccer clubs slipped from profits into deficits.

Manchester United was different because it had the smartest manager around. And then the 1958 Munich air disaster—in which eight players, three staff, and eight sportswriters died—created a global surge of sympathy for the club. The poignancy of so many young, brilliant players losing their lives touched hearts and created a well of support internationally. Take for example the story of Professor Andy Markovits, who is a leading scholar on the sociology of sport (among other things): he grew up as a German-speaking Hungarian Jew in the 1950s, later moved to Vienna, and then to New York. He now teaches at the University of Michigan, Ann Arbor. But in 1958, when he was a kid growing up in Soviet-bloc Romania, he was so moved by the newspaper reports of the tragedy that he became a Manchester United fan, which he remains, religiously, even superstitiously, to the present day.

The heroism of Matt Busby in his recovery from life-threatening injury (which kept him in the hospital for almost three months after the plane crash), his return as manager in the following season, and the breath-taking flair of his new team, led by Munich survivor Bobby Charlton and newcomers Denis Law and George Best, wove a tale of redemption that was irresistible (unless you already had a team); and so Manchester United became the best-supported English team both at home and abroad. After Busby retired in the early-1970s, the team went through an extended period of high spending with limited returns on its investment. But the club retained its popularity and so was still able to make money. All this in an era when English clubs made systematic losses almost regardless of their success on the field. In the early-1980s, clubs such as Bristol City, Wolverhampton Wanderers, Charlton Athletic, and many others entered legal insolvency proceedings, usually following relegation. United was relegated in 1974—and bounced back immediately, its fan base, and finances miraculously unaffected.

By this time, Louis Edwards was passing on control of the club to his son Martin. Martin Edwards was unquestionably an innovator, always looking for new ways to bring more money into the club. His schemes did not endear him to the fans—and in the end he decided to sell out. He agreed to sell the club in 1989 for £20 million (about $75 million in today's currency) to Michael Knighton, a schoolteacher turned property developer, but the deal fell through at the last minute after Knighton made a fool of himself by insisting on going on the field before the start of a game to kick a football into the net. It was probably the biggest favor he ever did for Martin Edwards, who was able instead to float the company on the stock exchange in 1991 and in the following decade realized more than £100 million (equivalent to about $230 million today) from his father's investment.

By the late-1990s, United had risen to become not only the most valuable soccer club, but also the most valuable club in any sport worldwide, worth more than the New York Yankees or the Dallas Cowboys.

The 1990s also saw Manchester United return to sporting success under the leadership of manager Sir Alex Ferguson. Ferguson's success on the field was extraordinary and unmatchable, but even without him the club's value would have skyrocketed during this era. Globalization of televised soccer put the international spotlight on the Premier League, and as the most glamorous club in the league it was inevitable that United would reap the benefit. It's not necessary to believe the club's claim that it has 700 million fans worldwide to accept that anywhere you go in the world the club is known, and you can probably buy a team replica jersey.

Here in the United States, many may have been surprised by the discovery that the world's most valuable sports franchise was not American. But surprise soon led to interest, and to a desire to have a piece of the action. During the last decade, five Premier League clubs have come under American ownership. In any country, foreign takeovers of treasured domestic assets are controversial. But the Glazer family takeover of Manchester United in 2005 generated far greater and more durable antipathy from fans than any of the others. It was not so much that they were Americans, but the way they did it. The family, led by Malcolm Glazer (who died in May 2014), presides over a real estate empire that ventured into sports in 1995 when it acquired the NFL's Tampa Bay Buccaneers, and won the franchise's first Super Bowl in 2003. After a takeover struggle with rival Irish bidders, the Glazers paid around £800 million ($1.3 billion) for Manchester United, almost all of it borrowed; they then unloaded a large fraction of the debt (about $800 million) onto the club. Fans went ballistic. Protests were launched and blogs started screaming that the Glazers would bleed the club dry and leave it on the scrapheap.

In the first seven years after the Glazer takeover, United won five league titles, won the Champions League, and appeared in two more Champions League finals—a spectacular performance even by United's standards and better than any other English team. Perhaps the crowning achievement of those years was the 2008 Champions League title. That final could not have offered a bigger contrast between two English clubs. On one side was Chelsea, the monster bankrolled by the billions of Russian oligarch Roman Abramovich. His team fielded the likes of Frank Lampard, Didier Drogba, John Terry, Claude Makélélé, Michael Ballack, and Ashley Cole. On the other side were the steely suits of Manchester United, which still retained Cristiano Ronaldo and Wayne Rooney—but by then there were almost weekly rumors that one or both were leaving. The rest of the team was aging, with Paul Scholes and Ryan Giggs still hanging on from the golden generation of the previous decade. Each team was led by a charismatic manager: Alex Ferguson for United and José Mourinho for Chelsea. Perhaps it isn't a surprise that the game went to a shootout, and that it took more than the regulation five penalties per team to settle it.[6] United won, even if you would be hard pressed to find one fan prepared to give the Glazers one iota of credit.

Manchester United may not be rated as highly as the Barcelona team of that period, but the English team would rank alongside anyone else. And in this period the Glazers reduced the club's debt by around a half while paying penal amounts of interest. Revenue has risen so fast that talk of financial problems has now faded. The Glazers floated part of the club on the New York Stock Exchange in September 2012, amid widespread claims that the stock would plummet, but by the spring of 2013 its value had risen by around 25 percent, placing a $3 billion price tag on the company as a whole.

Not that the Glazers changed the way the club was run that much—though they encouraged a commercial department to develop more international deals, which has produced a lot of extra revenue. In the early days, they made themselves even more unpopular by raising ticket prices, but prices have been more or less frozen since the United Kingdom went into austerity after 2008. They have benefited from huge increases in broadcast revenue both at home and abroad. But mainly the Glazers have made themselves richer simply by recognizing that United is one of the most powerful symbols of soccer in a world where demand for soccer is expanding.

FC HOLLYWOOD

Germany is the waking giant of club soccer,[7] a nation that is crazy about the game and about two teams in particular: the German national team and Bayern Munich. Often it is hard to tell them apart. Bayern, or FC Hollywood as the all-star team is jokingly referred to in Germany, has bossed the Bundesliga almost from the start. With twenty-three championships in half a century, no one else is even close. Other countries have at least two dominant teams (Barça and Real in Spain), many have at least three (AC Milan, Inter Milan, and Juventus in Italy), and others have several depending on the era. In England, teams have often switched places. Both Manchester United and Liverpool enjoyed extended periods of dominance, but even at their respective peaks they had close rivals: Manchester City, Chelsea, and Arsenal in recent times; Everton and Nottingham Forest in times past.

Bayern, by contrast, has no serious rivals in Germany. It has been associated with the dominant players in German soccer, not least Franz Beckenbauer, *der Kaiser*. It was a stroke of luck that he joined Bayern because he was a childhood fan of TSV 1860 Munich, the city's other professional club, and he had planned to join that rival squad. But after the youth team that Beckenbauer played for ended up contesting a bad-tempered game against 1860's youth team, he changed his mind and plumped for Bayern Munich. It is a conservative club: Bavarian, industrial—the soccer equivalent of BMW (although the carmaker does have serious competitors in Germany). Bayern is a magnet for talent: all the great German stars, except some of the radicals and the dreamers, end up playing for Hollywood.

Bayern's rise to dominance seems serendipitous. Germany did not even have a national league until 1963, and when the Bundesliga started, Bayern was not even included in it because the league preferred to take on the more successful TSV 1860 Munich. The early success of the club in the 1960s was not built on a strong financial base, and there were questions about its solvency right up until the end of the 1980s. No doubt, Bayern benefited from sharing the monumental Olympic Stadium (built for the 1972 Olympics) with 1860, and it no doubt benefited indirectly from Bavarian affluence. But these are not overwhelming advantages. Instead, Bayern just started winning games, and one thing led to another in that kind of virtuous circle that everyone talks about but seldom lasts. In Bayern's case, it did. Of course, all success is ultimately attributable to good fortune in the sense that we are endowed with skills and capabilities that we did not acquire by design or by merit. But somehow Bayern's success feels at times more like the blind luck of a coin toss that just keeps on coming up heads. The club would probably just say that it always makes good decisions—which its rivals do not appear able to match. For example, in the 2013 Champions League semifinal, Bayern routed Barcelona (7-0 on aggregate), a team that only a year before had looked invincible.

And there is little chance that Bayern's dominance can be challenged. Since it became the dominant power in German soccer, it has been protected from competition because of the organizational model of the sport in Germany. German clubs, including Bayern, are mostly member organizations with guaranteed fan control, thanks to something called the 50+1 rule, which prevents investors from buying a controlling stake. This makes the German system very conservative. There is no room for wealthy individuals to take over a club and buy their way to success, and so there is little chance that any club could ever challenge Bayern's place at the top of the German hierarchy.

The German organizational model has recently become popular internationally for a number of reasons. The current crop of German players is stellar, as witnessed by the national team's convincing victory in the 2014 World Cup. German ticket prices are relatively low and clubs play in large, well-appointed stadiums, many of them rebuilt and refurbished for the 2006 World Cup, partly at public expense. Average attendance at league games has risen rapidly in recent years, and is now the highest in the soccer world. The conservatism of the German system, however, also helps to sustain the long-term dominance of Bayern.

Dominance is often associated with the absence of competition, but that is not the case when it comes to soccer. There are, for example, twenty-seven professional soccer teams within a fifty-mile radius of Manchester United.[8] If fans don't like United, there are plenty of alternatives. Often, rivals play in the same stadium (Bayern and TSV 1860, Inter Milan and AC Milan are the two most notable examples). And if Spanish fans are looking for variety, there are four other professional soccer clubs in Madrid to choose from.

Dominance through monopoly, the absence of competition, usually occurs because the scale of the investment required is so great that competition just isn't feasible. Take the water supply and sewage systems for example. Competition would require individual households and businesses having access to not one, but two or more networks of pipes, a proposition that amounts to economic madness. Laying pipes is very costly, and water supply and sewage fees have to be set in such a way as to recover these costs. Any benefit that might arise from competition would be dwarfed by the cost of duplication.

But dominance also occurs in markets where competition is perfectly feasible. The beverage market is a good example. Any child can (and often does) set up a lemonade stand on the street and sell to passersby—this is not a business in which entry is difficult or particularly expensive. It remains to this day relatively easy in business terms to set up a production plant to bottle soft drinks, and yet Coca-Cola dominates this world, with a market share of around 42 percent in 2012, followed by Pepsi with 28 percent. Despite all that potential competition, these two firms dominate the market. Their hegemony is not explained by set-up costs but—according to the work of John Sutton, an industrial economist—by something different: advertising. Consumers tend to buy soft drinks that they recognize, and advertising is the way that they usually recognize the product. So when sellers compete against each other they compete not just on price, but also on recognition. Recognition is costly, and takes years to establish. Moreover, once you have it, and if you want to maintain it, you have to keep on investing. Is there anyone on the planet who does not recognize the name of Coca-Cola? And yet the company still spends around $3 billion a year on advertising. That is what it takes to fend off the constant threat of competition.

Sutton argues that soft drinks are a good example of an "advertising-intensive" industry in which a pattern of dominance can emerge. In the early days of such industries there are many competitors jostling for recognition, which leads to an arms race in advertising. Advertising expenditures precede sales, and so represent something of a gamble. For some companies they pay off and the business grows, while for others the sales don't follow and the business goes to the wall. In this way, a small number of successful firms grow into giants. A competitive fringe also survives, mostly consisting of small firms with small market share. In very large markets (such as the United States), the power of advertising conferred a huge advantage on companies like Coca-Cola. In Europe's smaller markets (which tend to be drawn along national lines), more small firms tend to survive, making the biggest firms less dominant.

BOX 1.4: JOHN SUTTON, SUNK COSTS, AND MARKET STRUCTURE

Economists build models of industrial structures in order to capture the salient facts about markets within a framework of rational decision-making. This does not mean that there is no luck involved or that no one ever makes a mistake; however, consumers are assumed to pursue their best interests, given what they know, and businesses try to take advantage of opportunities to make profits if they are there. The salient fact that John Sutton set out to capture in his landmark book *Sunk Costs and Market Structure* is that many industries are characterized by a small number of dominant firms and a "competitive fringe" consisting of large numbers of small firms. Dominance is easy to explain if there are very large set-up costs, which, once spent, cannot be recovered other than by operating in the industry—what economists call "sunk costs." For example, there are only ever a small number of electricity generators in a market because building them entails large sunk costs, which are essentially defined by the technology. The dominance of Coca-Cola seems more complex to understand because the set-up costs to manufacture soft drinks are not that high, and most of the sunk costs are incurred in the form of advertising, which is essentially at the discretion of the firm. Advertising is an example of "endogenous" sunk costs, meaning they are determined by the decisions of firms in the process of competition, as opposed to "exogenous" sunk costs, which are simply determined by technological requirements.

Sutton develops a model in which firms can pursue one of two types of strategy. One is an advertising-intensive strategy, which makes the product more attractive but at an increasing cost. The second is a non-advertising strategy, which limits the attractiveness of the product to the market but keeps costs down. He shows that an equilibrium is possible in which the market is dominated by a small number of firms that advertise intensively, and

CONTINUES

a potentially large number of firms that do not. How many fringe firms there are depends partly on how willing consumers are to switch to the high-advertising product. If fringe firms are willing to absorb losses persistently then in theory the number of fringe firms can remain high—although Sutton does not consider this idea in his model.

What determines whether you are in the dominant group or the fringe group? Two obvious mechanisms are first-mover advantage and tastes. First movers can establish a reputation and brand name that gives them a broader appeal than late-arriving upstarts. Tastes also matter. Once a product becomes fashionable it can build from this platform, and continually enhance its dominance through advertising. Note, however, that the profitability of being a dominant firm, which has to spend large sums on advertising to maintain its dominance, may not be much greater than that of a fringe firm that, although small, does not have to maintain the advertising outlays. In equilibrium, no one should be making profits above and beyond those required to keep the business going, otherwise new firms would be tempted to enter the market.

Applying Sutton's model to the world of professional club soccer, one should focus on player investment instead of advertising. The big clubs are the ones that spend heavily on players and achieve a potentially global following—there are only a small number of these large, dominant teams. These clubs were able to develop this image because they were first movers, because of their location, because of a specific event in their history, or because of their association with particular individuals or movements. But there is a very large competitive fringe that survives largely on local loyalty, which is intense. These clubs can never break into the dominant group, unless they receive substantial funding from an investor (who does not expect to see a direct financial return) or they are extraordinarily lucky.

This is essentially the story of soccer, too. Instead of advertising, think of league championships. Teams that win are the ones that attract the fans—the biggest clubs have the largest number of fans and the largest revenues. The big difference between soccer and soft drinks is that the pattern of dominance looks the same in small markets (Faroe Islands) as in the big markets (Spain). The reason for this is that in the soft drinks industry, and most other big markets, small firms trying to keep up with the dominant firms go out of business. In soccer, small clubs almost never disappear. Of the eighty-eight clubs in the English Football League in 1923, eighty-five still exist, and most of them still play in the four English divisions. Of the seventy-four clubs playing in the top divisions of England, France, Italy, and Spain in 1950, seventy-two still exist. Unlike most businesses in which loss-making firms are shut down or merged into other businesses, soccer clubs almost always survive. This does not prevent dominance, but unlike most industries, it does mean that the pattern of dominance tends to look the same everywhere.

DISTRESS

In the summer of 2010, the Italian soccer federation (FIGC) issued a ruling that twenty clubs in the second, third, and fourth tiers of the various leagues would be subject to sanctions, including exclusion from league competition, for failing to meet their financial obligations. Under the club-licensing rules in Italy, a club may be refused a license because of overdue payments on debts, payments owing to players or other clubs, or overdue payments to the tax authorities. Additionally, every club must disclose its full accounting information, and a license may be refused if the accountants deem that the club is "not a going concern" (a term of art in accounting that means the business is not commercially viable without making some additional assumptions, such as a commitment to further investment by the owners).[9]

As a result, eighteen clubs were liquidated—that is, the companies that owned the clubs were wound up. Out of these eighteen, twelve new clubs were born claiming the heritage and insignia of the defunct club. In three cases, other existing clubs sought to take over the history and identity of the old clubs—two succeeded, and the third, Ancona, is still in the process of doing so. In only three of the eighteen cases was there no successor club: Pro Vasto, Sanguistese, and Pescina. Of the twenty clubs sanctioned, seventeen have entities that have already replaced or will replace the old clubs by the 2014/15 season. One of these was operating three tiers lower than in 2010, seven were operating two tiers lower, seven were one tier lower, and two were actually playing at a level one tier higher than in 2010.

In May 2014, Spanish secretary of state for sport Miguel Cardenal revealed that professional soccer clubs in Spain's First and Second Divisions had accumulated debts of €3.6 billion ($4.5 billion). Seventy-four percent of this debt was owed by just eight clubs in La Liga's Primera División. According to Cardenal, money owed by clubs to the government amounted to €752 million ($940 million) in January 2012. The inability of Spanish soccer clubs to pay their debts has a long history. In 1990, the Spanish government passed a law requiring professional clubs to convert from members associations to limited liability companies in the hope that this would stop the clubs from acting irresponsibly, and at the same time canceled €192 million ($240 million) of debt.[10]

The reforms made no difference—throughout the 1990s, Spanish clubs continued to rack up debt until in 2003 a new law, the *Ley Concursal*, came to their aid. This was a reform of Spanish insolvency law, which was intended to save indebted companies from being shut down. Prior to that the only option for companies that could not pay their creditors was to close down the business, sell off the remaining assets, and repay as much of the debt as they could. Often this meant closing down viable companies, often with significant loss of employment, just to solve a short-term credit crunch. The *Ley Concursal* enabled companies to negotiate with their creditors with a view to keeping the business running while agreeing to pay back as much money as possible. Spanish soccer clubs have embraced the new law enthusiastically—between 2003 and 2011, twenty-two clubs took advantage of it to renegotiate their debts.[11]

Notwithstanding these restructurings, the Spanish government felt obliged to intervene in 2012 to devise a new plan to force the clubs to pay the backlog of taxes and other social security obligations. This process will take several years to complete, so as yet we cannot tell if this intervention will prove any more successful than the previous attempts.

There is a long history of insolvent soccer clubs in England. After World War Two, the first club to become insolvent while still competing in one of the top four divisions was Bristol City in 1982.[12] Since then, there have been more than seventy cases where clubs have undergone insolvency proceedings of one form or another while still playing in the four professional divisions. At the end of February 2010, Portsmouth Football Club became insolvent, the first club ever to do so while playing in the Premier League. However, at the time, Portsmouth was already nearly certain to be relegated, and that indeed happened a few weeks later. Insolvency is mainly a problem of clubs operating in the lower divisions.

Evidence of insolvency problems in England and Wales can be traced back even further by searching the records of the *London Gazette*, whose archives are now available online. Renamed *The Gazette*, it is the publication of record for any company based in England and Wales. All significant events relating to insolvency, such as a meeting of creditors or the winding up of the company, must be published in *The Gazette*. Between 1893 and 1935, a little over forty years, there were twenty-two cases notified to the *London Gazette* involving Football League clubs—about one every other year on average. The first case was the liquidation of Middlesbrough Ironopolis in 1893. Ironopolis was in fact a successful club, having won the Northern League three times and reached the quarter-final of the FA Cup, a single elimination tournament that is older than the league itself. The year it went into liquidation was also the year it entered the Second Division of the Football League (which only had two divisions at that time). The club ultimately failed because it was unable to afford the lease on the stadium it played at, which was adjacent to Ayresome Park—home of the more famous Middlesbrough Football Club.

The list of twenty-two includes some august names—Newton Heath, later renamed Manchester United, Arsenal, Aston Villa, and Wolverhampton Wanderers—all of which went on to win the Football League championship more than once. Only ten of the businesses actually collapsed—in all of the other cases some kind of resolution was found to the financial problem. Of these ten, only three have not reappeared in one guise or another: Ironopolis, Bootle AFC (which collapsed in 1893), and Leeds City, which was expelled from the League in 1919 after being found guilty of paying its players during World War One in breach of the Football Association's wartime rules.[13]

It has become popular in recent years to suggest that some countries, notably Germany, are better managed in this respect and that insolvencies are unknown in German soccer. Research by Daniel Weimar of the University of Duisburg-Essen shows that this is not the case. While it is true that clubs in the top division (1. Bundesliga) have not undergone insolvency proceedings, in the mid-2000s, both Borussia Dortmund and Schalke 04 got into considerable financial difficulties, the former being bailed out in part by a loan from Bayern Munich. Lower division clubs are not so fortunate—Weimar has identified eighty-six cases of soccer clubs in lower divisions entering insolvency since 1993, a rate of almost four per year.

BOX 1.5: DOMINANCE, SOCCER CAPITAL, AND PIKETTY

Thomas Piketty's book *Capital in the Twenty-First Century* was the publishing sensation of 2014. In the book, the French economist argues that there are some fundamental relationships in the capitalist system that lead inevitably to inequality, and that their influence was overshadowed by the horrendous consequences of two world wars. The key trend, which echoes the work of Karl Marx, is that over time capital plays a larger and larger role in the national economy, and that if ownership of this capital is concentrated in a few hands then income inequality may grow to extreme proportions. This argument is used to justify government intervention in the form of a minimum income, the provision of basic public services, and a tax on capital.

This narrative may sound oddly familiar to anyone who follows the public debate on soccer. The following statement comes from a 2003 decision of the European Commission on the sale of UEFA Champions League broadcast rights:

> The Commission understands that it is desirable to maintain a certain balance among the football clubs playing in a league because it creates better and more exciting football matches, which could be reflected in/translate into better media rights. The same applies to the education and supply of new players, as the players are a fundamental element of the whole venture. The Commission recognises that a cross-subsidisation of funds from richer to poorer may help achieve this. The Commission is therefore in favour of the financial solidarity principle, which was also endorsed by the European Council declaration on sport in Nice in December 2000.

On the face of it, Piketty's argument is somewhat different. Economic activity is generally the product of capital—owned by someone—and labor. Both need to be rewarded for their contribution, and Piketty is arguing that there is a natural tendency for the reward to capital to grow to the point where inequality becomes unsustainable. In soccer, the inequality is among clubs that do the same thing, and in competition with each other. However, there is a logical connection. Those who own capital were once like the rest of us—they relied on income from their labor—but they were so successful that they had lots of spare income that they were able to turn into capital, which then sustained them, their families, and their descendants. Likewise, the dominant soccer clubs of today are, for the most part, the descendants of some extremely successful clubs from the past, and are able to live off that capital today. Without their history, Real Madrid, Manchester United, and Bayern Munich would struggle like everyone else.

Moreover, there is a logic by which their dominance can become unsustainable (if the gap becomes too large then competition with lesser teams becomes unattractive), and the dominant clubs would be better off breaking away and forming their own superleague. This is a proposition that has been in the air since the 1980s, and indeed it was the motivation for statements such as the year 2000's Nice Declaration "on the specific characteristics of sport and its social function in Europe." Some say a breakaway superleague will never happen; others say that the Champions League is already a superleague in all but name.[1]

1. Back in 1999, I published an article with Tom Hoehn discussing the prospects of a superleague, see Hoehn, T., and S. Szymanski. "The Americanization of European Football," *Economic Policy*, 205–233.

These examples are drawn from the big four nations of professional soccer. According to Deloitte the seventy-eight professional clubs in the top division of these four countries had a combined income of €8.5 billion ($10.6 billion) in 2013, equal to almost half of the European soccer market by value. Yet this is only a tiny fraction of the total number of soccer clubs in Europe and farther afield. There are around 700 clubs in the top divisions of the member nations of UEFA, and hundreds, if not thousands, more clubs in the lower tiers. Clubs in nations that have smaller revenues are more likely to face the threat of insolvency. According to UEFA, in the financial year 2012, 39 percent of European top division clubs had negative equity—meaning that their liabilities exceeded their assets. This is usually taken as a sign of impending insolvency. However, this figure fell to only 31 percent when looking at clubs whose annual revenues exceeded €20 million ($25 million). In other words, larger clubs look more secure. Since the first club-licensing report for the financial year 2008, UEFA has issued figures on the number of clubs whose auditors raised a "going concern" qualification (i.e., that the clubs would need external financial support to survive). Between 2008 and 2011, the fraction of clubs whose accounting information was qualified in this way rose from 10 percent to 14 percent. In 2012, UEFA did not reveal the percentage.

Soccer, then, is a competitive enterprise characterized by both dominance and distress. These are not merely a consequence of accidents or misjudgments (although both are common in soccer as in other walks of life), but they are inherent to the structure of the game and its organization. They are also, at least in part, the reason that this is the world's most popular sport. In recent years there has been intense pressure from some quarters to regulate soccer more strictly, often through government intervention. Though much of this pressure is well intentioned, there is also a danger that regulation could undermine those characteristics that have contributed to making the game so popular.

2

PLAYERS

EVERY GAME IS A GAMBLE. OR AN INVESTMENT. OR BOTH. WHY? In order to put eleven players on the field, a professional soccer club must first spend money to get those players—win, lose, or tie. In order for a player to appear, the club must hold a valid registration for that player, which the club has to acquire with the consent of the player and, if necessary, with the consent of the club that previously held the registration. The player's consent is purchased with the promise of wages, and the consent of previous clubs with the payment of a transfer fee.[1] While there are several routes to acquiring players—transfers, free agent signings, loans, youth academy—all involve significant costs to the club in addition to the player's salary.[2] And all of these commitments are made before the game even starts.

The main activity of a professional soccer club is the acquisition of playing talent. Big teams maintain armies of scouts to seek out and buy up emerging talent. Today it is a global search. Managers are fêted for their ability to attract top stars to a club, but they do not act alone. In recent years, clubs have embraced data as a way of finding talent. Statistical departments have been established that not only assess players whom the scouts have not yet been able to see, but also analyze performance data on the field and off the field in search of any possible factor that might signal an emerging star.

And yet the outcome of every game remains highly uncertain (unless the match has been fixed), while the terms of employment are settled in advance. The central paradox of soccer is that no matter how much we know about each player, the outcome of every competitive game remains unpredictable. As Chris Anderson and David Sally put it in *The Numbers Game*, "half of all goals can be attributed to luck, and the better team wins only half of the time."[3]

Professional soccer amounts to a form of financial speculation. Whether one likes the idea of soccer "as a business" or not, making decisions about investing in players is in many regards exactly the same kind of decision-making process that any commercial organization has to undertake. The uncertain outcome of the investment in players influences the amount of revenue that the club can generate and therefore the capacity to recoup the investment cost. Success implies the capacity to keep on going, to invest again, possibly to achieve even further success. Failure can mean insolvency—the inability to repay debts incurred when investing. The financial health of a soccer club, as well as the mental health of its fans, depends on the success or failure of player investment.

THE PROBLEM OF CHOICE

Players

Everyone knows that the right blend of players on the field is important. But sometimes, those of us who do not do this for a living are tempted to think that there is nothing more to it than selecting the best eleven players each week—as if it were self-evident who those would be. In reality, the choice of players to field each week is a complex problem.

In the English Premier League, each team must supply the match officials with a team sheet no later than one hour before the game starts, listing the eleven starting players and seven players on the bench. These players must be drawn from the team squad of twenty-five, although the squad can be changed from game to game, so that the total number of players employed is much larger (according to its 2013 annual report, Manchester United employed eighty-two players throughout the year). So in a thirty-eight-game season the manager has to make 418 decisions on the starting line-up (38x11) and 684 decisions in total (38x18), as well 114 decisions about substitutes (38x3). That's a lot of decisions to make about just twenty-five players.

Take the example of Manchester United in its championship-winning 2012/13 season, the last under Sir Alex Ferguson. Some players made the cut almost all the time (e.g., Robin van Persie, 35 starts, Michael Carrick and Patrice Evra, 34 each), but most players appeared far less often. One way to think about this is by looking at the number of changes that occur over the course of the season. In the first game, the manager makes 11 decisions about the starters; in each subsequent game, he either keeps the same players or makes a change. In the season we are looking at, Ferguson made 270 changes of this kind. No doubt many of these were forced on him by injury, but many others were tactical. And these are just decisions about starting players—and that number does not even include games played in other competitions such as the Champions League or FA Cup. A total of 270 changes in thirty-eight games: that's an average of seven for every game played!

Manchester United is a big club, but the story is not very different if we look at a smaller one. Consider, for example, Queen's Park Rangers (QPR), who fired its manager Mark Hughes early in the season to replace him with Harry Redknapp and were ultimately relegated at the end of the season. They used only thirty players in total over the season. By coincidence, the highest number of starting appearances by any one player was also thirty. The club made a total of 207 changes to the starting line-up over the season (more than five per game). This mostly reflects the fact that QPR did not have as much depth in its squad, and so was unable to rotate its players in the way that Manchester United did without significantly limiting the performance of the team. But it still amounts to a lot of decisions over a season.

Performance

If the manager could predict how well each player were to perform, either in every game or over the course of a season, then the process of management would be much easier. But in reality players are inconsistent, and there's not much the manager can do about it. An indication of just how inconsistent they can be is provided by player ratings. There is a long tradition in the Bundesliga of expert panels rating individual players in each game, and these scores can be used to gauge just how variable player performance is over time—fascinating data even if the results might at times be skewed by individual bias. In a recent paper, Christian Deutscher and Arne Buschemann examined such player performance ratings in the Bundesliga between 2005 and 2010.[4] Ratings are assigned on a scale of one to six, with one being the best. Over the period they studied, the average rating for the 845 players in their sample was 3.62 and the standard deviation was 0.76. This translates into a rather big difference from game to game. According to these numbers, two thirds of the time an individual player's performance will rate between 2.86 and 4.38—that is a pretty big spread already. In addition, during one third of his appearances, the player will be ranked either better than 4.38 or worse than 2.86.

Imagine a team made up of eleven players, each of whom has the average rating of 3.62 with a standard deviation of 0.76 at the end of a thirty-four-game Bundesliga season. What should we expect of such a team? Let us first see how this would play out if we assume that the team performance is just the sum of the individual performances and that there is no correlation among the performances of the players on the team. Under those conditions, there will be less variation in the team performance than in the individual performances: randomly bad performances would cancel out randomly good performances. The ratio of an individual player's best-to-worst rating would be more than 2:1 with, say, a top rating of five and a bottom one of two. That is a very significant difference, but seeing that many of the variations in individual performances cancel each other out, the best performance for the team as a whole would only be 30- to 40-percent better than the worst one.

This makes the team sound fairly stable, even if individual performances vary wildly. But, in fact, we really can't assume that the performance of a team is simply the *sum* of individual performances. Precisely because it's a team game, a better performance by one player is likely to enhance the performance of the others—so the combination of player performances is more likely *multiplicative*, rather than additive. Of course, much depends on whether changes in player performances are highly correlated (e.g., all the team members go down with a stomach bug) or whether they tend to be independent of each other (e.g., each player's mood depends entirely on his private life). The more independent the individual variations are, the larger the effect on team performance will be. Under plausible scenarios, the best performance of the team could easily be twenty times better than its worst.

Anyone who has played fantasy soccer understands the process. You have a budget with which to put a squad together, you choose the players that you think will provide best value for money, and then you see how they do on the field. Everyone knows that you could do better if you were allowed a larger budget—because the better players cost more money. But even if you invested lavishly, on any given weekend your carefully chosen blend of superstars can fall flat on their faces.

In fantasy soccer the transfer prices of the players are based on supply and demand—if more gamers want to buy a particular player for their team, then the game organizer allows the price rise; likewise, the price of rejects falls. That is not so far from what happens in the real world except that (1) each player can only be on one team, and (2) players can only be traded at certain times of year. But imagine that managers in the Premier League could trade players on a weekly basis. In-form players would see their value rise, out-of-form players would see their value fall, and so the teams that spent the most money would be pretty certain that their spending would translate into weekly success.

As it is, the amounts teams spend on their players actually *do* translate into weekly success to a certain extent, but the correlation on a week-to-week basis is not very strong—expensive players frequently have lack-luster days. Some people conclude that the ways we measure player skills aren't very reliable and that a team's expenditure doesn't tell us all that much about their likely success. But they are and it does. What is the best indicator that we have of the outcome of a game before the event? The answer is the bookmaker's odds. The bookmaker makes money by taking a percentage of the money staked by gamblers, who generally have different opinions about the outcome. If most people want to bet that Manchester United will beat Chelsea, then the bookmaker needs to offer very low odds on this event—and so the payoff to every $1 staked is small. Of course, if Manchester United wins then the money paid out to these bettors is usually balanced by the losses of those who bet on Chelsea. There will be no bettors on Chelsea in the first place if the bookmaker doesn't offer very high odds, offering a high return for those willing to take a risk on what most people consider an unlikely event, hoping for a large payoff. In an ideal world—at least ideal for the bookies—the odds are calibrated so that the bookmaker's profits are the same no matter the outcome.

If the bookmakers set the odds appropriately, then they face no risk. In practice, however, many bookmakers take a gamble themselves by not balancing the book exactly. There is a small but significant literature in economics that examines how bookmakers set their odds. One important result is that they appear to be pretty good at it—at least, there are no simple ways to bet against the bookmaker that consistently make money. Occasionally, research shows that there are small imperfections in the market, but it provides little evidence to show that this could be exploited profitably.[5] This may be hard for many people to accept as a fact—but before discounting the evidence just remember how profitable bookmaking is.[6]

So let us engage in a very easy exercise and compare the bookmakers' odds with the probabilities derived from a one-dimensional mechanism—namely, that the team that spends more on its players is the one that is more likely to win. This is an unbelievably simple model. In fact, it sounds simplistic. It takes no account of managerial skills, injuries, form, psychology and morale, or any of the other countless factors that the media like to speculate on in relation to the outcome of a game. I estimated the probabilities based on this model for the Premier League in the 2012/13 season, using the club wage payments recorded in the Deloitte *Annual Review of Football Finance*, and then calculated the correlation between the win, tie, and loss probabilities for the home team from a reputable bookmaker (Bet365). Correlation is a statistical measure of the extent to which two sets of figures move in step with each other. By construction, correlation can vary between +1 (perfect positive correlation) and −1 (perfect negative correlation). In the middle is zero correlation (no relationship whatever). The correlation of the win probabilities was +0.83, of the tie probabilities +0.78, and the loss probabilities +0.83. Not perfect, but extremely close.

This doesn't mean that wages predict *individual* games perfectly. Far from it—when it comes to single games, the model does not perform a whole lot better than a blind guess. Nonetheless, betting odds, which are likely the best estimate we can get, are very close to the simple wage model. Spending on players really does tell us something about likely results. But what exactly and why?

Let us first look at the limits of the model when it comes to individual games. Despite the high correlation between wages and bookmakers' odds, the amount that a club pays the collection of players who appear on the field, or the amount that it paid for them in the transfer market, will be of limited help in predicting individual outcomes. This is because there are so many factors that can determine the result of a single game of soccer, many of them random. Frequently, the most expensive team simply will not win. In the 2012/13 Premier League season, the most expensive team won 187 times, tied 108 times, and lost to the less expensive team 85 times. In other words, the most expensive team failed to win more than 50 percent of the time.

That said, having the most expensive team nonetheless represented a clear advantage. In fact, the more expensive team was more than twice as likely to win than the less expensive team. In bookmaker's terms, the pricier team is the clear favorite if there is to be a winner—with odds of around two to one—and the odds of coming out on top get better the more often you play. For example, suppose two teams with these odds play a best-of-three series, with no ties allowed—in that case, the probability that the more expensive team wins the series is 74 percent. If, as in national championship playoffs of American baseball and basketball, the teams play a best-of-five series, then the probability rises to 79 percent, and if, as in baseball's World Series, the teams played the best of seven, then the probability is 83 percent. Any advantage for one team gets amplified by repetition. If two unevenly matched teams play often enough, it becomes almost certain that the stronger team will win more often.

This is an example of the law of large numbers. The law of large numbers states simply this: if you repeat a game of chance often enough, the frequency of the outcome will equal the probability of that outcome in each game. So if the probability that the rich team wins is two thirds, then they will, provided they play enough games, end up winning two thirds of them. While the possible outcome of each *individual* game is hard to predict, the outcome over many games is hardly uncertain at all—and with enough repetition, probability becomes certainty. If the team that has the best players has the highest probability of winning, and the law of large numbers turns this probability into almost exactly that share of wins, then it will also be the most successful team in the league. With the law on your side, you are highly likely to win the championship.

This mechanism is very clearly at work in soccer leagues. Over the last twenty seasons, the team spending the most money on player wages won the Premier League nine times out of twenty, the club paying the second most won seven times, the team with the third-highest wage bill won three times. In 1993/94, Blackburn Rovers won with the fourth-highest wage bill. No team paying less than this has won the Premier League since then. In most countries, the teams paying the highest wages usually win the league. Consider for example the Scottish teams Celtic and Rangers (until the latter was expelled from the Scottish Premier League in 2012)—they've always been dominant and always the most expensive teams. It also works across leagues. UEFA conducted an analysis of the wage bills of clubs across fifty-two European national leagues and found that the club with the highest wage bill won the national title twenty-nine times (56 percent), the second highest wage bill won eleven times (21 percent), the third highest won four times (8 percent), and the rest won 15 percent of the time. Not quite a guarantee, but rather close.

BOX 2.1: CORRELATION IS NOT CAUSATION

There is a very high positive correlation between the wage spending of soccer clubs and their league position. But that just means that when one is high the other is also high; when one is low the other is also low. Causation—the claim that higher wage spending will inevitably lead to a higher league position—is not so easily proven. Indeed, identifying causation is one of the biggest problems in social science. Natural scientists design experiments in order to identify causation. In the trial of a new drug, researchers will administer the drug to some patients, and something that looks like the drug (a placebo, which does not contain the active ingredient) to other patients, all the time ensuring that the two groups of patients are broadly similar before the trial starts. By carefully controlling the experiment in this way the researchers can measure whether the drug has a significant causal impact.

This is not possible in most social situations, including competitive league soccer. We only observe what the clubs do, and even if we treat the results like experimental data, we cannot control the experiment. It is possible that clubs that spend more also do other things that make them successful, or they are especially receptive to the positive effect from spending. It might even be that the successful pay more—the extra money they generate from success is paid out as a reward to players. After all, players do receive win bonuses.

Now there are some statistical tests that one can implement in order to get a better idea about whether a relationship is causal. Some (but not all) of these studies support the view that causation runs from wage spending to league success. But in my view it's also important to have a theoretical model in mind—and it's very hard to develop an argument to explain the data that does not entail causality from wages to performance.

What do we know about the market for players? There are many buyers and sellers; there is a lot of information available about players—it's possible to observe performance over many games to get a good estimate of productivity—and there are large numbers of people working on making this assessment (not to mention fans voicing their opinions for nothing). These sound like the conditions required for a competitive market to operate, and so we should expect the better players to command higher wages.

Of course, this does not rule out mistakes, or simply loss of form. Moreover, this is not an argument about incentives—you cannot turn donkeys into superstars by paying them more money. But a bigger checkbook will get you access to the superstars.

The law of large numbers also helps to explain why leagues are so popular. League competition typically involves many games in a season. The Premier League involves 380 games among twenty clubs, each team playing thirty-eight games. The FA Cup in 2013/14 involved 737 teams in total and 736 games—each team played an average of only two games, and even the winners played only six games. A cup competition can engage many teams, but no one teams plays that often; a league competition involves fewer teams playing more games.

Historically, cup competition came before the league. The FA Cup started in 1872, while the Football League did not start up until 1888. Most countries have a national league and a national cup. The most important international competitions—the World Cup and the European Championship—are essentially cup competitions. But even these, along with the most important international club competition—the Champions League—have in recent years developed an element of league play, having started life as purely knockout (single-elimination) cup competitions.

A cup competition is exciting because every team is in danger of elimination in every game. In some ways, the high stakes and the ensuing drama are more entertaining for the fans. But in other ways, the outcomes can appear to be excessively random. There's something not quite perfect about winning a knockout competition—the fact that you didn't have to play all of the teams in the competition leaves matters somehow unsettled. It also can make a knockout seem to be arbitrary—though in reality it is much less arbitrary than it seems. Over the last twenty years, the highest spending team in England won the FA Cup seven times, the second highest spender won five times, the third highest spender twice, and the fourth highest spender three times. Of the remaining three, only Wigan Athletic (ranked twentieth in spending) in 2013 was lower than seventh in that category. This is a little more random than league competition, but not by much. The point is this: while the law of large numbers will not work for any one team in a cup competition, it tends to work in favor of the strong teams collectively—the chances of the winner coming from outside their ranks is almost as small in a cup competition as the chance of the winner of the league coming from outside the top three spenders.

Depending on how you view it, the law of large numbers either helps managers or just stops most of them from making any difference at all. In other words, club managers are like pension fund managers who pick stocks for portfolios. Anyone who has a pension scheme is aware that the money they save for retirement needs to be invested, and that historically the best returns on an investment have come from the stock market. For that reason you want to be invested in the stock market, but that is, of course, risky. If you don't know how markets work, then you had better leave the management of your investment to someone else.

Fund managers are experts who are familiar with markets and can invest your money on your behalf, just like a soccer manager chooses players on behalf of the team owners. Some fund managers claim that their skill at picking stocks is such that they can consistently obtain a better return than other fund managers. Academics have studied this proposition over and over for the last fifty years and have reached the general conclusion that this is not the case. Sure, if you invest $1 billion the annual income from your investment will be greater than if you invest $1 million. But there is very little evidence that any fund manager can invest your $1 billion (or $1 million) better than any other fund manager. The same reasoning applies quite closely to soccer.

Companies on the stock market are not unknown quantities. They are well-known businesses about which much information is available. You can look up their history, you can obtain financial accounts, and you read about them daily in the financial press. The only reason you would not be well informed about any particular company would be that you had not bothered to gather the available information. Thousands, maybe tens of thousands, of expert investors do gather the information and invest on the basis of what is known. Some companies offer very high returns but also carry considerable risk—for example, high tech companies. These businesses are often small, can quickly grow to be very big, but can just as easily fail to live up to expectations: high risk, high reward. Some companies are very safe—think of your local water company. No one is going to stop wanting to have water, but growth is going to be slow. These businesses offer low returns that are very safe.

Because these facts are obvious to almost everyone who invests, the prices that you pay to buy the stocks reflects the risks you take. You could, of course, invest all your money in one very risky stock, and possibly produce a phenomenal return—but then you might also lose your shirt. Most investors (and you should hope that whoever is investing your pension money is doing this) can reduce the risk by buying a collection of different stocks. This is essentially another example of the law of large numbers at work. You cannot eliminate all risk—if the market crashes, all stocks will suffer—but you can eliminate some risk by buying a balanced portfolio. In this way, you will also tend to perform in line with the market—and that is what most fund managers do. They might get lucky some years and perform above average, and they might be unlucky other years and perform below average, but over time almost all fund managers perform more or less in line with the market average.

BOX 2.2: THE MARKET FOR PLAYERS

The market for players has changed considerably in the last seventy years or so. After World War Two, most players were tied to their club by a contract that would not let them play for another professional team without their present club's permission. This restricted the mobility of players and restricted their bargaining power when negotiating wages. It also limited the sensitivity of wages to performance. In England there was a maximum wage fixed by the league until 1961, which tended to compress wages—so the sensitivity of performance to wages was low. From the 1960s onwards, players won more freedom of movement and more freedom to negotiate their wages, and so the sensitivity also increased.

From the 1950s, the international market for players also started to evolve. By the early-1980s there were so many cross-border movements that UEFA tried to limit player mobility by restricting the number of foreign players that could appear on European teams. This restriction was outlawed for European players by the Bosman judgment of the European Court of Justice in 1995. As a result, international mobility increased substantially. A 2013 survey of thirty-one European leagues by the International Sports Study Center (CIES) Football Observatory found that on average 36 percent of the players were foreigners, and in six leagues the figure was over 50 percent—including England and Italy.

As the market for players has become more global, one should also expect to see the phenomenon of talent compression—first noted by Stephen Jay Gould in relation to baseball. He observed that there were fewer players with extreme averages because as the talent pool became larger the differences between top players got smaller. To the extent that this is happening in soccer, we should expect to see the same difference in ability produce a larger wage differential than it did in the past because it has become more unusual. And it does indeed appear that the salary dispersion in professional soccer has been getting larger over time.

If you swap the word "player" for "stock," that is more or less what happens in the world of soccer management. Clubs perform in line with the amount of money spent on players. Sometimes clubs are above average, sometimes below average, but over time most clubs are very close to the average. The fact that a team contains eleven players already diversifies the choices of the manager—he should not be overexposed to the weaknesses of any one player. Then the number of games played in the league over a season diversifies the risk yet further—the rotation of the squad enhances the diversity of choice—and so the team performs in close correlation with what is spent on the players.

All this gives rise to some very basic facts about the way league soccer works. While every game entails a good deal of uncertainty, over time, the performance of a team can be predicted quite accurately by the amount it spends on its players. To demonstrate the validity of this claim, we need a good data source. Researchers on financial markets examine data for thousands of companies over many years in order to assess the performance of fund managers. The best data source in the world of soccer is to be found in the published financial accounts of around one hundred English soccer clubs. I have collected this data back to 1958, a fifty-six-season timespan, and in the rest of this book this data source will be used many times to analyze the relationship between financial performance and performance on the field.

Figures 2.1 to 2.3 illustrate the relationship between pay (the amount each team spends on wages, a figure that can be found in the financial accounts of each club) relative to the average spending of all other teams

FIGURE 2.1 **The wage performance relationship in England 1958–1975.** (Source: Club financial accounts)

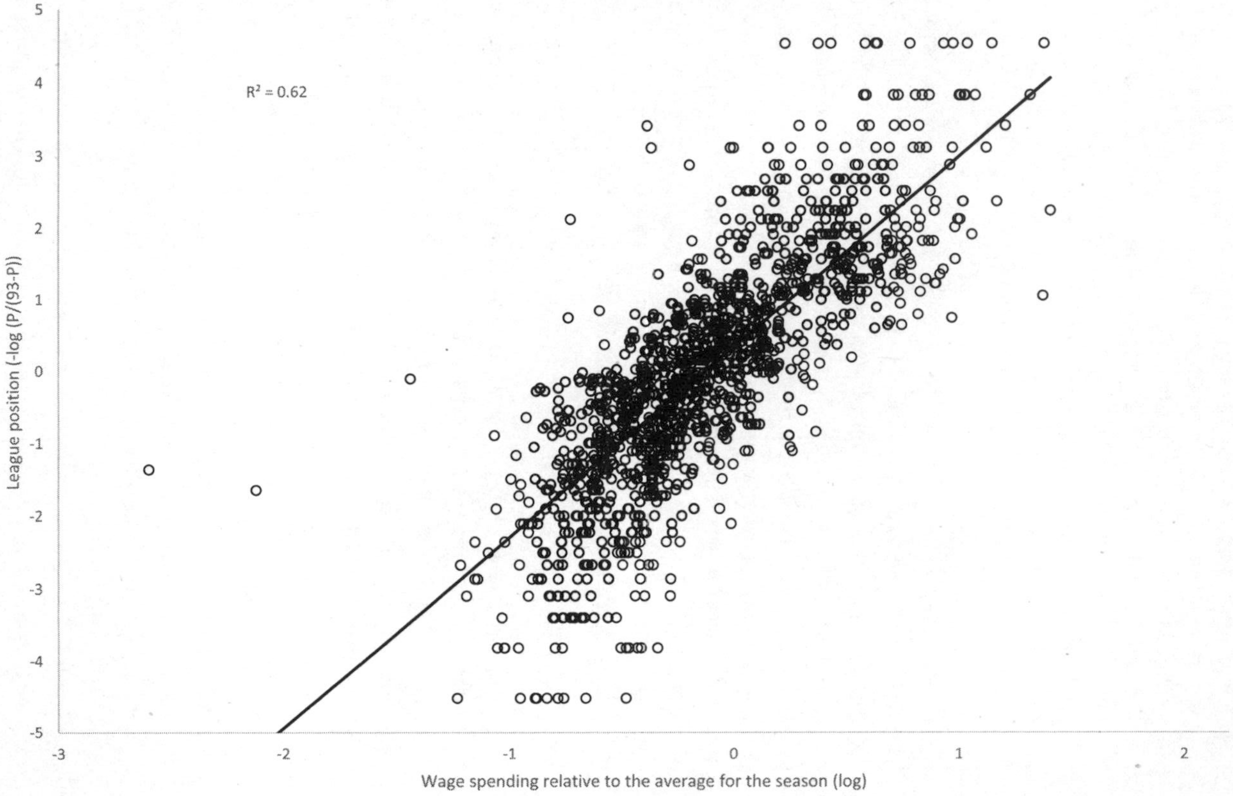
R² = 0.62
League position (-log (P/(93-P))
5
4
3
2
1
0
-1
-2
-3
-4
-5
-3
-2
-1
0
1
2
Wage spending relative to the average for the season (log)

FIGURE 2.2 The wage performance relationship in England 1976–1994. (Source: Club financial accounts)

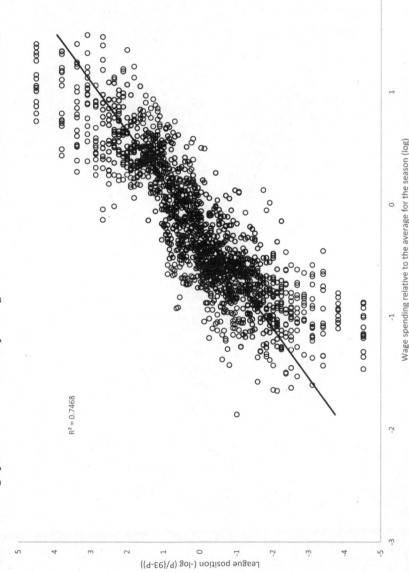

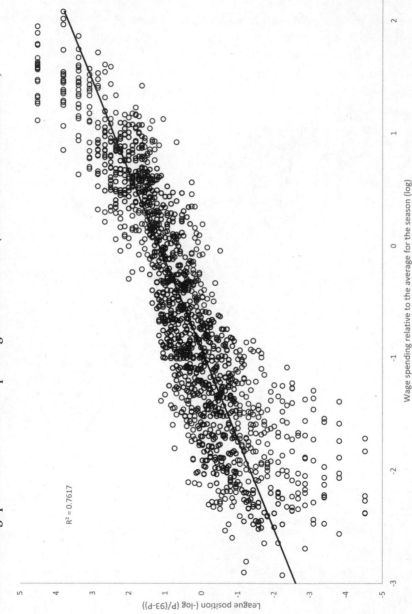

FIGURE 2.3 The wage performance relationship in England 1995–2013. (Source: Club financial accounts)

44

in the English leagues,[7] and performance, meaning the league position achieved. They do so for three discrete periods: 1958–1975, 1976–1994, and 1995–2013. These are really three distinct eras in English soccer. The first is the period when it started to go into economic decline, the second is the period of crisis, whose darkest days were in the mid-1980s, and the final period is the era of the Premier League (which started in 1992). On each of the charts, a circle represents the combination of wage spending and league position for a given club in a given year.

The relationship has been essentially the same over the entire period—the wages and league position of a club go in lock step. Although in each of the charts the dots are somewhat dispersed, they tend to cluster around a line going from the bottom left to top right. That line, known as the regression line, represents the best estimate of the relationship between wages and spending based on the data. In any given year, the performance of a team can be measured by the vertical distance from the regression line. Teams well above it have outperformed—done better than could have been expected on average given the resources at their command—while teams below the line have underperformed.

The closeness of the relationship is measured by the R^2 ("R squared"). This number must lie between zero and one. Zero means that none of the variation in position can be accounted for by the variation in wages. One means that 100 percent of the variation in position can be accounted for by wages. The R^2 in the 1958–75 period is 0.62. In the second period (1976–1994) it has increased significantly to 0.74, but in the Premier League period it has changed little, only a slight increase to 0.77. If money has become the root of club success, then the data shows that this has been the case for at least forty years.

BOX 2.3: DOCUMENTING THE
PAY PERFORMANCE LINE

The most complete source of data for estimating the pay performance line comes from England because English soccer club

CONTINUES

accounts are available for the four professional divisions going back for more than half a century. For other countries the data is more limited—both because there tend to be fewer professional clubs and because data does not go very far back in time, even if it is available.

In research with Thomas Peeters, we obtained some data for the top two divisions in France, Italy and Spain for around ten years. We found the relationship between wages and performance to be very similar.

The accounting data refers to the wages of all employees, not just the players, but for almost all soccer clubs the player wages account for the lion's share of wage expenditure.

In earlier research I have also looked at the relationship between player wages and team performance in American sports. In professional baseball the correlation between wages and team performance is also high, although not as a high as for the European soccer leagues.[1] In the case of American football there is almost no correlation, but this fact has a simple explanation. There is almost no variation in the player wage bills of NFL teams—they have both a cap on total spending and minimum spending limit. If wage bills do not vary between teams, then wages cannot explain the performance of teams, which obviously does vary.

1. Hall, Stephen, Stefan Szymanski, and Andrew S. Zimbalist. "Testing causality between team performance and payroll: The cases of major league baseball and English soccer." *Journal of Sports Economics* 3.2 (2002): 149-168.

These figures leave plenty of scope for factors other than wages to affect performance, especially just plain old luck (good or bad). They leave room for the effect of management, culture, history, and so on. But nothing is bigger than spending, and most of the other factors are likely to have a relatively small impact compared to wages. To a large degree, the effect of luck can be eliminated by simply averaging the performance of each club over time. When dealing with pure luck, there should be as much good luck as bad luck, and if one takes an average, then the positive and the negative should cancel each other out. This can be seen in Figure 2.4, which averages the performance of each club over all fifty-six

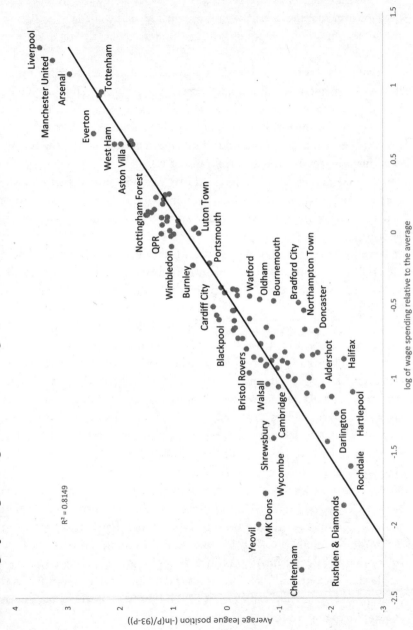

FIGURE 2.4 Wage spending and English soccer on average. (Source: Club financial accounts)

years of the data. Now the R^2 rises to a remarkable 0.81. Remarkable because over more than half a century, with so many changes in regime, the most important factor, on average, seems to be the total amount spent on the players.

These relationships can also be illustrated using only the more recent data and looking only at the English Premier League. Figures 2.5 and 2.6 include only Premier League clubs over the decade 2003–2012. In Figure 2.5, the dots seem very dispersed, but when we average each of the clubs over the decade, they are clustered much more closely around the regression line, and the R^2 increases from 0.61 to 0.90.

Once again, we are looking at an instance of the law of large numbers at work—when we consider each individual game, relative wages can account for only 5 to 10 percent of the variation in the outcome— less expensive teams always have a good chance of pulling off a tie (especially at home) and even a win. But the season irons out these effects. For example, there is no home advantage when you take the season as a whole—every team plays the same number of home and away games.

And we can go further. The relationship between money and success can at times look less strong than it is because a whole season can rest on the wellbeing of a single player. Manchester United famously won the Premier League title in the last season of Sir Alex Ferguson's tenure, and in the following season slumped to seventh under his chosen successor, David Moyes. No doubt much of this change of fortunes can be associated with the presence and absence of the great man. But a less commonly observed point is this: in the 2012/13 season Robin van Persie played in all thirty-eight league games and scored twenty-six goals, while in 2013/14 he was injured and so ended up playing only twenty-one games and scoring only twelve goals. It's not inconceivable that the club's results would have been reversed if Van Persie had been fit in 2013/14 and injured in 2012/13. We cannot be sure, but it is not hard to see that highly specific factors such as these can have a big effect on a single club's season and therefore upset the relationship between pay and performance—after all, Van Persie's pay in each season would have been roughly the same.

FIGURE 2.5 Premier League position and wage spending relative to the average 2003–2012. (Source: Club financial accounts)

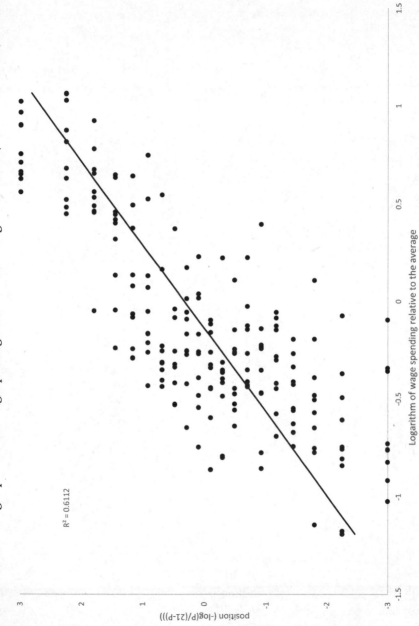

FIGURE 2.6 Premier League position and wage spending relative to the average 2003–2012 (clubs with four seasons or more in the league) (Source: Club financial accounts)

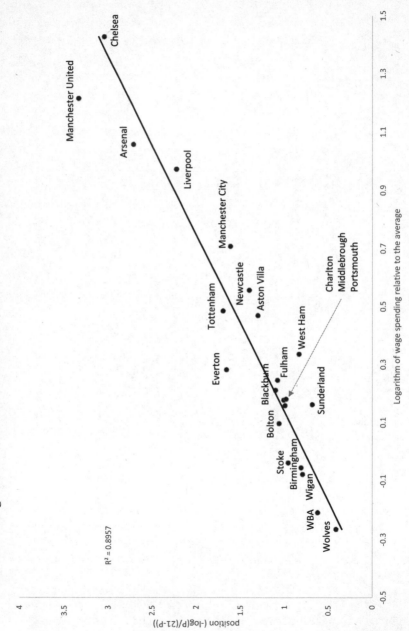

But once we move to the long term—a period of a decade—the relationship between spending and performance approaches perfection; 90 percent of the variation in the average league position of a club over time is explained by the amount spent relative to the other teams, on average. This does not mean that spending guarantees championships, but that wage spending dominates in any explanation of the relative status of clubs over time. High-spending clubs seem inevitably to achieve higher positions on average and low-spending clubs seem condemned to lower positions on average.

Over this particular decade, for example, Chelsea consistently spent high amounts and Fulham consistently spent low amounts—so their relative position on average has remained stable throughout. Manchester City, by contrast, was a relatively low-spending club until the takeover by Abu Dhabi's Sheikh Mansour bin Zayed Al Nahyan in 2008, which turned it into the highest spending club in the Premier League. When it was a low-spending club, it achieved low positions, and when it became a high spending club, it achieved higher positions—indeed, winning the league in 2011/12, and then again in 2013/14.

BOX 2.4: THE POWER OF MONEY

There is no better example of the power of spending in soccer than the performance of Chelsea and Manchester City over the last decade. Chelsea was acquired by Roman Abramovich in 2003 and City by Sheikh Mansour in 2008. The charts plot the relationship between each club's annual wage spending (relative to the league average) and its league position since 1958. Over this period each club has moved up and down a lot, both winning the Premier League and both experiencing relegation to a lower division. Chelsea's worst position was eighteenth in the second division in 1983, City's was third in the third tier as recently as 1999.

Both charts illustrate a fairly reliable relationship between wage spending and league position. Sixty-six-percent of the variation of Chelsea's position over the period can be accounted for

CONTINUES

by its wage spending. The cluster of points in the top right-hand corner show the three titles won and four second places achieved with Abramovich's money. At no other time in the club's history has it been able to outspend its rivals by so much.

The picture for Manchester City is even starker—the last five seasons represent the highest spending compared to the average in the club's history, and by some margin. However, the correlation between relative wage spending and league position is not as high as it is for Chelsea due to a single outlier—the league title win in 1968. Manchester City was not a favorite to win the title that year and the club ranked only seventh in wage spending. If that outlier were to be taken out, the R^2 would rise by ten percentage points. Only five teams have won with lower relative wage spending, three times before 1968 and then in 1970 and 1975. No winner of the Premier League has ranked lower than fourth in wage spending.

Manchester City 1958-2013. (Source: Club financial accounts)

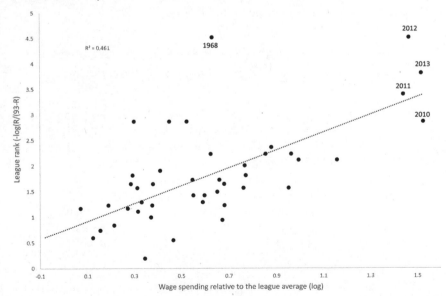

Chelsea 1958-2013. (Source: Club financial accounts)

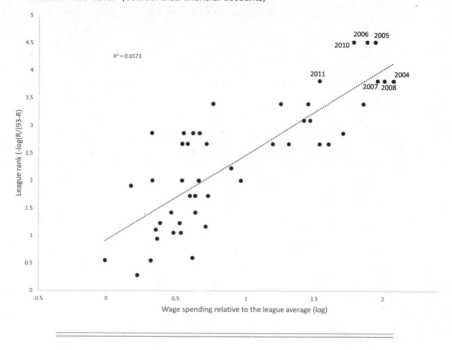

This is exactly like looking at the performance of stock prices over time. If we look at a collection of risky firms (i.e., those which tend to have very large variations in annual performance), they will tend to have higher returns on average than those firms that have relatively stable returns over time. This is the risk reward trade-off of modern portfolio theory. The centerpiece of this theory is the capital market line—which relates the expected return of any portfolio of assets to their riskiness. Investors can identify their optimal portfolio by simply working out the capital market line and then choosing the level of risk that they wish to bear. Essentially, investors can choose to be at any point they want along the line. Likewise any soccer club can choose to be at any point on the regression line depending on how much it is willing to spend. Just like the capital market line, the pay-performance line works because there *is* a market—in the former case, the market prices the relationship between risk and reward, in the latter case the relationship between player talent and success.

BOX 2.5: MEASURING PERFORMANCE

One of the great paradoxes of soccer is that while in the long run the correlation between spending and performance is very close, in the short term, performance seems very unpredictable. Not only does performance seem highly variable, but analysts have also struggled to find good measures to quantify individual performance in the way that they have in baseball and, at least to some extent, in basketball. Many statistically minded soccer fans are searching for the "*Moneyball* moment"—the killer stat that enables a team to outperform the market.

There is good reason to search—we know that humans are subject to "cognitive biases," rules of thumb in decision-making, which lead us to systematically under- or overestimate ability. For example, the bandwagon effect, where we tend to believe something just because others believe it, or optimism bias—many humans tend to believe things will turn out better than they actually do. A *Moneyball* moment would overturn some widely believed but ultimately unsupported bias in the industry.

So far, the results have not been encouraging. There are now enormous amounts of data available—often millions of individual items for a single game. But because we are usually interested in things that happen very infrequently—one or two goals in a game—we face the problem of overdetermination: the data is consistent with almost an unlimited number of possible explanations. If we had hundreds of millions of games and a big enough computer the data might be able to resolve this, but while there are thousands of games played every year at the highest level, this is still in fact too few to cope with all the data we have. Books such as Chris Anderson and David Sally's *The Numbers Game* have pointed to statistics that seem important—but there is little to guarantee that reproducing these statistical patterns will win games.

Some researchers have focused on relatively simple metrics —such as Gerrard's shots on goal.[1] And while it is true that teams that shoot more often tend to win more often, you probably didn't need a detailed statistical analysis to know it.

Another interesting approach is to model the outcome of the game as a function of the contribution of individual players, on the theory that players who are on the field when goals are scored must be contributing to that outcome. The Goalimpact blog run by Jörg Seidl contains a good explanation of this approach.

In recent years, many professional clubs have hired statisticians who work to produce information in preparation for games. Ironically, there is no easy way to measure the performance contribution of these analysts. Before modern sciences such as physics and chemistry became the rigorous disciplines they are today they were synonymous with alchemy—a strange mix of experimentation and mysticism. It may be that performance analytics in soccer is still at the alchemy stage today.

1. Gerrard, Bill, "Is the *Moneyball* approach transferable to complex invasion team sports?" *International Journal of Sport Finance* 2.4 (2007): 214–230.

Does all this sound too good to be true? Well, I am certainly not suggesting that anybody can obtain any given result with perfect certainty. Moreover, nothing says that a club might not run out of money when trying to buy success. Over recent years, Chelsea and Manchester City have demonstrated rather convincingly that monumental spending is an effective formula for winning championships. But being the most expensive team cannot *guarantee* you the championship. Recall that all the things I have said about the relationship between success and spending are only true on average and over time. Neither fans, players, nor owners tend to celebrate their achievements *on average*—the joy of success is always specific.[8]

3

STADIUMS

WHILE THE ESSENCE OF RUNNING A SOCCER CLUB IS THE PROCESS of investing in players, a club is also synonymous with its stadium in the minds of the fans. Like the players, the stadium is an investment, but obviously one that is much longer term. A player contract is typically for three years, while the expected life of a stadium is usually assumed to be around forty years—and it often lasts much longer than that before being rebuilt. The question, then, is what can the stadium—in particular its size—tell us about the success of the club?

Most people are familiar with the line from the baseball film *Field of Dreams*: "If you build it they will come."[1] In this beautiful (if somewhat schmaltzy) movie, a farmer builds a baseball stadium in the middle of cornfields, and by the end of the movie people are coming from miles around to watch baseball being played there. This notion corresponds to a decidedly unromantic economic proposition known as "Say's Law," which is often stated in the form: "Supply creates its own demand." Jean-Baptiste Say, an eighteenth century French economist, asserted not exactly this, but something that more or less amounts to this.[2] For more than two hundred years, economists have argued the validity of his claim. The essence of the proposition is that the act of building a stadium (supply) will give rise to payments to suppliers and workers who carry out the construction. When they spend their income, this will in turn create demand for products and services. Some of that demand will be channeled into buying tickets to watch games played at the stadium. So, indirectly, the building (the supply) of the stadium has created demand, including the demand for its own services.

The South Africa World Cup of 2010 exposes one problem with the theory. Of the ten stadiums used for the competition, five were built from scratch, each with an average capacity of nearly 50,000. Yet today the average attendance in the South African Premier League is a mere 6,722 per game. This is a lower number than the average attendance in the year before the World Cup (which was 7,639). They have built them, but no one has come. The very fact that the stadiums are so empty is off-putting for fans—in this case, supply actually seems to be destroying demand.

However, the South African case is something of an exception. With the economist Bastien Drut, I examined attendance in domestic leagues following six World Cups and four European championships and found that average attendance increased in the top division in each host country by 15 to 20 percent. And the effect was a lasting one—it persisted for at least five years after the event. By far the largest effect was at the stadiums of clubs that hosted games in the World Cup—either in stadiums that were specially built or had been refurbished for the event. There have been a number of studies that have identified the "honeymoon effect," the tendency for attendance to increase at newly built stadiums. For example, Christopher Clapp and Jahn Hakes found that attendance increased by between 32 and 37 percent in the year that a new baseball stadium opened in the United States, with the effect persisting for six to ten seasons.[3]

Stadium size is important for a club because it has a large effect on the team's potential. Larger stadiums can accommodate more fans and generate more revenue. On the other hand, investing in a large stadium is expensive and if the fans do not come then the stadium can become a white elephant. It's not an easy decision to make.

In the English Premier League, the average stadium capacity is more than 37,000; in the Championship it is 26,000; in Football League One (third tier) it is 16,000; and in Football League Two (fourth tier) it is 11,000. But more successful clubs also use more of their capacity. The Premier League sells over 90 percent of its seats each season. In the second tier,

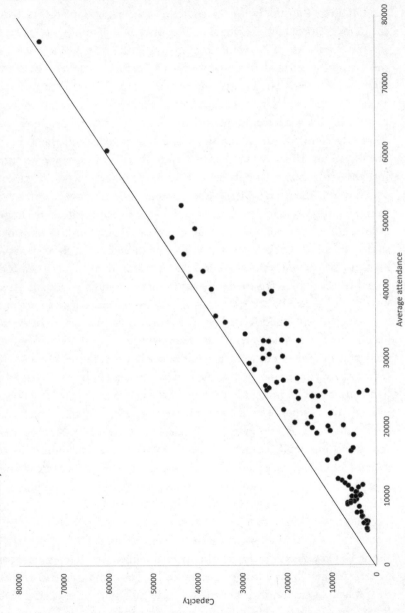

FIGURE 3.1 Attendance and stadium capacity Premier League and Football League 2009/10. (Source: Sky Sports Football Yearbook)

only 68 percent of the seats are sold, 54 percent in the third tier, and 39 percent in the fourth. The relationship between capacity and seats sold is shown in Figure 3.1. The closer clubs are to the diagonal line, the more of their capacity they are using.

The graph shows that clubs with smaller capacity also tend to use less of the capacity that they have. There is also a high correlation between stadium capacity and success measured by league position. If we call the top of the Premier League "rank 1" and bottom "rank 20," and then label the top of the Football League Championship "rank 21" and the bottom "rank 44," and so on down the third and fourth tiers (so that the lowest rank is 92), then the correlation between capacity and league rank in any given year is about -0.75 (there is a minus sign because rank 1 is a high rank but a low number and rank 92 is a low rank but a high number. The larger the rank number, the lower the stadium capacity). Teams with big stadiums tend to do well.

Correlation, yes, but surely not causation. If that were the case then the "build it and they will come" theory would really work—you would just build a larger stadium, attract lots of fans, and have the money to spend on a successful team. It is spending money on attracting a high-quality collection of players that determines success, and the amount spent is highly correlated with stadium capacity—also around +0.75 (a plus, this time, because higher wages go with higher capacity). Again, this is not a causal relationship. Higher wage spending doesn't cause you to have a big stadium, and having a big stadium doesn't cause you to pay high wages. Rather, a club has to be in position where it can successfully fund the maintenance of both a big stadium and high quality squad. This depends in part on the local market conditions and in part on what all the clubs are doing.

You need two things to have a successful team: good players and a large stadium. In a world where there are many teams and few good players, the talent that you need to win will be priced accordingly. To cover the costs of wages you will need a large stadium to hold the fans who pay to watch their team. Large stadiums also cost a lot to build and, something people often forget, a lot to maintain. If you borrow money to build the stadium you will need to pay your debt out of the money coming in from the fans.

So why doesn't everybody just build a very large stadium and have lots of fans and a very successful team? The ultimate problem is attracting the fans. Your club needs to be located in a place where there are large numbers of people interested in soccer who are willing to follow you. And they need to be nearby. For example, research on English soccer by David Forrest, Rob Simmons, and Patrick Feehan has shown that most fans travel from within a ten-mile radius of the stadium.[4]

The most obvious requirement, therefore, is to be located in a large city (this is the economic weakness in the *Field of Dreams* proposition and the location of several of the South African stadiums).[5] Almost all of the successful teams around the world are located in, if not *the* largest, then one of the largest cities in the country in which they play. This is true whether we are talking about Real Madrid (Madrid's population of 3.2 million is 7 percent of the population of Spain's 47.7 million) or HB Tórshavn (the population of Tórshavn is 18,000, which amounts to 36 percent of all Faroe Islanders). Manchester, Munich, and Milan are not the largest cities in their respective countries, but they are among the largest metropolitan regions.

Teams based in smaller towns still build the largest stadium that they can afford, but there is little point in building a stadium whose size is greater than the population of the city.[6] There is a clear correlation between the number of people living within a given distance of a stadium (e.g., five to ten miles), the size of the stadium, the spending on players by the team, and the success of the team.

The correlation between city size and dominance is powerful. In smaller countries the dominant teams usually come from the largest cities—such as Olympiakos, Panathinkaikos, and AEK Athens in Greece; Celtic and Rangers in Scotland; Ajax in the Netherlands; and Galatasaray, Fenerbahce, and Besiktas in Turkey. All these teams hail from the nation's largest city. In Portugal, two of the three dominant teams come from the capital (Benfica and Sporting) and the other (Porto) comes from the second largest city. For larger nations the pattern is more mixed—but Madrid and Barcelona are the two largest cities in Spain, while Milan (Inter and AC Milan) and Turin (Torino and Juventus) are the second and fourth largest metropolitan areas in Italy. In England, eighty-seven out of 115 league titles (76 percent) since 1888 have been won by clubs from the five largest metropolitan areas: London, Greater Manchester, the West Midlands, West Yorkshire, and Liverpool.[7] In Germany—perhaps the most decentralized of all the major European nations—the thirteen largest cities have carried off forty-two out of fifty-one Bundesliga titles (82 percent), despite accounting for only 16 percent of the present German population. Six of the thirteen cities have not won one, and Munich alone accounts for twenty-three, so within the dominant group there are large variations. Being a large city is not sufficient to have a strong soccer club. Nor is it necessary, but it does seem pretty unlikely without it.

This correlation is not perfect. Munich has a smaller population than Berlin, but Bayern plays in the Allianz Arena, which now has a slightly higher capacity for league matches than the Olympic Stadium in which Hertha BSC plays. More importantly, Bayern (twenty-three Bundesliga titles) is much more successful than Hertha (none). Rome has a larger population than Milan, but Milan's Stadio Giuseppe Meazza, in which both Inter and AC Milan play, is larger than the Stadio Olimpico in which AS Roma and Lazio play; and the Milan clubs (thirty-six titles) have been far more successful than the two Roman clubs (five). Marseille is smaller than Paris, but Olympique Marseille's stadium is much larger than Paris Saint-Germain's, and until recently they have been much more successful (ten titles against four). Liverpool and Manchester are much smaller than London, but the combined capacity of the Liverpool, Everton, City, and United stadiums is 215,000, almost 25-percent larger than the combined capacities of London's four largest club stadiums (Arsenal, Chelsea, Tottenham Hotspur, and West Ham United). The two northern cities have also won fifty-one national titles compared to only nineteen for the Londoners.[8]

BOX 3.1: MARKET SIZE AND COMPETITIVE OUTCOME

In a paper published in 2007, Tunde Buraimo, David Forrest, and Rob Simmons[1] analyzed the relevance of the market size of a club to its success in English league competition. They used census

CONTINUES

data from 2001 to measure the number of fans within a five- and ten-mile radius of each stadium. They found this was highly correlated with the club's league position, although in densely populated cities where the catchment areas of clubs overlap, this effect was slightly diminished.

Of course, they acknowledged that market size cannot directly cause a club to win, so they hypothesized a model in which market size created revenue (more fans), revenue funded higher wages, and higher wages ensured better league performance. This last relationship was discussed in the previous chapter, and the revenue-performance relationship will be discussed in the next chapter.

Their analysis found that there were powerful correlations in all three stages of the model, but as with all such models there is a problem of causality. My own view is that the first link is the weakest to justify in its own right—putting a team in a large city does not guarantee large revenues (consider, for example, smaller London teams such as Leyton Orient and Brentford). However, in the context of John Sutton's model of competition, a large market ensures that a club can support a wage bill that will generate league success. However, this is only a slight difference in interpretation—the important point is that these correlations are very powerful.

1. Buraimo, B., Forrest, D., and Simmons, R. (2007) "Freedom of entry, market size and competitive outcome: evidence from English soccer." *Southern Economic Journal* 74 (1): 204–213.

There are two reasons for these exceptions. Firstly, much depends on culture. Professional soccer was always much more popular in the industrial centers of northern Italy, southern France, and northwest England than in those countries' capitals, Rome, Paris, and London. Berlin suffered from being a divided city just at the time when professional soccer was developing in West Germany. These are accidents of history—there is no iron logic of sport and capitalism that says that the bigger city gets the bigger stadium and the bigger team, and it is not so everywhere. But there are also many capital cities whose clubs dominate their nation, including Madrid, Lisbon, Athens, Istanbul—and Tórshavn—which have all produced one or more dominant teams from the capital city. A city with a smaller population can produce a dominant team if that city can supply enough fans. Moreover, intense support, once it has developed, tends to last for a very long time. Once a city has an established soccer culture and had a successful team with a large stadium for some period, the support tends to persist, even if the club experiences a period in the doldrums. Perhaps Manchester City is the best example—a club that struggled to compete with cross-town rivals for decades, and yet still retained an intensely loyal fan base, which has ultimately been rewarded with the injection of riches from Abu Dhabi.

The second reason why city size and team success do not correlate perfectly in soccer is that there is no geographic restriction on club locations. London is a big city but it also has a lot of professional soccer teams, among which support is divided. Imagine that every city was permitted only a single team. In such a world it would be likely that the largest cities would be able to finance the largest stadiums, the largest spending on players, and produce the most successful teams—and consequently generate the largest amount of revenue. As it is, Arsenal has to compete for fans with neighboring Tottenham, West Ham has to compete for fans with Millwall, and Chelsea has to compete with Fulham. Smaller cities also tend to have more than one team, but generally the larger the city, the greater the number of its professional soccer teams.

At this stage, the reader will be asking a number of questions: What about TV money and sponsorship? What about rich individuals who pour money into a club in order to make it successful? And, ultimately, what about teams that overinvest and cannot pay their bills? The world I have described here fits more exactly with the way that the finance of soccer clubs worked up until about 1990 (i.e., for more than a century in England, and more than half a century in most of Europe and South America). Without question, television changed the economic structure of soccer in some fundamental ways. However, the long-established patterns have not changed. Setting aside a few peculiar examples—such as TSG 1899 Hoffenheim, a German team based in a village of 3,300 people that has played in the Bundesliga since 2008—the big, successful clubs have continued to be those from the larger cities. The dominance that is characteristic of soccer has changed very little, and the identity of the dominant clubs has been largely unchanged. But before going on to look at the revenue breakdown, I want to consider the cost of the stadium in more detail.

It costs a lot to build a stadium. Depending on how grand you want it to be you can work from a basic figure of between $1,600 and $3,200 per seat—so a stadium with a 20,000 capacity might cost between $32 million and $64 million. At the luxury end of the market, Arsenal's Emirates Stadium cost around $10,400 per seat. So suppose a club borrowed the money to build an entirely new stadium, how would the finances work? It would depend on a number of factors, but you can get the basic idea by thinking about the following:

- The cost per seat built
- The interest rate paid on the money borrowed
- The life of the stadium
- The number of tickets sold
- The average revenue from each ticket

Let's imagine the club's ambition is to be a fairly consistent team playing in the second tier of English soccer. A reasonable target would be an average gate of 15,000 for which a capacity of 20,000 would be sensible. At a modest price of $2,400 per seat, the construction cost would be $48 million and the expected stadium life should be around 40 years. If the funds for this long-term investment can be borrowed at an interest rate of 5 percent, we can work out how much the club would have to repay every year. This calculation is just like the mortgage on a house—every year your debt accumulates interest, and every year you have to pay back enough to cover that interest plus a little bit so that the debt diminishes over time. To pay off $48 million over 40 years would require an annual payment of about $2.8 million (for the sake of argument I'm ignoring the effect of inflation here).

Given that the team might play thirty home games in a season (say twenty-four in the league and the remainder in cup games) this amounts to 450,000 tickets sold every season. Then for every ticket sold the club would need to pay $6.20 to the lender. In the 2011/12 season, the average revenue of English Championship clubs was $32 million, so this level of debt would amount to 10 percent of revenue for an average club—and for some clubs significantly more. Over the last twenty years, the median wage spending of a second-tier club has been 78 percent of its revenues.[9]

So, in order to finance a stadium, about half of the club's revenue left after paying wages would typically need to be spent on servicing stadium debt. Clubs have operating expenses other than wages, not least those of maintaining the stadium itself. These other costs are likely to amount to at least 20 percent of revenue. Already, it seems, a stadium cannot be financed out of revenues generated by a club operating in the second tier. And there are further risks: revenues tend to decline when performance is poor, not only because fewer fans turn up for each game, but also because there are likely to be fewer cup games.

There are many complicating factors left out of this equation. Taxation is complex, but generally the tax system will work in favor of capital investments such as stadium building, so that the after-tax cost would probably be lower. On the other hand, a stadium cannot usually be built in a year, and any gap between borrowing the money and starting repayments will add to the interest burden.

But the most important issue in thinking about the financing is the risk entailed in the system of promotion and relegation. Premier League clubs have revenue that is about five times larger than Championship teams. Going lower down, Football League One clubs have revenues that are less than half that of Championship clubs. Relegated teams face a near impossible situation—they have to cut back spending on players in any case, but if they prune too much then they will get relegated again and see their revenues cut in half again. Halving annual revenues would mean that debt repayments alone would account for about 20 percent of revenues. The temptation is to borrow yet more in order to maintain player spending as far as possible, in the hope that promotion will ensue. Well-run clubs might use the windfall of promotion to accelerate the repayment of their debts and insulate themselves against rockier times that might lie ahead, but that is not always easy given the pressures to invest in a team that can compete at the highest level.

Without promotion and relegation, the financing of the stadium looks difficult, but feasible. With promotion, and especially relegation, it looks extremely risky. All lending involves risk but lenders usually try to insure themselves against the risk that the borrower will be unable to repay their debt by taking security over the asset. Taking security means that if repayments are not made on time, the lender can seize the asset that the borrower invested in and sell it off to someone else in order to recover what they are owed. Better still, the lenders can take security over the entire business of the borrower, so that if debts are unpaid they can take over the entire business and sell it off to take what they are owed.

Which finally brings us to the question of what a stadium is worth. The only time anyone really wants to know the answer to this question is when a club cannot repay its debts, and the creditors step in to recover their money. If the club were able to repay the money it owed, it would essentially be worth whatever revenue could be generated by selling tickets, less the cost of paying the players and the costs of administering the club. But if the club cannot repay its debt because there is nothing left after paying salaries and operating costs, does this mean that at this point the stadium is worthless? The answer must be yes—*so long as* the stadium continues to be used for the purpose of operating a soccer club.

And here is where we encounter perhaps the fundamental difference between soccer clubs and ordinary businesses. Failures of this kind are typical in all kinds of businesses, and lenders step in all the time to recover their money when these businesses can't repay their debts, but mostly these businesses do not continue to operate. Instead, they are closed down, and the assets sold off individually and used for completely different purposes, realizing some return for the creditors. But in soccer that almost never happens. Not that there would not be plenty of alternative uses for the stadium—or at least for the land on which the stadium stands. Because most stadiums are in large towns or cities (and often in the center of these towns and cities), it would be easy to tear down the stadium and redevelop the land to build houses or a supermarket. If the stadium were auctioned off on this basis it would be quite likely that the lenders would get back almost all of the money that they were owed. But in the world of soccer this almost never happens. As the soccer sociologist Rogan Taylor famously said, no one ever asked for their ashes to be scattered in a supermarket. Soccer grounds are hallowed grounds, and religion trumps economics.

In most developed countries there is a planning system for the uses of land. You can't build a skyscraper or start digging for oil in your backyard unless you comply with the planning regulations, and these tend to impose fairly strict controls. This makes sense: cities need a certain amount of logic and order to function properly, and unregulated use of land can create an enormous nuisance for neighbors. Towns and cities are places where large numbers of people live very close to each other, and without a system of rules and restraints they would be in danger of descending into chaos. Any plan to significantly change the use of a plot of land requires planning permission. Planning systems are administered by local politicians, who depend on voters for their position. The political status of the land—how people feel about its current use, and how they might feel about any new use—matters a great deal. A large proportion of voters generally like soccer, and their own local club in particular. Usually, it would be political suicide to allow a local soccer stadium to be turned into a supermarket—and indeed this almost never happens.

So if a club cannot repay the loans used to fund its stadium, and the stadium cannot be sold off for use in some alternative business, then what is the stadium worth? The answer seems to be "precisely nothing"—at least to anyone who lent money to have it built in the first place. This might seem paradoxical, but remember we are only talking about value in the sense that something can be bought and sold, and what someone might be willing to pay in order to buy it. I wouldn't put my life savings into buying the stadium of a failing soccer club because I could never expect it to return any money to me. But that does not make it worthless to the fans who go to watch soccer in that stadium—they may value it very highly, in the way that one might value a local park that is going to be turned into new houses, or a historic monument that is about to be demolished to make way for a highway. You might value these things but not be willing to pay enough to prevent the land use being changed. Soccer fans generally have the guarantee that the use of the land on which their stadium is built will not be allowed to change, which makes the stadium practically worthless to anyone else if the soccer club cannot cover its costs.[10]

BOX 3.2: UEFA ON STADIUMS

The UEFA *Club Licensing Benchmarking Report,* published annually since 2008, provides a valuable insight into the finances of

CONTINUES

European soccer. It has published a lot of information about stadiums—here are some of the key findings based on the 600 to 700 clubs that play in the top divisions of the fifty-four UEFA member associations:

- Only 17 percent of clubs own their own stadium, while 66 percent are municipally owned (i.e., by the local government). The remainder are not directly owned by the club but the club often has some interest in the business that owns it (as is the case, for example, in Germany). Only in Britain, Norway, and Spain is direct ownership the most common form (2008 Report).
- Clubs that own their own stadium have "significantly larger" gate receipts. Of the top fifty clubs in Europe by gate receipts, twenty-seven clubs owned their stadium, seven had an indirect interest, and only sixteen were municipally owned (2009 Report).
- The average stadium age is forty-seven years. Out of 447 top division club stadiums, 214 were older than fifty years, 131 were between twenty and fifty years old, and 102 were less than twenty years old. However, stadiums had been subject to significant investment on average only seven years earlier (2009 Report).
- Only 50 percent of stadium capacity was covered, 88 percent of capacity was seated, and only 3 percent used artificial turf (2009 Report).
- The average capacity of top division clubs was 18,000. UEFA broke down the capacity into different ranges:

More than 50,000-	35 (7%)
40-50,000-	17 (3%)
30-40,000-	44 (8%)
15-30,000-	157 (29%)
8-15,000-	124 (23%)
3-8,000	119 (22%)
Less than 3,000-	45 (8%)

Source 2009 Report

- Only three associations had capacity utilization in excess of 80 percent (England, the Netherlands, and Germany). Twelve had capacity utilization of 50 to 80 percent, eighteen were between 30 and 50 percent, and sixteen were below 30 percent. The average capacity utilization was 48 percent—so, on average, stadiums in Europe are half empty. The highest utilization was the Premier League at 92 percent (2009 Report).

- Stadiums account for the largest share of fixed assets owned by clubs, but given that relatively few clubs own their stadiums, the ownership of fixed assets is concentrated in the hands of relatively few clubs. Out of 665 top division clubs, 60 percent of the fixed assets were accounted for by just twenty clubs (2010 Report).

Who would choose to invest in something that might turn out to be worthless? Nobody who expects to turn a profit. If we look at the history of stadium investment around the world the most common answer is: "the government." It is not just in soccer that public subsidy has been the preferred method. In the free markets of the United States, taxpayers have subsidized the construction of stadiums for professional sports teams in baseball and football to the tune of $30 billion or so over last two decades.[11] While the United States has some of the most profitable sports businesses in the world (which we will discuss in chapter 9), these same businesses have nonetheless claimed that without a public subsidy they would not be able to repay the cost of construction. Skeptical economists have pointed out that these subsidies are not really necessary, and that often the teams are blackmailing local politicians by threatening to relocate to another city (relocation is accepted, if not liked, in American sports). In many cases, governments have held referenda allowing voters to have their say, and often enough the voters have been willing to pay for the stadium. In each of the major sports there are only thirty or so franchises to serve the hundred or so metropolitan areas in the United States with populations exceeding one million people. When demand exceeds supply by this much, blackmail pays.

Another non-profit source of investment in stadiums in the United States is a university. The third largest stadium in the world, after North Korea's 150,000 May Day Stadium and India's Salt Lake Stadium (120,000), is the University of Michigan's "Big House" (110,000), followed closely by the stadiums of Penn State, Texas A&M, Ohio State,

Tennessee, Louisiana State, Alabama, and Texas—all over 100,000. These stadiums now tend to seem somewhat dated. They are often very simple bowl arrangements, open to the elements and somewhat daunting to attend at the end of November when winter is setting in. Nonetheless, they are almost always sold out. They have also been the driving force behind alumni giving and the massive endowments that these universities generate (Michigan $8 billion, Ohio State and Penn State $3 billion each). The directors of the universities' athletic programs are responsible for managing all sports, but focus primarily on gridiron and basketball. These people tend to describe the stadium as the front door to the university. And there is statistical evidence to show that when the football team does well, endowments and enrollments really do increase.[12]

In the rest of the world, the main source of funding for soccer stadiums has been the government. According to UEFA, around two thirds of the stadiums of clubs playing in the top divisions in Europe (some 700 clubs) are owned by municipal authorities. In the lower divisions the proportion is almost certainly larger. It would be hard to overstate how much this acts as a guarantee of survival for most clubs. The municipal government is extremely unlikely to go bankrupt and have to sell off the stadium for redevelopment. Even if it did decide to sell off the land on which a stadium was built, the deal would almost certainly entail providing another home for the team. Moreover, as owners, the municipal authorities usually contribute most of the funding for construction and maintenance.

Most soccer stadiums are old. Across the world, many clubs play in structures that were built more than fifty years ago, and in Britain many are more than one hundred years old. Back in those early days, both governments and private investors were optimistic that the stadium would prove to be a profitable investment, even if subsequent experience showed that this was rarely the case. Since those early days, the owners of stadiums have tended to pay for renovations only when it became absolutely necessary, knowing that these investments would rarely pay back. This state of affairs led to a number of stadium disasters over the years, as decrepit facilities often literally collapsed under the weight of the fans.

BOX 3.3: STADIUM DISASTERS

The problem of underinvestment in soccer stadiums is best described by looking at the history of injury and death caused by inadequate facilities. Britain seems to have had more than its fair share of disasters, although this may in part reflect the fact that professional soccer has a far longer history there than anywhere else, and that there are many more professional teams per capita than in most countries—England and Scotland combined had six professional divisions consisting of 128 clubs in 1923, at a time when most nations did not even have one professional league.

The first documented stadium disaster was in 1902 at Ibrox Stadium, the home of Rangers Football Club, where 26 people died after an overcrowded wooden stand collapsed. Other notable disasters in Britain include Burnden Park (home of Bolton Wanderers) in 1946, when 33 people died, and Ibrox again in 1971, when 66 were killed. At Valley Parade (Bradford City) in 1985, 56 fans died. At Hillsborough in 1989 (FA Cup semifinal between Liverpool and Nottingham Forest), 96 people were killed. In each case the disaster can be directly attributed to design flaws that rendered the stadium unsafe, consistent with a history of underinvestment. Only since Hillsborough, and thanks to government intervention, have standards been established that ensure further fatalities are unlikely. It should also be noted that while the biggest disasters in Britain were contemporary with the hooligan era that made attending league matches there a fairly risky activity, none of these disasters were attributable to hooliganism or indeed any misbehavior on the part of the fans.

This is in contrast with the Heysel stadium disaster at the 1985 European Cup Final in Brussels when 39 Juventus fans were killed by the collapse of a wall while being pursued by Liverpool fans. In this case, hooliganism interacted with inadequate facilities. Similar stories can be told about other stadium disasters. At the Estadio Nacional in Lima, Peru, 300 people were killed at a Peru versus Argentina game in 1964. At Accra Sports Stadium in Ghana, 127 were killed at an Accra Hearts versus Asante Kotoko game in 2001. Deaths attributable purely to inadequate facilities are also known in other countries. At the Luzhniki Stadium in Moscow, 66

CONTINUES

were killed at a 1982 UEFA Cup game between Spartak Moscow and Haarlem. At Stade Furiani in Corsica, France, 18 people were killed in a 1992 game between Bastia and Olympique de Marseille. And there are also a smaller number of disasters that seem wholly attributable to fan-initiated violence, most recently at Port Said in Egypt, in 2012, when 79 were killed in a game between Al-Masry and Al-Ahly.

The problem of underinvestment in stadiums seems to be longstanding and almost universal. It also seems obvious why. The main short-term driver of success is the quality of the team—which depends on spending on players. Setting money aside for investment in the stadium might improve long-term success, but most clubs and most fans seem resolutely focused on the short term.

In more recent years governments have found new reasons to invest public money in stadiums. Hosting major events such as the World Cup and the European Championship finals used to be a surefire way to buy popularity with the public. And there is no doubting the feel-good factor that envelops the host nation, albeit for a short period. Governments have gone further and suggested that building stadiums will lead to increased economic growth through the stimulus to the construction sector and through increased tourism. Economists have raised the same objections to these arguments as they have in relation to stadium investments in the United States. Judging by the public protests prior to the 2014 World Cup in Brazil, such objections are also starting to register with the public. UEFA has taken the revolutionary step of not awarding the 2020 European Championship to any specific nations, with a view to spreading the burden across Europe as a whole. The final and semifinals will be played at Wembley Stadium in London, while the other sixty matches will be played in cities in a dozen different countries: Munich (Germany), Baku (Azerbaijan), Saint Petersburg (Russia), Rome (Italy), Copenhagen (Denmark), Bucharest (Romania), Amsterdam (the Netherlands), Dublin (Ireland), Bilbao (Spain), Budapest (Hungary), Brussels (Belgium), and Glasgow (Scotland). In almost all these cases, the stadiums will not require major refurbishment, let alone new construction. This seems to represent a recognition that the economic case for investing billions in the construction of a dozen 50,000-seat stadiums does not make sense for most countries.

Nonetheless, public funding has been a major benefit for many clubs. Not only does the club get a subsidized facility, it also usually sees a big jump in attendance thanks to the exposure effect of the event. The problem with government support is that government often also wants to have a say in the running of the stadium. Italian clubs in particular seem to have struggled in recent years because municipal owners have wanted to keep ticket prices low. Juventus actually bought the stadium that the local government built for them for the 1990 World Cup and tore it down because it was such a poor place to watch soccer. AS Roma is developing a similar plan, but the finances of most Italian clubs are so weak that they are unlikely to have the capacity to fund the construction of a new stadium.

The Hillsborough disaster of 1989, in which ninety-six Liverpool fans were crushed to death in the Sheffield stadium, was the result of antiquated facilities and negligent crowd management. The subsequent government report[13] also concluded that the practice of standing to watch games had contributed to the scale of the tragedy, and so this led to legislation in Britain mandating all-seat stadiums. Capacity at English stadiums had been falling for some time because of safety issues, but the new legislation caused a further significant drop. Comparing the total capacity of the eighty league clubs present in both 1974 and 1991, it had fallen from 3.1 million to below 1.8 million—a 44-percent decline. Hillsborough also caused clubs to reconsider what they were offering fans. The government made between $160 million and $320 million available, to be divided among the ninety-two league clubs to help comply with the new laws. But many clubs decided to go much further than this, and in the 1990s there was an investment boom in English stadiums. Some of this was funded by local government. Examples include new stadiums in Wales built for Swansea City and Cardiff City, and the conversion of the stadium used for the 2002 Commonwealth Games into the home of Manchester City—which was cofunded by the Greater Manchester authority with the central government. But of the twenty-four new stadiums built by league clubs since the 1990s, three-quarters have been privately funded. According to accounting and consulting firm Deloitte, along with stadium upgrades, this amounts to a total investment of around $4.8 billion. There has even been an expansion in capacity—the same eighty clubs that were present in 1991 now have a capacity of 1.9 million, an increase of 7.5 percent.

BOX 3.4: CHANGING CAPACITY AT ENGLISH SOCCER STADIUMS

In the last fifty years, English soccer has been on a roller-coaster ride. Between 1960 and 1986, league attendance fell from 32.5 million to 16.5 million. This was an era of stadium disasters, hooliganism, and the seemingly terminal decay of the national game. Between 1986 and 2010, attendance bounced back to more than 30 million.

This is reflected in the changing capacity of English soccer stadiums, which was declining from the 1970s as safety legislation reduced overcrowding and eventually forced clubs to have all-seater stadiums. Capacity in England reached its nadir around 1991, after publication of the Taylor Report into the Hillsborough tragedy.

Since then, capacity has also increased but not by as much as attendance—with the obvious result that more stadium capacity is being used than ever before. Premier League teams have been playing to mostly sold-out stadiums for the last twenty years or so. Even in the lower divisions capacity utilization has risen. Comparing 1991 to 2010, it has risen from 49 to 69 percent in the second tier, from 32 to 57 percent in the third tier, and from 26 to 35 percent in the fourth tier. Capacity utilization is important not only for the extra money it generates to fund the team, but also to make the spectacle more attractive.

Another important trend has been the increasing concentration of capacity in the biggest teams. If we look at the eighty teams that have been in the four divisions continuously since 1974, the five largest stadiums accounted for 10 percent of capacity in 1974; it had increased to 13 percent by 1991; and to 15 percent by 2010. Similarly, the ten largest stadiums accounted for 19 percent of capacity in 1974, 24 percent in 1991, and 26 percent in 2010.

In recent years the economics of austerity has placed increasing pressure on government budgets, and the willingness to invest public money has diminished. Not everyone is a soccer fan and there is growing resistance to public subsidies. This has triggered a search for new ways to justify stadium investment, with or without public finance. And the flow of private money has increased. How did investors come to see stadiums as profitable investments again? In most cases, the key is ancillary developments that have been tied to the stadium construction. Many clubs have learned to take advantage of their location and to tie their investment plans with property development. There are several options for a club if it can control enough of the space around the stadium—perhaps a hotel, a gym, a supermarket, or even a shopping mall.

BOX 3.5: STADIUMS AND ECONOMIC DEVELOPMENT

Soccer teams often try to obtain subsidies for stadium development from government on the grounds that the investment will attract consumers and businesses into the local area, and provide an economic benefit that goes well beyond impact on the soccer club itself. These arguments have been studied intensively by economists over the last twenty years and the research generally does not support this proposition—the evidence is that the economic impact of new stadiums is largely neutral.

Most of the research has been conducted on stadiums in the United States. This is because in the closed professional leagues of North America (no promotion and relegation) there is a shortage of teams and many cities would like to attract a team—which they hope to do by building a stadium ("build it and they will come"). Moreover, the United States is a more homogeneous region than Europe, and so it is possible to make comparisons between cities that have built stadiums and those that have not in terms of economic growth, job creation, and so on.

Research by Dennis Coates and Brad Humphreys[1] shows that cities with new stadiums enjoy few observable benefits in terms of growth or employment. In a well-known paper, Siegfried and

CONTINUES

Zimbalist[2] provided a number of reasons that this is likely to be the case.

First, for all their cultural significance, sports teams are not very big businesses and so their economic impact is small in most cities of any size. Second, if local residents tend to spend more at the stadium, they are likely to reduce spending elsewhere, which will take money away from other local businesses (e.g., shops, restaurants, cinemas). Third, a stadium may attract more visitors from outside the area who inject spending into the local economy, but the knock-on (multiplier) effects are likely to be small because many of the services they consume will actually come from outside the area (e.g., food and beverages may be shipped in from elsewhere).

Much the same results have been found when analyzing the impact of events such as the FIFA World Cup or the UEFA European Championship, which have often caused new stadiums to be built.

So why do governments pay for stadiums? They may not generate a quantifiable economic benefit, but there is little doubt that a proper stadium and a successful local team generate pleasure and pride in the local community. That should be reward enough.

1. Coates, D., and Humphreys, B. (2003) "Professional sports facilities, franchises and urban economic development." *Public Finance and Management*, 3 (3): 335–357.

2. Siegfried, J., and Zimbalist, A. (2000) "The Economics of Sports Facilities and Their Communities." *Journal of Economic Perspectives*, 14(3): 95–114.

Obtaining planning permission from local government to build hotels, supermarkets, and luxury apartments is increasingly difficult in the densely populated cities of Britain, and tying these investments to a popular public amenity such as a soccer stadium has become a very good way to get the local government on board. This approach has also become increasingly popular in the United States, where ballparks and arenas are increasingly tied to the development of the downtown area.[14] In previous decades, people had deserted city centers to go to the suburbs and their new shopping malls. Cities such as Baltimore and San Diego have used baseball stadiums in particular as attractions to lure people back to downtown. In London, Chelsea added a restaurant, hotel, and gym to the redevelopment of its Stamford Bridge stadium in the 1990s. More modestly, northern England's Chesterfield Football Club (average attendance 6,000) built its stadium (currently called the Proact stadium) as part of a new development that included a superstore for food retailer Tesco. Almost all British stadiums now boast extensive conference facilities, capacity to host concerts and other sports teams (including rugby clubs), and often restaurants and bars that open throughout the week. Increasingly, the way to fund the construction of a stadium today is to find someone who wants to build a supermarket.

4

REVENUE

In June 2000, a new broadcasting company, ONdigital, agreed to pay £315 million (just over $500 million) for the right to broadcast games played in the English Football League—which represented the second, third, and fourth tiers of English professional soccer. This amount equaled the total revenue of the seventy-two clubs involved in the year 2000. Even though the payments would not start until the 2001/02 season, and would be spread over three years, the contract represented a bonanza. It was a lot less than the £1.2 billion (almost $2 billion) contract that rival broadcasters were paying for Premier League rights—but, still, many observers were asking if ONdigital had overpaid.

Second-tier soccer is a lot less attractive than first-tier soccer, and lower tiers have very limited TV appeal. At the time, the Premier League had average attendance of almost 31,000 per game, while the Football League First Division averaged less than 14,000 per game, Division Two 7,000, and Division Three 4,000. At least fans who go to the game tend to have some loyalty to their team even if it is playing in a lower division; TV viewers tend to be heavily influenced by the perceived quality of the soccer. Below the Premier League, the perception was that standards were not high.

Sure enough, once ONdigital started showing the games, the audience was not large. ONdigital's main rival, the established pay TV broadcaster Sky, offered a better quality service, more choice, and lower prices.

ONdigital's owners were two of the UK's largest private TV channels, Carlton Television and Granada TV, and in early-2002 they went into overdrive trying to save their venture. The company was relaunched as ITV Digital and heavily advertised. Because the games were not attracting enough viewers to justify the price, they tried to renegotiate the broadcast contract with the Football League. The League, however, while recognizing the problem, was not inclined to negotiate because Carlton and Granada had guaranteed the contract and were very stable and profitable businesses. Even if ITV Digital went bust, the League reasoned, the clubs would still get their money.

To no great surprise, in March 2002 ITV Digital announced that it would not be able to pay its debts—the Football League would have to rely on the parent company guarantees. As lawyers started to pore over the contract, a terrible realization dawned: the contracts with Carlton and Granada had never been signed! Surely, they thought, these reputable corporations would honor their promises? Sadly, the law insists on a signature for a valid guarantee. Carlton and Granada insisted on the law. And so, while the first season's installment had been paid, the Football League clubs suddenly developed a $320 million hole in their income statements.

Since the 1980s, soccer clubs had been experiencing financial problems that have led them into legal insolvency proceedings. This process is known in Britain as administration. It entails an independent manager being put in charge of the business and seeking to keep it going while finding as much money as possible to pay the creditors what they are owed. In the 1990s, out of the one hundred or so clubs in the four professional divisions, clubs had been going into administration at an average rate of two per year. In 2002, nine clubs entered administration; in 2003, a further eight clubs had to. Not all of these insolvencies were necessarily precipitated by the ITV Digital collapse, but most of them were. As must by now be obvious, the clubs had spent the TV money before they had received it.

Most English clubs operate on a financial year that coincides with the soccer season and typically ends on either May 31 or June 30. Even though the ONdigital contract was only agreed in June 2000, in the financial year to the end of May/June 2000 the average wage spending of Football League Division One clubs had increased by 36 percent (in that season actual revenues received had increased by only 10 percent). In the financial year that ended in mid-2001—still before any of the contracted games had been shown on TV—wage spending had risen by another 24 percent. So in the two years before the contract came into effect, salaries rose by two thirds. Eight months into the contract, ITV Digital went bust.

This might sound like a cautionary tale about not counting chickens, and, indeed, if someone offers you a guarantee it is a good idea to make sure you see the signature on a contract before acting—but that is not really the point. All businesses work on the principle that expenditure goes before revenue. All business is based on credit—in fact, all productive activities are based on credit. You make something first and then you sell it. Farmers plant seeds, harvest, and then sell what they have produced at the market. Car manufacturers build cars, which are then displayed in showrooms and sold to customers. Hollywood makes movies, and then we buy tickets to watch them in theatres. I had to write this book before you could buy it. Growing food, building cars, making movies, and writing books are not costless activities—time and resources have to be devoted to their production, and meanwhile the producers have to live. Without credit in some form or another, none of this could happen. And all of this is true for soccer clubs too. They have to invest in a team and a stadium before they can sell tickets and broadcast rights to watch games, which is what soccer clubs really produce.

Soccer club revenues come from four main sources: ticket sales (match-day revenue), broadcast rights, merchandising, and sponsorship. This chapter will examine all four of these, but first we start with an examination of the growth in total revenues in England over the last fifty-six years. In 1958, the average annual revenue of teams in the highest division in England was £127,000 (just over $200,000), equivalent to about two and a half days of Wayne Rooney's salary in 2014. In 2013, the average Premier League club received revenue of £126 million (just over $200 million)—that's almost one thousand times as much. This is not quite a fair comparison because inflation has meant that £1 today ($1.60) will buy you little more than a shilling (or 5 pence, equivalent to 8 cents) would in 1958—so one pound sterling is worth one twentieth of what it was then. But even after adjusting for inflation, the growth of soccer club revenue has been remarkable. Inflation-adjusted revenue in the top division has grown at an average compound rate of 7.3 percent per year so, over fifty-six years, revenue has increased almost fifty-fold (see Figure 4.1). Even in the lower divisions the growth has been very rapid. Both the second tier and the third tier have seen revenue growth of 4.6 percent per year after inflation, which amounts to an almost twelve-fold increase over fifty-six years. Growth in the fourth tier has also been positive, but at a more miserly 2.6 percent per year on average, meaning that after inflation revenue has increased around four-fold. For the purpose of comparison, real incomes over this period in the United Kingdom have grown at 2.2 percent per year—less than revenues in the fourth tier. Now 2.2 percent a year might not sound like much, but even this level of growth has made some very big changes in people's lives. In 1958, most British families didn't own a car, rationing of food had ended only four years earlier, only about half of the nation had a television set, and there was no league soccer on TV anyway.

One feature of the growth of soccer revenue is that there is only a limited correlation with the growth of the wider economy (the correlation coefficient is +0.12). During the major recessions of 1974–1975 and 1980–1981, soccer revenues were affected, and the second of these recessions did have a major impact on English soccer. But the even bigger recession of 2008–2009 (the economy shrank by 6 percent) did not seem to touch the Premier League. Its revenues grew by 20 percent in 2008 and 9 percent in 2009.

Some of the difference between soccer and the wider economy is easy to explain. The year 1967 was an average year for the UK economy but a great year for English leagues, which enjoyed a surge in popularity following England's victory in the 1966 World Cup. Four of the nine biggest annual increases in revenues over the last fifty-six years have coincided with the start of new broadcasting contracts (1993, 1998, 2002, and the recession year of 2008), whereas one of the worst years for soccer was 2005 (a good year for the economy), when the new broadcasting contract was worth 7-percent less than the previous one.

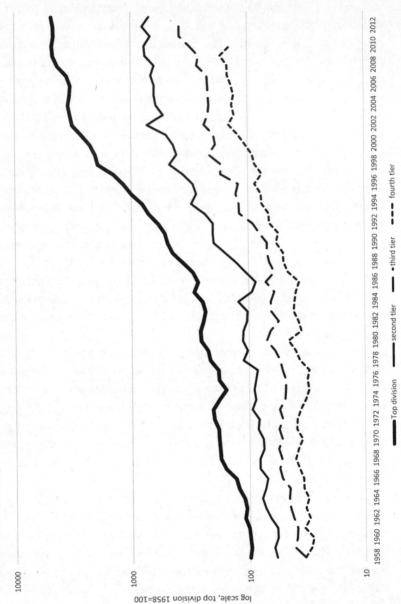

FIGURE 4.1 Inflation adjusted revenue growth in English league soccer by division 1958–2013. (Source: Club financial accounts)

Looking at Figure 4.1 one might be fooled into thinking that soccer clubs deliver fairly steady annual growth—there don't appear to be many wild swings either up or down. This is only true on average; individual teams see much greater revenue variation from year to year, not least because few clubs remain consistently in the same division, a consequence of promotion and relegation. This also means that the teams that compose the average in any division change from year to year. Figure 4.2 compares the growth of revenues of the "average top division club" with two specific clubs: Manchester United and the Bolton Wanderers.

In 1958, both clubs were in the top division—Manchester United finished ninth and Bolton fifteenth, with only five points separating the two teams. United might actually have won the league that year: they were in third place on February 1 after beating Arsenal 5-4 at Highbury that day in what some people have said is the best game they ever saw in the English leagues. Six days later, a plane carrying United's team home from a European Cup match in Belgrade crashed on takeoff at Munich Airport killing eight players and forcing the team to play with a hastily assembled team of replacements. They lost eight of their last fourteen league games. Manchester United did still make it to the final of the FA Cup that season, losing 2-0 to Bolton.

Since 1958, the two clubs have traveled on different trajectories. Manchester United has been almost ever present in the top division since 1958—it had one season in the second tier back in 1974/75. Only Arsenal and Everton have a better record (and Tottenham is the only team other than United to have been out of the top division for only one season, namely 1977/78). Bolton, by contrast, was relegated from the top division in 1964, and in the following thirty-one seasons reached that level again only twice, and in the meantime visited all three of the remaining divisions. The club's fortunes revived again in the mid-1990s, and since 1995/96 it has spent most of its time in the Premier League.

These different trajectories are reflected in the revenue generated by the two teams. Back in 1958, Manchester United already generated twice the revenue of the average club in the top division. Until the 1980s, the club typically generated revenues that were 50-percent higher than the top division average, and in the last twenty-five years it has typically generated two to three times as much as the average. Bolton saw its revenues

FIGURE 4.2 Inflation adjusted revenue growth in the top division, Manchester United and Bolton Wanderers 1958–2013. (Source: Club financial accounts)

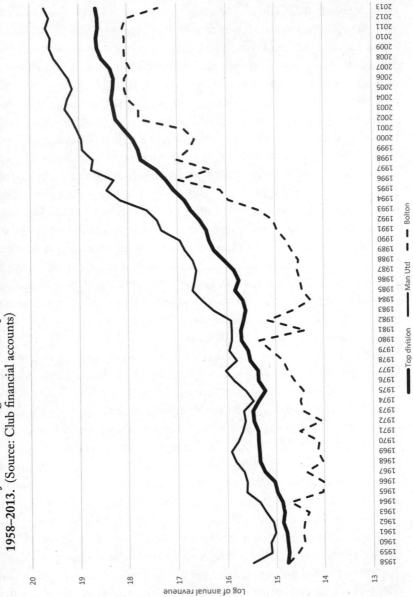

Log of annual revenue

Top division — Man Utd ---- Bolton

fall (after allowing for the effect of inflation) in the 1960s, and apart from the occasional good year, remained below its 1958 levels right up until 1989/90. Since the revival of the club and its more frequent participation in the top tier, revenues have also climbed, but not to the level of the Premier League average (at the time of writing Bolton was out of the Premier League again).

Most people are aware that financial inequality among soccer clubs has grown over time. The data for English clubs reveals by just how much. Figure 4.3 shows the ratio between revenues in the top division and the three lower tiers.

Back in early-1960s, average revenues were about 50-percent higher as you moved from one division to the next one up the ladder. While this ratio has increased a little between the lower divisions, the greatest increase in the gap has emerged between the top division and the second tier. Even by 1985, the gap had increased to three-to-one, and then from the mid-1990s rose steadily to the current level of around seven-to-one. This divergence has significantly affected the experience of promotion and relegation. In particular, relegation involves such a large loss of revenue that many clubs have struggled to adjust.

While the gap *between* the divisions is important, competition itself takes place *within* a division, and many people worry that inequality of resources within divisions will undermine the attractiveness of league competition. Figure 4.4 shows the variability of revenues within the top two divisions. The measure used in the figure is the coefficient of variation. This measure takes account of the increase in average spending within each division, so that we can focus only on the changing dispersion of revenues among clubs. The pattern we see is a bit different to the one we observed between the divisions. Although the variation has increased (more or less doubling since 1958), it appears that most of that increase in variation arose in the years before 1990. In other words, the financial gap between a team at the top of a division and a team at the bottom has hardly changed in recent years. In the last twenty years there has been very little increase in the dispersion of revenue, either in the Premier League or in the Football League Championship.

The explanation for what we see in Figures 4.3 and 4.4 is that the gap between the Premier League and the other divisions has been driven by

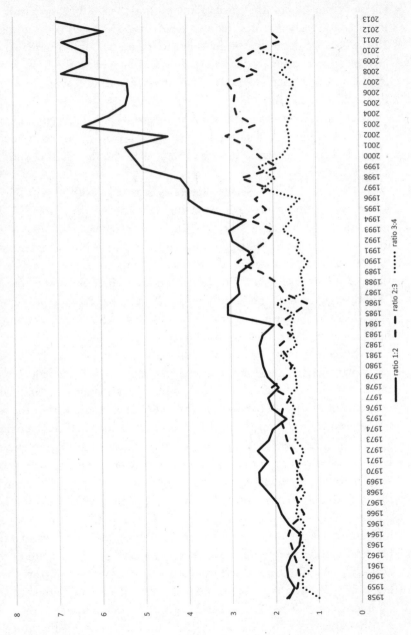

FIGURE 4.3 Ratio of average revenues between English soccer divisions. (Source: Club financial accounts)

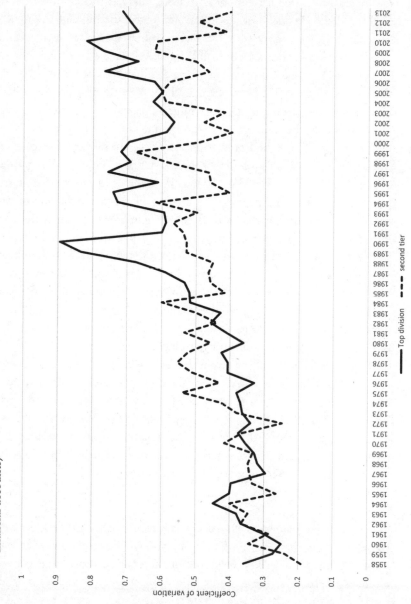

FIGURE 4.4 The variability of revenues among clubs in the top two English divisions 1958–2013. (Source: Club financial accounts)

the increases in broadcast money. Indeed, this was the rationale for the creation of the Premier League in the first place: the big clubs wanted to keep the broadcast money for themselves rather than sharing it with all ninety-two clubs in the old Football League. While TV revenue in the top division has skyrocketed in recent years, the distribution formula has not changed, so that revenue distribution in the top division has changed little.[1]

Perhaps less familiar is the story of growing revenue inequality within divisions before the foundation of the Premier League in 1992. This was the era when clubs relied almost entirely on gate money. Between the wars ticket prices at all soccer clubs were more or less identical, regardless of the division, but after World War Two some differentiation started to set in. In 1960, the price to see a game in the top division was still only 25-percent higher than the price of a game in the fourth tier[2], but from then on the gap started to grow and by 1990 the difference in price had almost doubled. Price variations within divisions became significant as some clubs exploited their popularity by developing their marketing capabilities, something that the government had been calling for since the 1960s as a way to improve the financial management of professional soccer[3]. In the top divisions, variability in attendance also increased. This was an era of generally declining attendance at soccer. From 1950 to 1986 crowds fell annually in twenty-seven out of thirty-seven seasons as fans became disillusioned with poor facilities and the growing threat of hooliganism, and on average across the four divisions attendance dropped from almost 20,000 per game to just above 8,000. Not every club was equally squeezed and in the top two divisions the variability among clubs increased. As a result, soccer club revenues had been diverging long before the advent of the Premier League and broadcasting.

There are two fundamental statistical relationships in soccer: first, the more you spend on players the more successful you will be on the field (on average and in the long run). The second fundamental relationship is between revenues and success. The second relationship is as simple as the first: more successful teams on the pitch generate more revenue on average. The extent of this relationship is demonstrated in Figures 4.5 and 4.6. Using accounting data on one hundred English clubs over fifty-six years, yielding more

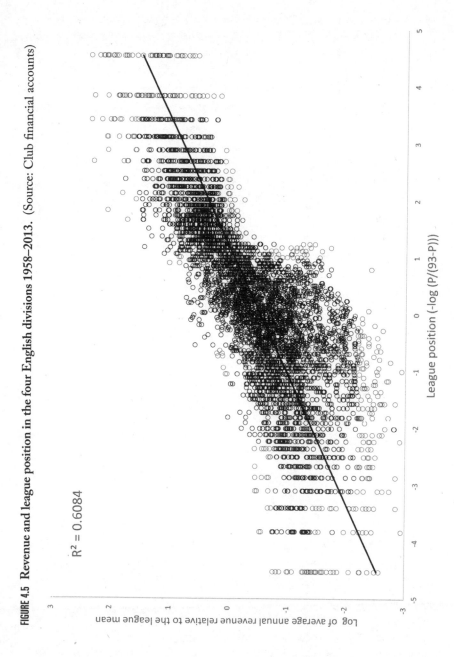

FIGURE 4.5 Revenue and league position in the four English divisions 1958–2013. (Source: Club financial accounts)

FIGURE 4.6 Revenue and league position in the four English divisions 1958–2013. Club financial accounts)

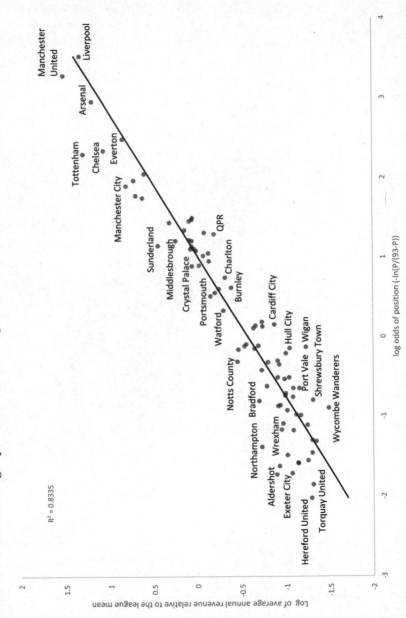

than 4,000 separate observations of league position and revenue, Figure 4.5 shows that the correlation is very close. Despite all the changes in the world of soccer over this period, league position alone is capable of accounting for over 60 percent of the variation in club revenues. No other single factor is anywhere near as closely correlated. Revenues have risen dramatically, but the relationship between revenues and league performance across the leagues has remained in step. This is all the more remarkable when one considers all the potential sources of revenue to which a club has access— not least from participation in other competitions such as cups (domestic or international). League status alone accounts for the lion's share of the differences in revenues among clubs in any one season.

In Figure 4.5, the revenue of each club is expressed relative to the average revenue of clubs in the league in a given season, which we know has risen rapidly over the last half-century. For Figure 4.6, the relative revenue of each club is averaged over fifty-six seasons, together with its league position. League position ranges from one to ninety-two, and many clubs have roamed across the range over this period. For example, the difference between the highest and lowest rank for Bolton is sixty-seven—signifying that the club has moved across all four divisions in this period. Even for Manchester United the range is twenty-three. The average range for all clubs is fifty-three—spanning at least three divisions. Take a long enough period of time and there is a lot of mobility up and down the leagues. The average position for each club across this range can explain 83 percent of the revenue generated by clubs relative to their rivals over this period. It is, and always has been, virtually impossible to be rich without being in the top division, and being in the bottom division more or less guarantees that your club is poor. Better performance on the field is eventually rewarded with higher revenues.

BOX 4.1: DATA TRANSFORMATIONS

Readers may have noticed that the axes on the charts do not say "position" and "revenue" but "minus log odds of position" and "log of revenue." The data has been transformed in order to demonstrate clearly the relationship. This does not change the underlying relationships; it just helps give some visual clarity.

Taking logarithms is common practice in economics whenever the data involves very large differences—for example, between the very rich and very poor. It makes the gaps look smaller even though the gap is still there.

I have also expressed revenues (and wages in chapter 2) relative to the average of other clubs in a given season. The average has risen dramatically in recent years thanks to the increased popularity of the game and the demand for broadcast viewing, but the relative differences between successful and unsuccessful clubs have remained relatively stable.

For position, there are a number of transformations to bear in mind. First, I put a negative sign in front, so that a low position (-10) is smaller than a high position (-1). Second, for the case of England, teams are ranked from 1 to 92, with 20 being last place in the Premier League, 21 being first place in Championship and so on, with 92 being last place in the fourth tier.

Finally, I could simply have used the logarithm of position, but have always used the "log odds" of position, which has a similar effect but makes the average for the league as a whole zero, and enlarges the gap between positions as you move to the extremes. It is certainly the case that we think the gap, in sporting terms between, say, rank 40 and rank 39 is smaller than the difference between rank 2 and rank 1.

It is also clear why this should be true. Fans are attracted to more successful clubs. Even if many fans are loyal, some desert when results do not go their way. When a team is relegated, the quality of the opposition also declines, making games less attractive. Between 1974 and 2010, 88 percent of clubs relegated from England's top division experienced a fall in attendance, and the average decline was 16 percent.[4] Relegated teams also find it hard to attract new fans, while promoted teams create a new generation of supporters.

Successful teams will attract bigger crowds that pay higher ticket prices. More successful clubs sell more merchandise. More successful clubs attract better sponsors who are willing to pay more money to be associated with the club. And better clubs appear more often on TV and therefore receive larger payments from broadcast companies. It is therefore not surprising that greater sporting success generates larger financial rewards. This explanation suggests a clear line of causality from success to revenues. At the same time higher revenues can be used to buy better players and so generate even more success. And we observe wealthy individuals subsidizing clubs to become successful. But for most clubs, most of the time, the level of revenue that they generate depends primarily on success on the field.

BOX 4.2: LEAGUE POSITION AND ATTENDANCE

The basis of inequality in soccer has always been the capacity of successful teams to attract more fans. The chart below shows the relationship between league position and attendance in England between 1948 and 2010. Small teams have the ability to attract larger crowds if they can only achieve a higher league position. But for teams in the lower tiers this means acquiring a winning

League Position and Attendance in English Football, 1948–2010.
(Source: Sky Sports Football Yearbook)

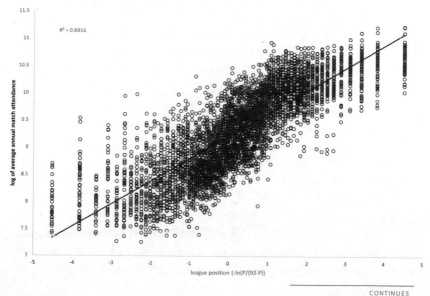

CONTINUES

team, which is now very expensive, and also finding the stadium capacity to house a larger number of fans, which is usually a substantial long-term investment. Achieving both at the same time is almost impossible without a benefactor. Banks are usually unwilling to lend large sums against this risky proposition, which may take years to pay off, if at all.

The argument above should make it clear that a dominant club investing more in talent or in a better stadium is actually raising the bar for any would-be rival. As the wages of players have risen, so the chances that a smaller club could afford to buy a team to compete at the highest level have diminished.

A quarter of a century ago, soccer clubs derived 90 percent or more of their revenue from fans spending money at the stadium, mostly in the form of tickets. For more than a century in England, and more than half a century in other countries, the primary source of revenue was gate money. But for the world's leading soccer leagues this is no longer the case. According to analysis by Deloitte, only 23 percent of revenue in the German Bundesliga and English Premier League comes on match day. In Spain's La Liga, the figure is 22 percent, and in Italy's Serie A and France's Ligue 1 the figure is a mere 11 percent.[5] This is a major break with tradition.

The roots of modern soccer lie in the mass support of working class fans living in cities. The communities of shared emotion created by men and women going to the game on a Saturday or Sunday afternoon is an abiding cultural image. And traditionally it was cheap—poverty was no barrier to buying a ticket. The sociologists who wrote about the emerging phenomenon of hooliganism in the 1970s also focused on the working class origins of the sport.[6] By this time, however, significant shifts in the structure of industrial economies were starting to impinge on the culture of soccer as well. Figure 4.7 illustrates the evolution of attendance in the top divisions of England, France, Germany, and Italy.

There are three identifiable eras in this data.

The Golden Age (1964–1978): In the 1960s and 1970s attendance was relatively stable across the four countries. England enjoyed a substantial boost after 1966 thanks to hosting (and winning) the World Cup, but those gains were soon lost; (West) Germany likewise enjoyed a large

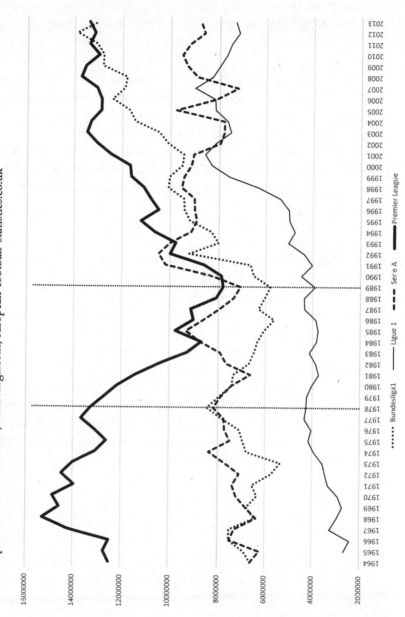

FIGURE 4.7 Total attendance in the top divisions of England, France, Germany, and Italy 1964–2013. Sources: Sky Sports Football Yearbook, bundesliga.com, european-football-statistics.co.uk

boost after hosting the 1974 World Cup (and also winning); France saw some growth during this period, but from a relatively low base. Between 1964 and 1978, attendance across the four leagues grew at a modest 1.5 percent per year.

The Dark Ages (1978–1989): In the 1980s, attendance declined significantly. The global recession of the early-1980s hurt everyone, although the collapse was most noticeable in England, where the combination of decrepit stadiums and hooliganism provoked an existential crisis. Hooliganism may have been noticed first in England, but by the 1980s it had become a universal problem. Between 1978 and 1989, attendance fell by 41 percent in England, 32 percent in France, 28 percent in Germany, and 14 percent in Italy.

Soccer's Renaissance (1989–present): The renaissance in attendance at soccer has been remarkable across most of Europe. The combined annual attendance at top division games in England, France, Germany, and Italy has risen from 24 million in 1989 to 42 million in 2013—an annual average increase of 2.3 percent. Each country has its own story, which accounts for some of the variations—the success of the Italia 90 World Cup was undoubtedly a boost for Serie A, while the victory of the German national team in Italy may have helped boost demand for the Bundesliga. Similarly, France hosting and winning the 1998 World Cup was even more of a boost for Ligue 1. In England, the aftermath of the 1989 Hillsborough tragedy helped to spur a recovery. In Italy, the boom of the early-1990s was not sustained and the combination of financial mismanagement, match-fixing scandals, and rising hooliganism undermined the popularity of the game to some extent.

BOX 4.3: HOOLIGANS AND BUSINESS

The phenomenon of "football hooliganism" first started to be talked about at the end of the 1960s in England and has often been called "the English disease"—but nowadays it is recognized as a global soccer problem (see, for example, Carnibella et al [1996]).[1] Spectator sports have always provoked violent outbursts by the overexcited, but hooliganism refers to something more structured: groups of fans fighting with each other, or with the police, and terrorizing the neighborhoods of stadiums on game day. Occasionally there are deaths.

By the mid-1980s, the police were collecting statistics on the frequency of hooligan incidents at stadiums and the number of arrests. In a recent paper Todd Jewell, Rob Simmons, and I looked at the relationship between the revenues of English soccer clubs and the frequency of arrests.[2] One can imagine two possible effects. Arrests and violence at stadiums is likely to deter some fans from going to the game, but on the other hand, the aggression of home fans might help to intimidate players of the visiting team and the referee, making it more likely that the home team will win, be more successful, and generate more revenue. We found that during the 1980s, when the hooliganism problem in England was at its peak, clubs that experienced higher arrest rates also suffered from lower revenues, suggesting that hooliganism was bad for business.

In the last two decades, hooliganism has largely been brought under control in England. The use of CCTV cameras at stadiums, and better organized policing, has halved the number of arrests at the same time as attendance has doubled. We also found no relationship between arrests and revenues in more recent years. The relationship between the renaissance of English soccer in the last two decades and the decline of hooliganism is controversial. Hooliganism is generally associated with younger men who have largely been priced out of the Premier League since the 1980s, a process sometimes described as "gentrification." Critics argue that soccer in England has lost touch with ordinary people and become the preserve of the relatively wealthy. Whether or not that is the case, there is no arguing with the fact that English stadiums have become safer places to watch soccer.

1. Carnibella, Giovanni, Anne Fox, Kate Fox, Joe McCann, James Marsh, Peter Marsh. "Football violence in Europe: A report to the Amsterdam Group." Social Issues Research Centre (1996).

2. Jewell, R. Todd, Rob Simmons, and Stefan Szymanski. "Bad for Business? The Effects of Hooliganism on English Professional Football Clubs." *Journal of Sports Economics* (2014).

But beyond these individual factors, the era since 1989 has been one in which the cultural centrality of soccer has been affirmed and mostly expanded. To some extent the explanation is to be found in the changing structure of society. The working class shrank and more people came to see themselves as middle class. With the decline in manufacturing and the shift toward a more service-based economy, many traditional elements of day-to-day life have disappeared, but soccer remains a constant. People may not go to church anymore, but the soccer stadium has survived as a place of a different kind of worship. Showing support for the local team became essential for aspiring politicians, and the national soccer team became subsumed into the national identity. For example, Angela Merkel, the popular German chancellor, became the mascot of the German national team, regularly being photographed with the players in the changing room, something that one could not have imagined of her predecessors.

What is striking about the growth in attendance—and 2.3 percent per year may not sound so spectacular on its own but it is faster than the European economies have grown on average over this same period—is that it took place against the backdrop of astronomical ticket price increases. Since 1989, ticket prices across Europe have risen at an annual rate of anywhere between 5 and 10 percent. Part of this reflects the fact that personal incomes also rose, and soccer clubs found themselves catering to a wealthier clientele. Since 1990, the global economy has benefited from the economic ascent of China, the revolution in computing, and the Internet, as well as relatively cheap energy prices for most of the period. The great recession caused by the banking crisis of 2008 has barely touched soccer.

But there have also been significant changes in the commercial practices of soccer clubs. Put bluntly, they have tried to squeeze as much money out of the fans as they can. When clubs in Europe thought about pricing they looked to the experience of professional teams in the United States. Executive boxes became more important and the range of prices offered increased. Clubs tended to preserve some cheaper ticket options, but prices for the better seats rose. This was only possible against a background of increasing demand.

Rising ticket prices has been a source of complaint from fans all over the world. To a large extent, young men with limited incomes were priced out of soccer in many countries in the 1990s. The average age and income of people going to matches increased. People often think that rising prices were driven by the rising costs of players, but if anything the logic works the other way around. Clubs always want more revenue with which to buy players so that they can be more successful. The growth in the popularity of soccer in recent decades has led to increasing demand for tickets, bigger crowds, and increasing prices.

BOX 4.4: SEASON TICKETS

Given the extent of risks involved in financing a stadium and the playing squad, one way that a club can insure itself against risk is by selling season tickets. Season tickets for the following year typically go on sale right after a season ends, providing an important source of cash flow. Indeed, since most clubs have a financial year-end during the summer break, their accounts typically report relatively large sums of cash held, which can be misleading. Season-ticket revenue is used to finance player wages over the season, and the temptation to overcommit during the summer transfer window, when there is plenty of cash at the bank, has been the ruin of many a club.

Most clubs aim to sell about half to two-thirds of seats in the form of season tickets. The benefits include getting the money upfront, ensuring that fans have an incentive to attend all games, not just the attractive ones, and maintaining a long-term relationship with fans. However, this comes at a cost. Season tickets are attractive not only because they guarantee a seat at the most important games but because they offer a discount to the normal ticket price, assuming you attend all the games. In other words, fans get a discount for buying en bloc and in advance.

In the Premier League about 63 percent of capacity is sold in the form of season tickets, whereas in the Bundesliga the proportion is about 55 percent. In the Football League Championship, season ticket sales in 2013/14 accounted for only 44 percent of capacity, but since on average stadiums in this division were only 65-percent full, season-ticket sales accounted for about 67 percent of all seats sold.

Club policies in relation to season tickets vary significantly depending on the overall state of demand for soccer. In England,

CONTINUES

the average attendance at soccer clubs fell dramatically from the 1950s to the 1980s—falling in 1985 to roughly one-third of their 1950 level—and against this backdrop season tickets were usually easy to obtain. In the 1990s and early-2000s, when demand increased and stadiums started to fill up again, season-ticket waiting lists grew longer, especially at the more popular clubs. The clubs responded to this by raising their prices, which have risen quite dramatically over a number of years.

Back in 1985, when attendances were still falling, a ticket for a top division game cost £2.80 ($4.50), and a season ticket for Manchester United cost only £70 ($112). When ticket prices were low, attendance fell. Since then prices have risen at an average annual rate of more than 10 percent to a level of about £35 ($56) for a typical (median) Premier League ticket, and between £513 ($821) and £930 ($1,488) for a Manchester United season ticket. For the sake of comparison, had ticket prices increased only with the rate of inflation, an average ticket today would cost £6.60 ($10.56), and a Manchester United season ticket £166 ($266).

As a result of these price increases, the waiting time for a season ticket has fallen in England. Arsenal, which has the most expensive tickets in England and is highly criticized for it, has a waiting list of around 45,000, of which it can satisfy around 7,000 every season—implying a wait of six to seven years (although in fact the wait is shorter than that since people often lose interest after a few years on the list). For almost every other club in the Premier League a season ticket can be obtained without any waiting, although many clubs still require you to buy tickets for cup games as well as league matches. In Germany, by contrast, where average ticket prices are lower, season ticket waiting lists tend to be longer.

Back in the mid-1980s you could buy a ticket for a top division soccer match in England for about £3 ($4.80), and in the Bundesliga for about 15 Deutschmarks, which would be something like £4 ($6.40). Nowadays the average (mean) price of a Premier League ticket is around £43 (about $70), while in the Bundesliga average ticket prices are around 36 euros (about $45). Even after allowing for inflation, these are very large price increases.

Yet since the 1990s real incomes have risen very little *on average*, either in the United Kingdom or Germany. In both countries inequality has also grown significantly since the 1990s—the better-off have seen their incomes grow, while the worse-off have seen their incomes fall in real terms. Much the same story can be told about soccer ticket prices and incomes in Spain, Italy, France, and elsewhere. The term "gentrification" is sometimes used to describe the process by which soccer has moved away from its working-class roots to a wealthier clientele. In truth, it is often the sons and daughters of working-class parents who have moved into better paying middle-class jobs who now fill soccer stadiums.

Ticket pricing in England has been controversial; many fans have accused clubs of profiteering and point to significantly lower prices in countries like Germany. There's no doubt that prices have been high in England, but the gap between England and Germany is not as large as many imagine. Because there are so many different prices charged, depending on the quality of the seat, it is difficult to make overall comparisons. But in terms of what people pay *on average*, the best approach is to take the total match-day revenue of a league and divide it by the total attendance. Annual attendance figures can be found on the web, while Deloitte has published an estimate of match-day revenue for each league going back to 1997.[7] Table 4.1 compares the evolution of attendance and match-day revenues for the two leagues between 1997 and 2013.[8]

Annual changes in attendance at soccer leagues need to be interpreted carefully because of the effects of promotion and relegation. If a club with a large stadium capacity is relegated and replaced by a club with a small stadium capacity then it might appear that demand is declining, when in fact the general popularity of the league has not changed. Bearing this in mind, the data suggests there are two distinct periods in the data. Until 2003, attendance at the Premier League was growing thanks to investment in stadium capacity (up 25 percent over seven seasons), while attendance at the Bundesliga was static. Since 2003, attendance at the Premier League has stagnated as investment has fallen off, while attendance at the Bundesliga has grown significantly (up 25 percent over eleven seasons).

Because clubs in both leagues sell out most of their games, the only way attendance can increase is by investment in new capacity. Investment in England slowed down mainly because of the financial crisis of 2008.

A good example is the case of Liverpool. The club was acquired by two American investors, Tom Hicks and George Gillett in March 2003. Hicks is a Texas businessman who once owned a baseball team, a hockey team, and a rodeo; Gillett (no relation to the razor blade family) made his fortune in media, food processing, and Colorado ski resorts. The financial accounts of Liverpool published in February 2008 stated that the club had obtained planning permission to build a 76,000-seat stadium at a new location in Stanley Park that would start to generate revenue in 2011/12. Hicks and Gillett had borrowed money to buy the club in the first place and intended to raise the finance for the new stadium by raising debt. During the financial boom that lasted from the early-1990s until 2008, raising debt had been easy. But within six months of Liverpool revealing the Stanley Park plan, Lehman Brothers in New York had gone bankrupt. The ensuing subprime crisis revealed that banks across the world had lent vast sums to borrowers who were never likely to pay it back. That left a huge hole in the balance sheet of the biggest banks. Almost no one was immune from this crisis; all of a sudden, banks did not want to lend to anybody. Liverpool still doesn't have a new stadium (but in December 2014 construction began on increasing the present capacity of its Anfield stadium by 13,000 seats).

Given that both the Premier League and Bundesliga play to sold-out stadiums, the only way for either league to increase revenue, short of building larger stadiums, is to increase prices. Table 4.1 shows that in the mid-1990s Premier League prices were already much higher than in Germany, but that they continued to rise in England until the mid-2000s—the ratio reaching a peak in the years after 2003 when investment in new capacity was slowing down. Without extra capacity, the English clubs responded to growing demand by raising prices. However, the 2008 banking crisis, which hit the UK economy hard, also hit the demand for tickets in the Premier League and clubs responded by freezing or even cutting prices. Match-day income per fan fell by 14 percent between 2007 and 2013, after allowing for inflation, while attendance was unchanged.

TABLE 4.1 Attendance, match-day revenue, and match-day revenue per fan ($) in Germany and England

Season ending	BL attendance	BL 2013 $ per fan	EPL attendance	EPL 2013 $ per fan	Ratio of ticket prices	Ratio of annual attendance
1997	9,442,825	24.26	10,804,762	40.61	1.67	1.14
1998	10,096,422	24.29	11,092,106	41.93	1.73	1.10
1999	10,022,784	24.63	11,620,326	46.65	1.89	1.16
2000	9,541,144	31.57	11,668,497	48.88	1.55	1.22
2001	9,459,002	25.42	12,472,094	50.15	1.97	1.32
2002	10,107,063	26.91	13,043,118	52.23	1.94	1.29
2003	10,464,649	26.59	13,468,965	56.25	2.12	1.29
2004	11,469,167	26.52	13,303,136	61.15	2.31	1.16
2005	11,568,788	28.91	12,878,791	64.72	2.24	1.11
2006	12,477,001	34.28	12,871,643	69.41	2.02	1.03
2007	12,226,610	35.11	13,058,115	79.71	2.27	1.07
2008	12,069,824	37.75	13,708,875	75.17	1.99	1.14
2009	13,016,848	37.50	13,527,815	77.39	2.06	1.04
2010	13,006,489	38.74	12,977,251	72.40	1.87	1.00
2011	13,051,796	40.84	13,372,614	69.77	1.71	1.02
2012	13,805,496	40.57	13,148,465	68.76	1.69	0.95
2013	13,042,590	44.95	13,653,908	68.55	1.53	1.05

Source: Deloitte

By 2007 ticket prices in England had risen to more than double those in Germany. Since 2007 this process has gone in to reverse. As ticket prices in England have fallen, in Germany they have risen following the refurbishment of stadiums for the wildly successful 2006 World Cup. Attendance has risen 13 percent (since 2005), but prices have risen four times as fast (55 percent). As a result, the price ratio in 2013 fell below the levels of the late-1990s. It seems that clubs in both leagues respond in fairly predictable ways to changes in demand. In the long term, they increase capacity when demand rises, and when demand is below capacity they tend to keep price increases down. However, when demand is increasing and getting close to capacity, prices increase rapidly.

TABLE 4.2 Match-day revenue per fan ($) in the top divisions of five countries

Season ending	England	Spain	Germany	Italy	France
2007	79.71	44.27	35.11	27.88	21.35
2008	75.17	49.49	37.75	28.57	22.21
2009	77.39	51.90	37.50	28.57	25.20
2010	72.40	55.47	38.74	29.93	23.68
2011	69.77	51.92	40.84	27.93	22.55
2012	68.76	51.16	40.57	28.01	21.84
2013	68.55	46.78	44.95	25.87	23.75

SOURCE: Deloitte

Table 4.2 compares average match-day revenue per fan across the top five European leagues since 2007. It shows that there are big differences in ticket prices across Europe, although in all cases they are all much higher than the four or five dollars you would have paid in the 1980s. The recession that followed the banking crisis of 2008 seems to have put a lid on price increases for the time being. But it would be fair to guess that prices will start to grow again when economic growth in Europe resumes.

When the English Premier League was founded, its first broadcast contract starting in 1992/93 was worth $80 million per season, or about $4 million per club. Several observers questioned whether the satellite TV broadcaster Sky would be able to recover such a huge investment in the form of subscriptions to its pay TV channels. From the 2013/14 season, the Premier League broadcast contracts will generate about $2.9 billion, or $145 million per club. The current contract round is the seventh since the foundation of the league, and apart from the 2004/05 setback, each one has generated significant increases over the last. In February 2015 it was announced that the three-year domestic rights contracts would be worth $130 million per club per year, starting in 2016/17, with the potential for overseas rights to generate as much again.

The value of broadcasting rights has risen rapidly in most countries, but the impact has been greatest in the larger nations with established soccer leagues. Until the 1980s, soccer broadcasting was generally restricted to the highlights of league matches in the top division, games played in the national cup competition, and international games, either of the national team or in UEFA club competitions. By 1966, watching the World Cup on TV had already become an international phenomenon—that final in England attracted an estimated 400 million viewers globally. In Europe, the midweek games in the various UEFA club competitions drew large audiences and introduced fans to players and clubs of other nations. But until the late-1980s, the clubs resisted more extensive coverage, for reasons that had to do with the nature of technology.

Traditional analogue broadcasting involved transmitting a signal from TV masts that could be picked up by any aerial within reach. The technology gave the signal for free, and the number of channels that could be broadcast was limited. Moreover, in Europe, most countries had followed the model of the United Kingdom, which licensed a single, publicly owned, national broadcaster (the BBC). While some private channels started to be allowed from the 1960s, for a long time there was relatively little competition. With a scarce spectrum and a wide range of potential content, broadcasters were unwilling to pay large sums for the right to show soccer matches. Clubs in turn feared that soccer on TV would provide a more comfortable alternative to going to the game and so cannibalize their most important revenue source, the money at the gate. The outcome was relatively little league soccer on TV in Europe, at least in the country where the games were played. English clubs were willing to sell their games to overseas broadcasters so that, for example, a generation of Scandinavians grew up in the 1960s watching live games from England that English viewers could not see!

By the 1980s, the digital revolution began to make it feasible to broadcast dozens of TV channels in the same bandwidth formerly occupied by only two or three. The technology also made signal encryption easy, and so making a subscription model feasible, unlike the old free-to-air analogue technology. The signal could be delivered by cable or by satellite, but in either case the business model was essentially the same. Building the infrastructure to manage the subscriptions entailed huge fixed set-up costs, and the profitability of the enterprise depended almost entirely on the number of subscribers that could be enrolled.

Two types of content were attractive for this model. The first was blockbuster movies, preferably from Hollywood, that would turn the home into a movie theatre. The other type of content was sports, especially attractive to men aged 18-34, a target audience with significant disposable income and notoriously hard to reach with most programming. Sport in the United States means football, baseball, basketball, hockey, NASCAR, golf, and more besides. In Europe, sports mean soccer, almost exclusively. In virtually every country in Europe soccer is the most viewed sport and the most attractive content for pay TV.

And so a technological revolution loosened an avalanche of cash that transformed clubs from essentially tiny local businesses—little bigger than a local building company—into multimillion-dollar enterprises participating in a global market. Back in 1990, the revenues of European clubs were dwarfed by those of the major league franchises in the United States. American sports benefited from TV exposure, even in the analogue era, because there was always competition in national network broadcasting. From the 1990s, European soccer started to catch up. It is now starting to overtake the American major leagues in purely financial terms. In 1990, the combined revenue of the major US leagues was almost $4 billion, compared to around $1 billion for all of Europe's soccer leagues. European soccer is now estimated to generate an annual revenue of $27 billion, compared to $23 billion for the US majors.[9]

Most of the European growth can be accounted for by broadcasting. Today, television accounts for about 60 percent of the revenues of Italy's Serie A; in England, France, and Spain it accounts for about 50 percent of the revenue of the top division, and in Germany about one third. Most of this revenue derives from the rights to broadcast the league domestically, but increasingly leagues are looking to attract fans from abroad. Already the Premier League obtains nearly 50 percent of its broadcast revenue from overseas sales; Barcelona and Real Madrid command global TV audiences; and the Champions League seems as popular in the Far East as it is in Europe.

Back in the 1990s, many clubs still feared that broadcasting would drive away fans from attending the game. Yet as we have seen, attendance has risen significantly despite rapidly increasing ticket prices. To a significant extent this can be explained by the exposure that TV has given to soccer. The broadcasting companies that used soccer to drive their subscriptions had enormous incentives to promote the sport. Not only did they invest in better presentation of the games, but they also advertised their product heavily, giving soccer the kind of platform that it had never had before. Broadcasters wanted subscriptions not just from households but also from bars, and bars liked soccer as a way to sell more beer. Co-ca-Cola set out to be, and generally is, "within an arm's length of desire." By the same token, it can be said that nowadays soccer is always within the eyeline of desire. The promotion of soccer by TV made people keener to go to a game. The soccer clubs worried that if games were shown on TV the fans would rather stay at home than go to the game, especially if it was cold and raining. However, generally it is only the most attractive games that are shown on TV. As a result, interest in attending the stadium for the live event has increased and not diminished.[10]

For the clubs, the main issue has been how to divide the money. The impetus toward increasing exploitation of TV opportunities came largely from the bigger clubs whose games are the most attractive to broadcasters. Looking at the US model, these clubs generally wanted to negotiate a collective deal as a league in order to prevent broadcasters playing off one club against another. That was the benefit of unity. On the other hand, in the United States the broadcast money was shared equally among all the members of the league and the big clubs of English soccer did not like this model. This is easy to understand. The big difference is that in the States the leagues are closed, there is no promotion and relegation. The owners of the teams therefore have a greater stake in the collective success of the league, even if this sometimes comes at the expense of their own team. In Europe, where there is a big divide between the big clubs and the small clubs, the big clubs are largely immune to the threat of relegation thanks to their superior financial firepower. If they shared revenue equally then their advantage would disappear, and they might too end up getting relegated one day.

As a result, most soccer leagues agreed to a compromise formula that shared some of the money equally but still reserved a larger share for the more successful teams. Typical of these sharing rules was the Premier League's. Money from domestic rights sales was divided 50 percent on the basis of equal shares, 25 percent on the basis of league position, and 25 percent on the basis of number of times shown on TV—something that tends to favor the bigger clubs. For example, in 2012/13,

Manchester United won the title and the Queen's Park Rangers finished at the bottom of the league. Both charged similar ticket prices (despite their poor performance, QPR played in front of a wealthy fan base in London), but Manchester United's capacity was four times larger. The club accounts show that United made more than thirteen times as much as QPR from match-day income: £109 million (almost $175 million) versus £8 million (about $13 million).[11] From the domestic broadcast contract, both teams got a basic payment of £13.8 million ($22 million), although United got a larger merit payment of £15 million ($24 million) compared to less than £1 million (about $1.5 million) for QPR, and a facility fee of £13 million (almost $21 million) compared to £6 million (almost $10 million) for QPR. So the domestic TV deal paid Manchester United only twice as much as QPR, which is a much more equal distribution than from gate revenue. In addition, both clubs received £19 million (just over $30 million) from the overseas broadcast rights because this revenue is divided equally.[12] As a result, Manchester United made only 50 percent more than QPR from the sale of Premier League broadcast rights: £61 million (about $98 million) compared to £40 million ($64 million).

Where Manchester United did much better than QPR was in revenue from playing in Europe—Manchester United was in the Champions League and QPR did not qualify for any European competitions that season. Manchester United's revenue from playing in the Champions League that season was £30 million ($48 million). But this still means that Manchester United's total broadcast revenue was only double that of QPR's—again, a much more equal distribution than the gate money.

If the Premier League broadcasting contract and most other domestic TV broadcasting contracts have tended to promote equality, then the Champions League has done much to increase the inequality of revenue distribution in soccer. Between 2003 and 2012 almost half of all prize money paid out by UEFA from the Champions League went to just ten clubs: Real Madrid, Barcelona, Manchester United, Chelsea, Arsenal, Liverpool, Bayern Munich, Internazionale, AC Milan, and Olympique Lyonnais. And it has largely been the traditionally dominant clubs that have benefited most from the unequal distribution of the new European TV money.

BOX 4.5: THE UNEQUAL SHARE OF CHAMPIONS LEAGUE BROADCASTING REVENUE

Between 2003 and 2012, UEFA paid out €5.6 billion ($7 billion) in prize money to teams competing in the Champions League. Some 45 percent of that prize money went to just ten teams, which competed in almost every season and received an average €256 million ($320 million) each over the decade, or €25.6 million ($32 million) in every season (see table below). By contrast, there were another eighty-five clubs that participated over the decade but only for 2.7 seasons on average and they received only €3.6 million ($4.5 million) on average for each season they played. This means that these clubs received only €10 million ($12.5 million) on average over the entire decade. To put it another way, each of the big clubs *every year* gets more than two and a half times as much Champions League broadcast revenue as each of the remaining teams can expect to make *in a decade.*

Club	*average Champions League revenue per season $m*	*seasons*
Chelsea	40.4	9
Manchester United	40.2	10
Barcelona	34.4	9
Arsenal	32.9	10
Internazionale	32.7	10
Bayern Munich	31.5	9
AC Milan	30.1	9
Real Madrid	29.3	10
Olympique Lyonnais	28.2	10
Liverpool	21.2	7
The rest	4.5	2.7

SOURCE: UEFA

CONTINUES

Revenue is also quite skewed among "the rest." A few clubs, such as Juventus, Porto, and PSV Eindhoven, appear quite often and generate substantial revenues. About 40 percent of clubs appear in only a single season and receive a tiny fraction of the amount paid to the big clubs. These small amounts, however, may still appear quite large relative to the annual budgets of the smaller clubs, and may still be enough to give them a significant edge in domestic competition in the smaller leagues.

As in the case of the Premier League, these two forces—domestic TV rights and Champions League revenues—seem to have canceled each other out (see Figure 4.4). While Arsenal, Chelsea, and Manchester United have obtained a significant advantage over their Premier League rivals thanks to the Champions League, the growth of revenue from Premier League broadcasting has ensured that weaker clubs have not become even weaker. This seems to have been the pattern in most countries.

The one big exception is Spain. Spanish clubs negotiate their broadcast contracts individually. Barcelona and Real Madrid have therefore been able to extend the advantage that they have over domestic rivals in gate revenue into TV broadcast contracts, which has helped to make them the two richest clubs in world soccer and also to make Spain the most unequal nation in terms of revenue distribution. For example, in England, the ratio between the highest revenue and lowest revenue in the top division rose from around 3:1 in the 1950s to around 10:1 by the end of the 1980s, but has since fallen and presently stands at around 6:1.

Long-term data for Spain is not available, but by 1998 the ratio already stood at 12:1 in La Liga. By 2007, it had risen to 20:1, and in 2014 it was still rising. La Liga must rank as the most unequal of any major sports leagues in the world: a surprising fact for those who think that inequality makes sporting competition less attractive to fans. La Liga has acquired a huge global following in recent years, second or maybe even equal to the Premier League's. It has also produced some of Europe's best teams. In 2014, Atlético Madrid, despite vastly inferior financial resources, beat Barcelona and Real Madrid to win La Liga, and reached the final of the Champions League where it was defeated by Real Madrid. Could it be that even the smaller Spanish clubs benefit from the dominance of the big two?

BOX 4.6: INEQUALITY AND LA LIGA

The Spanish league has always been one of the most unequal, dominated for most of its history by the two giants, Real Madrid and Barcelona. Economists often illustrate inequality by showing the cumulative share of income accounted for as you go from the poorest to the richest (the Lorenz Curve). If income is equally distributed then the Lorenz Curve will form a diagonal line rising from left to right on the chart. The more "bowed" the curve, the more unequal the distribution. The Lorenz Curves below compare the distribution of league revenues in 2011 for La Liga and the Premier League.

Income equality in La Liga and the Premier League in 2011.
(Source: Club financial accounts)

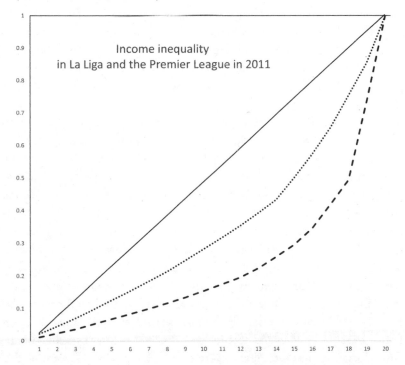

CONTINUES

The fact that the line for La Liga is far more bowed out than the Premier League shows that income is far more unequally distributed.

The degree of inequality can also be summarized by the Gini coefficient. This is a number between zero and one, with zero meaning perfect equality and one meaning all income is in the hands of one individual. The Gini coefficient for the Premier League is 0.38, while for La Liga it is a much larger 0.61. For the sake of comparison, the Gini coefficient for personal incomes in the Spanish economy is 0.46, exactly the same as it is for the United Kingdom. So income distribution in the Premier League is a little bit more egalitarian than income distribution in the UK economy as a whole, whereas income distribution in La Liga is far more unequal than it is in Spanish society taken as a whole.

Both domestic and Champions League broadcast money has helped to promote a different sort of inequality—inequality among the nations. The development of the Champions League in the 1990s not only gave more places in competition to clubs from the bigger countries, but also gave more weight to teams that come from the biggest broadcast markets (a.k.a., the bigger countries). Many people object to the fact that the Champions League no longer represents the best teams from each country but allows second-, third-, and fourth-ranked teams from some countries to compete. Whether you think it is acceptable for a team to become the champion of Europe without also being its own country's champion seems (to me at least) to be a matter of taste. But the argument, sometimes heard, that this penalizes the small nations does not seem warranted. If anything, the big nations are slightly underrepresented: the ten largest nations in UEFA accounted for 74 percent of the population in 2012, and 68 percent of the places in the group stages (the last thirty-two) between 2005 and 2014. To be sure, there are some countries that seem underrepresented relative to their population size—including Russia, Poland, and Turkey—and some that seem overrepresented—England, Spain, and Portugal—but then the Champions League is not intended to be a pure quota system. Teams have to qualify on merit.[13]

However, the revenue distribution formula for the Champions Leagues is strongly skewed toward the clubs from the biggest broadcast markets: England, Germany, Italy, and Spain. When teams from these countries win, they earn more money from winning than do clubs from smaller broadcast markets. Because the revenue from winning is larger, the capacity to fund a winning team is greater, so the teams from the larger countries do indeed win more often. There has always been dominance, and teams from these four nations/markets have always produced a disproportionate share of the champions. Out of fifty-nine winners of the Champions League/European Cup between 1955 and 2013, three-quarters came from one of these nations, and so did three-quarters of the runners-up. But the dominance of these four nations has increased somewhat in the last twenty years and now 90 percent of the winners and runners-up come from these nations.

The uneven sharing is a consequence of the economic bargaining power of the clubs from these countries. Their populations are not only large but also rich and fanatical about soccer. If UEFA did not give the big clubs from these countries the lion's share of the revenue, there would be enough of them to leave and form their own competition. UEFA prefers to promote an uneven competition than lose the participation of the biggest clubs.

Soccer clubs are remarkably focused activities. Unlike most businesses, few clubs undertake any significant commercial activities other than trying to win soccer matches. Diversification is not unknown in the soccer world—from making jerseys and cleats and building ticket machines to lotteries and bingo nights—but these enterprises are seldom a success and clubs usually return to their core business. In much of the world, soccer clubs are part of larger multisports clubs—notably Barcelona and Real Madrid, which boast teams in sports as diverse as basketball, handball, hockey, and even rugby union. But these activities impinge only to a limited extent on the financing of the soccer club.

The most important sources of revenue for clubs outside of gate money and broadcasting are sponsorship and merchandising. The amount of revenue that these activities can generate is almost directly proportional to the success of the team on the field. A team with lots of fans attending the stadium and watching on TV can sell lots of jerseys and attract lucrative sponsorship contracts from brewers, car manufacturers, and the like.

As with broadcasting, the growth in these sources of revenue is relatively recent, and now accounts for 30 percent of revenue in the largest leagues. The potential from these sources diminishes quite rapidly as you move to smaller leagues, and so this has been another factor creating inequality between divisions within countries, and between large countries and small countries. For the biggest clubs there still remains a lot of untapped potential. While they have a global presence, they have historically had limited capacity to negotiate local sponsorship contracts in faraway places, and piracy of merchandising has been rampant. As the global market becomes smaller, these clubs can be expected to exert more control and so secure an even larger revenue stream.

Merchandising mostly takes the form of soccer jerseys, and while they seem to have become ubiquitous in recent years the soccer clubs lag far behind the US sports leagues. One study by the consultants PwC[14] estimated that three-quarters of all sports merchandising is sold in the United States. This reflects both a higher level of spending on sports in the States, and perhaps a different approach to dressing. Europeans in particular still tend to dress more formally than Americans, and seem less willing to reveal their preferences through what they wear. In the long term, this is likely to change and soccer merchandise sales should grow rapidly in the future.

One aspect of merchandising that often puzzles Americans is that soccer jerseys also carry advertising logos for sponsors. Many Americans think that this devalues the jersey and no major league sports team has yet agreed to sell any of this valuable real estate.[15] This reflects a different cultural experience in relation to jerseys and uniforms. In American sports, teams have used logos on their uniforms since the earliest days of sport. This has not always been true of soccer clubs. They may have had crests and logos, but they were not always displayed on the jersey. For example, if you go back to 1970, Ajax, AC Milan, and Manchester United did not have their logos on their jerseys. This suggests that the jersey has a more malleable image in the soccer world than in the United States.[16] Soccer sponsorship on jerseys was not widely adopted until the 1980s, and developed first in England largely because at that time the league was in danger of complete financial collapse. With the future of the league at stake it was no time to be sentimental.

Sponsorship is a form of revenue that was developed first by US sports organizations but is rapidly growing in significance in the world of soccer. While sponsors have always wanted to associate themselves with successful players, and examples of players being linked to products go back to the nineteenth century, sponsorship of clubs is a more recent phenomenon. Even in the early-1970s the firms that made soccer jerseys and shoes actually sold them to the players and clubs rather than paying for the right to be the exclusive equipment supplier. Over time, sponsorship has grown and today PwC estimates that it accounts for about 25 percent of the total revenue of sports organizations. The company also estimates that while merchandising revenues in the United States are larger than sponsorship revenues, in the rest of the world (which mostly means the soccer world) sponsorships generate about five times as much revenue as merchandising.

A large part of the sponsorship market is associated with broadcasting. Businesses can pay to advertise their products on the boards that cover the perimeter of the playing field, but a sponsor can get its name onto the jersey that the star player is wearing—which is a seemingly more personal endorsement. It is striking that while the English and Spanish clubs have been more closely associated with the commercialization of sport, it is the clubs of the Bundesliga that have had the most success in attracting sponsorship. Around 30 percent of Bundesliga revenue comes from sponsorship alone, while in the Premier League the share may be as little as half of that—total commercial revenue, including sponsorship and merchandising, accounts for 30 percent of Premier League revenue.

One reason advanced for this is that Bundesliga broadcast rights have not migrated to pay TV to the same extent as they have in other countries. Free-to-air TV channels generate larger audiences than pay TV, so sponsors get more exposure. Germany is also the largest and wealthiest nation in the European Union, and hence the value of sponsoring popular clubs in this market may be greater than it is anywhere else. Alternatively, it may just be that the men (it is mostly men) who run German corporations like German soccer and so like to sponsor German clubs. Most corporations claim that they derive a great deal of value from sponsorship. It's clear that successful sponsorship can lead to increased recognition of a brand name; what is more difficult is showing that sponsorship translates into higher profits.

Returning to an important theme of this book, revenues from merchandising and sponsorship are very closely linked to league performance. Any well-run club can significantly increase revenue from these sources by better league performance, and no matter how well run, any club will see a dramatic decline in revenue from these sources if league performance deteriorates. However, some clubs have been more successful than others at developing merchandising and sponsorship revenues. In recent years, Manchester United has been at the forefront of developing sponsorship deals—in 2013/14 the team's commercial revenue was £189 million (more than $300 million), compared to only £77 million (some $123 million) at Arsenal, which finished higher than them in the league. United's model has been to develop local sponsorship deals across the world. Relying on the fact that you can watch the Premier League in almost every country in the world today, United has looked for a commercial sponsor (e.g., a mobile phone company) in every country. Because there are about two hundred nations on the planet, even if each of these deals brings in only a small amount of money, the collection of small deals adds up to be a big deal. We can expect to see the other big clubs imitating this strategy over the next few years.

Another source of revenue for clubs remains to be considered: player sales. Unlike the other sources, however, player sales are unlikely to be a stable, long-term source of revenue for most clubs. Most clubs do not have the capacity to develop players, sell them, and maintain their position in the league at the same time. Selling good players almost always entails a deterioration in league position unless new players are bought as replacements. Selling players without replacement is like eating into your long-term savings—it may bring a temporary respite in times of economic difficulty, but it is best seen as an emergency measure. Usually the reason for selling players without replacement is financial distress brought about by debt.

5

DEBT

THE BASIC OPERATING COMPONENTS OF SOCCER CLUBS ARE PLAYER costs, stadium costs, and revenues; and, as we've seen, performance on the field is fundamentally connected to what is spent on the team. Simply put, in soccer you get what you pay for because there is a market for players that functions more or less efficiently. Every player is a gamble, and individual performances are highly unpredictable, but clubs employ so many players, and players perform in so many games that these uncertainties tend to cancel each other out, leaving only the overwhelming effect of financial power. One only has to look at the rise of Chelsea, Manchester City, or Paris Saint-Germain in the last decade to see the reality of this power. Equally, success on the field turns reliably into revenue.

But the soccer market as a whole is highly competitive, which leads to the following conclusion: for every position in the league, the level of spending required to achieve that position is almost exactly matched by the revenues that can be earned. Over the long run this must be true if soccer markets operate more or less efficiently. At every position in the league, the expected profit (which is just the difference between revenues and spending on players and stadium) must be (1) roughly the same, and (2) roughly equal to zero.

If the market worked perfectly then this would be exactly true. In such a perfect world, imagine that profits were not exactly the same at all levels. If higher league positions were more profitable, then it would clearly make sense for lower-ranked teams to compete to hire the better players. But increased competition for the services of those players would bid up their cost, and this would reduce the profitability of the higher positions. Alternatively, if lower-league positions were more profitable then new teams would enter league competition from below in order to compete for these profitable league positions.

Unless there is some barrier to entry, then competition will also drive profits down to the lowest sustainable level. In most industries this is zero because loss-making firms will go out of business. In soccer, because owners may be willing to tolerate losses, the floor might actually be a level of profit less than zero. This is an idealized description of a competitive process at work. If there were barriers to entry—for example, new teams could not automatically enter the league because there was no promotion and relegation—then it would be possible for incumbent clubs to make sustained profits because there would be few rivals to compete them away. But promotion and relegation creates an open market, and the openness of the league system in soccer ensures that the competitive mechanism can work.

In a perfectly competitive market all businesses would be at zero-profit equilibrium. One way to think of the meaning of equilibrium in markets is that it is the state of the world in which all opportunities have been exploited and no one is making a mistake. Clearly, this is not a state of the world that we are ever going to reach—even if it is possible (depending on the market) to get quite close to it. Adjustment is difficult if some businesses corner the market, or if the assets required for success are difficult to identify. Efficient markets ease the adjustment toward equilibrium by ensuring that if an opportunity exists (e.g., to make money by achieving a higher league position) then it is easy to obtain the assets required by paying the appropriate price. But much as we try to avoid mistakes, they seem to happen. Maybe to some people more than to others but, even then, many of us may end up paying for the mistakes of others. For example, one investor who wrongly imagines there is money to be made by buying expensive players raises the market price so all the other investors have to pay more too.

The reality of markets is a process of constantly "groping" toward equilibrium, and it is in that process that we find the real decision-making problems of soccer. In equilibrium, revenues and expenditures match, but in the day-to-day operation of a club there is always the problem of timing. Spending comes first—spending required to put the team into the field. Revenues are the rewards for that investment. There is a gap between outlays and receipts that needs to be bridged. In essence this is the subject of finance: the different ways of bridging that gap. One of the most important ways to make that bridge is borrowing.

> Debt has become a somewhat dirty word in some quarters of football. However, people's perceptions are often created from, and reinforced by, negative generic headlines, whereas, in principle, debt is not necessarily a bad thing. If debt is sustainable and the repayment schedule is manageable within the cash generated from the club's operations, it can be used to facilitate and fund a growth strategy.
>
> Deloitte's *Annual Review of Football Finance* 2012/13

> In practice, the term 'football club debts' has been used in many different ways with a great deal of flexibility, references range from the very broad, totaling allliabilities that a club has, to the narrow definition of debt financing either including or excluding interest free owner loans.
>
> UEFA's *Club Licensing Benchmarking Report 2008*

Germans use the same word to describe both "debt" and "guilt"—*Schuld*.[1] Many people feel this way about incurring debts—it seems to have a slightly immoral character to it. And yet modern economies, with all that they deliver in goods and services, health, education, life expectancy, and wellbeing, have been delivered by extensive networks of credit and debt. The foundations of Europe's wealth were laid by a long process of trade and investment that stretches from the Middle Ages to the Industrial Revolution. At the heart of this process lay ever-more complex methods for creating credit and debt.

BOX 5.1: WHERE THE MONEY COMES FROM

The investments that clubs make in players and stadiums can come from revenue generated by the business of selling tickets, broadcasting rights, and so on. The gap between spending and revenues can be bridged by short-term finance (e.g., bank overdraft).

But in its 2013 *Annual Review of Football Finance*, Deloitte attempted to explain where extra money invested in the Premier League over its first 20 years had come from. It pointed out that the real debt of the Premier League, once soft loans from owners were discounted, added up to no more than $1.6 billion, only 40 percent of the annual income of the league. One of the successes of the Premier League has been its ability to attract capital investment from outside:

- *The stock exchange.* During the 1990s, clubs raised about $280 million in total from investors seeking a financial return from owning a soccer club—though most of these owners never saw any return
- *Media investment.* At the end of the 1990s, Sky, the satellite broadcaster that had done so much to finance and promote the Premier League, attempted to buy Manchester United. The company was blocked by the UK competition authorities but its bid triggered a spate of investments by media companies thinking that they needed to own part of a club in order to get better access to its broadcast rights. The fad petered out after the collapse of ITV Digital, but not before media companies had invested about $480 million in clubs, again with no obvious return.
- *New owners.* In the last decade, around $4 billion of new money has been brought in by new owners of clubs, most notably Roman Abramovich and Sheikh Mansour, who between them have accounted for about $2.8 billion. This has made a huge contribution to bringing some of the world's most talented players to the Premier League. But will these investors ever see a return?

The modern banking system grew out of the financing of trade ventures half a millennium ago or more. Ships traveling from Europe could bring back goods that could not be produced locally—spices, silk, porcelain, and the like—but these voyages were both time consuming and risky. Venturers willing to take the risk were not hard to find, but they seldom had the capital to invest. And so lenders emerged who would advance the costs of the voyage in exchange for a large share of the returns in the event of success. Ventures often failed because the goods purchased might turn out to be worthless or, worse still, the ship sank or was captured by enemies or pirates. The profits on the ships that successfully returned with valuable cargoes had to be large enough to cover the losses on those that did not. Wealthy individuals specialized in organizing this kind of lending, working out which ships and which captains were most likely to succeed, how much to charge for their services, and spreading their risk across many different voyages.

In later centuries these prototype banking services extended to industrial businesses. Established businesses borrowed money from industrial banks to finance the acquisition of equipment, raw material, and money to pay wages, to be paid back out of the revenues when the goods were produced and sold in the marketplace.

BOX 5.2: DEBT AND THE MODIGLIANI-MILLER THEOREM

It is a longstanding view among bankers and soccer fans that too much debt is bad for business. Back in the 1950s, two finance professors considered the issue in the following terms: a business can finance itself from equity (selling shares) or from debt (loans), but how is the value of the firm affected by the share of debt in the total financing package?[1] Their answer, which still surprises many people, is that in general it makes no difference.

So what is wrong with the commonsense intuition that debt is bad? Well, as is often the case, it all depends on what assumptions you make. The difference between debt and equity is that lenders usually insist on fixed repayments at fixed intervals, while

CONTINUES

shareholders receive whatever is left after paying off everything that is owed—which could be a little or could be a lot, and in some years could be nothing at all. So debt is usually considered less risky than equity.

However, many investors own both debt and equity—especially the large pension funds and insurance companies that account for a lot of investment in businesses. They might invest in debt with a safe and steady return, and in equity with high but variable returns. If one option were clearly better than the other, then they would invest in only debt or only equity. The fact that they invest in both tells us that the returns must be equalized—the higher return on equity compensates more or less exactly for the added riskiness.

Now consider what happens when a company increases the share of debt in its financing: since the debt has to be repaid on time, the equity becomes more risky as the residual left over for the shareholders gets smaller and smaller. But the overall variability in the profits generated by the business is unchanged. This is the crucial point: since the value of the profits themselves is unchanged, we are just arguing about how the profits are shared out. So the financing of the company can change the riskiness of the equity, but cannot change the value of the business.

Of course, as the share of debt increases the debt becomes riskier too—the chance of being unable to meet fixed repayments increases, and so the interest rate on the debt must also go up. Why? Imagine it did not, then the company shares would become much more valuable since the risk would be with the debt holders, but the upside returns would still go entirely to the shareholders. In the 1980s, the financial markets started to buy risky debt as just another financial product: junk bonds.

So is the value of a soccer club really independent of the proportion of its business that is financed by debt? Not really. Merton Miller and Franco Modigliani listed a number of assumptions required for their M&M theorem to be true. One is that debt and dividends (the shareholder returns) are taxed in the same way. But in general they are not. It's actually advantageous from a financial point of view to have more debt, since this tends to reduce the amount of tax due.

The second important assumption is that there are no transaction costs. If a firm issues a lot of debt and can't meet its repayments then it is in default and the business falls into the hands of the creditors. They can then obtain the money they are owed by reselling the business or running it themselves. In theory, this changes nothing about the business itself, and so should not affect the value of the company. In practice, though, insolvency is often an expensive and disruptive process that can affect the value of the firm.

1. Modigliani, Franco, and Merton H. Miller. "The cost of capital, corporation finance and the theory of investment." *The American Economic Review* (1958): 261–297.

In Shakespeare's *Merchant of Venice,* the business of Shylock is to lend money to fund trade voyages. His money is used to pay for ships, crew, supplies, and the goods to be bought abroad, and he is then repaid from the profits on the sale of goods after the ship returns safely home. When Antonio, a young merchant, seeks funding, Shylock agrees to lend him the money, but on condition that if the voyage fails to produce a return then he will still be compensated. Given his dislike for Antonio, who has insulted him in the past, he demands the unusual compensation of a pound of Antonio's flesh if Antonio cannot repay the money lent. This is an unusual example, but still illustrates the basic method by which lenders insure themselves against loss—in the event that the borrower cannot repay the debt, the lender is allowed to seize something of value belonging to the debtor.

"Pound of flesh" passed into the language as a metaphor for an excessive compensation in the event of the borrower's default. But until not so long ago the reality of failing to repay a debt was scarcely less onerous. Up until the late-nineteenth century, borrowers could be sent to debtors' prison if they did not repay debts exactly on time, and meanwhile all their assets could be seized and sold off to repay the debt. This system encouraged lenders to cheat their borrowers in order to take control of their assets on the cheap. In Charles Dickens's novel *David Copperfield,* Mr. Micawber lives on the edge of poverty but is always borrowing to fund a lifestyle that is beyond his means. He spends a good deal of time in debtors' prison.

Toward the end of the nineteenth century, governments and businesses started to realize the importance of credit for economic growth.

This led to changes in legislation. Debtors' prison was abolished, and while severe sanctions remained for those who entered personal bankruptcy because they were unable to pay their debts, the possibilities for businesses to engage in borrowing were expanded dramatically. Indeed, a new kind of "person" was invented within the legal system: the limited liability corporation. Until then, corporations had been few and far between, and were usually created explicitly by the monarch in order to grant special privileges to some. Before the limited liability corporation, businesses were either run by a "sole trader"—someone who typically owned and managed his or her own business—or a partnership. In either case, those who owned the business were totally liable for the debts of the business.

The concept of the limited liability corporation, introduced in England in 1855, revolutionized business. It allowed the company rather than the owners directly to borrow money, and if the business failed only the company was liable, not the owners. This still meant that in the event of failure the lenders could seize all of the assets of the company in order to get some or all of their debts repaid, but the individuals who invested in the business were no longer putting all of their wealth at stake. Put simply, they were no longer risking their own homes and the shirts on their backs.

The Football Association was founded in 1863. It is an odd coincidence of history that organized soccer developed just at the time when the new type of corporation became popular. English soccer clubs were some of the very first enterprises to take advantage of the opportunity. In 1888, thirteen years after its foundation, Birmingham City Football Club became company number 27,318 on the Companies House Register (these numbers being allocated in order of registration). Clubs such as Newcastle United, Notts County, West Bromwich Albion, Grimsby Town, Liverpool, Everton, Middlesbrough, Gillingham, and Preston North End all obtained company numbers lower than 40,000. Fifty clubs in total were given numbers below 100,000. The following statistic gives some idea of how early these clubs came in the history of limited liability. When, in 2007, Tom Hicks and George Gillett bought Liverpool Football Club and Athletic Grounds Public Limited Company (registration number 35,668, incorporated in January 1892) they created a new company called Kop Football Holdings Limited, with registration number 6,032,200.

The relatively novel limited liability corporation has become the dominant form of business organization in the last one hundred years. The main benefit to soccer clubs of this organizational structure is the same as it is for most businesses—insulating those who own and run the company from liability for the company debt in the case of default. Back in the 1870s and 1880s, English clubs were starting to build stadiums to meet the increasing demand for the new spectator sport. Until then, clubs had been just that: membership organizations run by a committee elected by members who paid an annual subscription fee. The problem was that, under English law, if the club borrowed money to fund the construction of a stadium and the debt could not be paid, the members of the club committee would be personally liable. Adoption of limited liability status avoided this problem. By 1923, almost every single professional soccer club in England was also a limited liability company. (Technically speaking, the limited liability company owns the club, which is a separate entity—this is important when dealing with insolvency as we will see in chapter 8.) The only holdout was Nottingham Forest, which did not become a limited liability company until 1982.

When we think of debt, most of us think of money borrowed from the bank or other professional lenders. In the corporate world, banks lend to businesses over a fixed term—say five or ten years—specifying the interest rate and repayment dates. Large corporations like Sony or Ford or Coca-Cola can sell large amounts of this debt to the markets in the form of bonds and then investors can trade it among themselves. Such corporate bonds are a reliable form of savings for investors. Big businesses such as these are unlikely ever to go bust, and so they are deemed safe investments. If they were unable to repay their debts, then in principle the company assets could be seized to ensure repayment. Even though this is very unlikely, the investors have the added reassurance that these assets would be worth something and could easily be sold off to another business in order to ensure at least partial repayment.

Most smaller businesses do not have the kind of reputation that would allow them to sell bonds to the market. However, they can still borrow from individual banks with which they have built a relationship. Typically, banks will lend to the same companies many times over. Their ideal is to build a long-term relationship with growing businesses (and in the process sell them lots of services). To protect themselves in the event of default, the banks will take security over the assets in which the company invests. For example, if a company buys a building in order to house a factory, the bank can lend the money, and if the business fails the bank can repossess the building, which can in all likelihood be sold off to another business. That will minimize any loss to the bank. The bank might not get back all of its money, but it is not called "security" for nothing.

This model of lending does not really work for soccer clubs. Most spending by clubs is on players, who cannot be owned, seized, or directly controlled in a world without slavery or indenture. Clubs do have some control over player careers through the player registration on which the transfer system is based. However, banks have shown little interest in lending to clubs so that they can buy players whose registration might one day be sold. Few clubs have found ways to consistently generate the profits in the transfer market that would be required to make the lending pay off. In any case, a club needs to retain enough players to make up the team.[2]

Stadium investment is also an unusually risky business for banks. A stadium does generate ticket and related revenues, which can repay money borrowed to build it, but these are highly contingent on the success of the team. If that success does not materialize, the bank can't just repossess the stadium and sell it to another club—local fans would not be willing to support a new club bused in to occupy "their" stadium. Banks also can't easily take possession and sell off the land to build houses or a supermarket. Local planning authorities controlled by local politicians usually place significant restrictions on changing the use of the land on which a stadium rests. They know that demolishing the local stadium would not go down well with voters.

BOX 5.3: THE FINANCING OF ARSENAL'S NEW STADIUM

Arsenal is one of the most stable and financially conservative soccer clubs on the planet. Based in the now wealthy area of Highbury in North London, it has been in the top division since 1919 and was known as "The Bank of England" in the 1930s. In the last 25 years, Arsenal has won the league title four times and its lowest finishing position was twelfth. From the 1990s, its stadium's capacity was only 38,000; every game was sold out and there was a long waiting list for season tickets—despite having the highest prices in the Premier League. As a result, the club wanted to build a new stadium and in 2002 obtained permission to start construction on derelict land very close to the old stadium.

At the time, the revenue of the club was just over $160 million per year, and the cost of the redevelopment was expected to be in the region of $560 million. The start of the project was delayed by problems with the financing—the club either didn't want or was not able to obtain bank loans for the full cost, and it needed to fund part of the cost out of player sales, a bond issued to fans, and the redevelopment of the old stadium as luxury apartments. Given that many clubs with far weaker financial positions than Arsenal have built new stadiums in recent years, it seems that the main concern of the club was to avoid risk.

The club raised £260 million (about $416 million) in commercial debt—meaning the debt could be traded on the market by investors, ensuring they obtained a relatively low interest rate of 5 to 7 percent. Only a handful of clubs are able to borrow on such favorable terms. The debt was securitized against future revenues of the club—one of the few cases in the world of soccer where securitization seems to have worked well.

Construction started in February 2004 and was completed by September 2006, and although financial constraints associated with the construction were blamed for team manager Arsène Wenger's reluctance to buy in the transfer market, the club remained ever-present in the Champions League—and even made it to the final in May 2006. From the company accounts, the investment ended up costing in the region of £400 million (about $640 million), measured by payments to acquire tangible fixed assets

CONTINUES

between 2003 and 2007. The financing was also hit by concerns
in 2008 that the global financial crisis would undermine the value
of the luxury apartments and so create a shortfall in revenues.

In any event, the London property market did not collapse,
the club never dropped out of its position in the top four of the
Premier League, and while the annual financing cost of around
$32 million will be with the club for the next twenty years, gate
revenues leaped from $70 million in 2006 to $146 million in 2007
thanks to the increase in capacity to 60,000. Despite carrying
more debt than almost any other soccer club in the world, there
is hardly any risk that it will not be able to repay its debt while
maintaining its position as one of England's and Europe's biggest
clubs. An investment worthy of the Bank of England.

During the 1990s a novel form of lending called "securitization" became popular in the capital markets. Generally, this meant combining
lots of small loans, such as mortgage loans made by banks to individuals
to buy a house, into a large pool—which could then be treated as an
asset like a bond and sold to investors who would receive fixed-interest
payments. The idea behind this was that the pool of small loans, which
individually could be quite risky, became safer when combined in the
pool, because the risk of default on any one loan would not prevent the
interest payments being paid out on the entire pool. In time, people realized that any revenue stream generated by an asset could be securitized in
this way—for example, car loans and tax revenues. In 1997, David Bowie
sold off the right to future royalties on his music as a securitized bond. By
the early-2000s as much as 10 percent of all bonds issued in the market
were in the form of asset-backed securities.

Starting in the 1990s, soccer clubs got in on the act too. Because
many soccer fans are loyal, the argument went, they could be relied upon
to generate the revenue to repay the bond in future years; and if they
didn't, so the argument went, the stadium was the asset that the bondholders could seize in order to ensure repayment. By 2003, a number
of English clubs had securitized ticket revenues, including Everton, Ipswich Town, Leeds United, Leicester City, Manchester City, Norwich,
Southampton, and Tottenham Hotspur.[3] FIFA, the governing body of

world soccer that owns the rights to the World Cup, raised $420 million in 2001 by securitizing the sponsorship and broadcast rights to future World Cups. Italian clubs Lazio, Fiorentina, and Parma also joined in on the fun, and even in financially conservative Germany, Schalke 04 issued a securitized bond in 2002 (Borussia Dortmund pulled out of an issue at the last moment in 2003). The problem in most of these cases is that the money raised was spent on buying players, which might increase success in the short term, and therefore increase revenues to meet current interest payments, but sustained success requires sustained high spending, which becomes harder if future revenues are already committed. Proponents of securitization pointed to the sustained revenue growth in soccer, but conveniently ignored the evidence of sustained wage growth.[4]

The problem with asset-backed securities came to a head in the soccer world when clubs such as Leicester City and Leeds United collapsed financially. Relegated teams do not have enough loyal fans to maintain fixed-repayment schedules while maintaining a competitive team. Taking over the stadium was not the solution that the investors had hoped it would be, since there were few realistic alternatives to using the stadium to run a soccer team. It took the rest of the world until 2008 to see the potential risks of asset-backed securities, whose defaults lay at the heart of the subprime crisis and the subsequent meltdown of Western economies.

This does not mean that banks never lend to soccer clubs, just that clubs often find it difficult to raise money from this source. Traditionally, the relationship between a local bank and the local club was more about day-to-day business. Soccer clubs typically have significant cash revenue during the summer break as fans pay in advance for season tickets. Some of this money is spent on transfers but the rest is set aside for player wages. As the season progresses, the cash balance of the club decreases as wages exceed weekly ticket revenue, until by the end of the season the club is running out of cash. At this point, a bank is often willing to tide the club over with an overdraft facility until the season ends and the next round of season-ticket revenue is received. Another way in which banks are prepared to lend to clubs is against revenue that it's guaranteed to receive—broadcast revenue in particular (though even this can turn out to be very risky lending because broadcasters can collapse).

Generally speaking, bank-lending to soccer clubs is small, and has been diminishing as a share of total club borrowing for some time. Deloitte estimated that the total debt owed by Premier League clubs in 2012/13 amounted to £2.5 billion ($4 billion), but that less than 40 percent of this total was owed to banks—most of which was owed by just three clubs: Manchester United, Arsenal, and Aston Villa. At the next level down (the Football League Championship), clubs had debts of around £1 billion ($1.6 billion), of which about 60 percent was owed to banks and similar institutions. Most of the money owed by clubs in the top two divisions—almost £2 billion ($3.2 billion)—was actually owed to the owners of the clubs. These are generally called "soft loans."

BOX 5.4: CHELSEA DEBT AND EQUITY

Russian oligarch Roman Abramovich bought Chelsea Football Club at the beginning of the 2003/04 season. In the following five years he spent $800 million on player transfers, which was only partly offset by $387 million of sales. By the end of the 2008/09 season, he had paid out $1.3 billion in wages, which together with the net transfer costs was almost exactly equal to the $1.7 billion of revenue that the club had generated from the soccer business. But any business has more operating expenses than just wages, and the club accumulated a large deficit, funded from Mr. Abramovich's gigantic personal fortune.

Until 2009, he chose to show this investment divided roughly 50-50 between equity investment (issuing himself new shares in the company) and debts owed to other companies he owned—which stood at $544 million in the accounts for June 2008. Although that sum was described as a loan the club paid no interest on it. Then the accounts for June 2009 suddenly showed this debt reduced to a mere $22 million because the debt was shifted to equity—which now stood at almost $1.2 billion—not real money but simply a reflection of what he had invested in the club. It would only be "real" if someone were willing to pay him $1.2 billion to buy the club—not very likely in the aftermath of the 2008 global financial crisis.

So why did he do this? In the summer of 2009, Michel Platini, the president of UEFA, was working hard to get clubs to agree to a new form of financial regulation: Financial Fair Play. A key moment in the negotiations was when Platini was able to announce that he had Abramovich on board and that the Russian was willing to wipe out the club's debt. Again, in the post-subprime-crisis atmosphere, fans were more frightened of club debt than ever. We will probably never know what Abramovich received in return for giving Platini his publicity coup. Some speculated that it was intended to help limit the rise of Manchester City, which at the time was busy emulating Abramovich's strategy at Chelsea. No doubt, having powerful friends within UEFA is useful. But whatever he obtained in return, it's important to recognize that he was just moving the numbers on the balance sheet from one column to another, a gesture that really cost him nothing.

One might wonder whether these soft loans should be considered debts at all. Roman Abramovich bought Chelsea Football Club for £140 million ($224 million) in 2003 and then injected £984 million (just over $1.5 billion) into the club over the following decade. For a long time, part of this investment was represented in the company accounts as a loan. Would he ever have been able to recover this loan? If he liquidated his investment today and sold off the club he would be unlikely to get back the £1.1 billion ($1.8 billion) he would need to break even on his investment (without even considering interest). In May 2014, *Forbes* placed a value of £572 million ($915 million) on the club, substantially less than his investment. In 2009, Abramovich decided to convert the debt into equity. In many cases, owners have "lent" large sums of money to their club and never seen a penny.

The 2008 UEFA Club Licensing Report found that less than one third of the money owed by the top division clubs in Europe related to bank and commercial debt. Moreover, of that third, more than half (56 percent) was owed by English clubs—and at that time a large fraction would have been accounted for just by Arsenal and Manchester United. In other words, when we talk of debt and soccer clubs, we are usually talking about something much broader.

BOX 5.5: MANCHESTER UNITED, THE GLAZERS, AND DEBT

In 2005, the Glazer family bought Manchester United in a bitter takeover battle, eventually paying a price of just under $1.3 billion. Exactly how this was financed is not clear, but within a year the club had gone from a position of having no debts to a total debt of $800 million, about two and a half times the annual income of the club. Moreover, the lenders had demanded very high interest rates that accounted for about 20 percent of club revenues.

Many of the fans were outraged and launched persistent protests against the Glazers and their financial strategy. Some of this had to do with the means that the Glazers were using to repay the debt, notably a sharp increase in ticket prices. But more generally fans were worried by the seemingly excessive risk that had been imposed on the club (what would happen if the debt could not be repaid?), and the way this would probably undermine the performance of the club. It's not hard to sympathize with the fans—the Glazers had bought the club with other people's money and were using the loyalty of the fans (and their willingness to pay money to the club they love) to pay for their investment.

There were also significant concerns in 2010 that the interest costs would spiral out of control and lead to financial collapse. Andy Green, an investment analyst and passionate fan, wrote extensively in his excellent blog, Andersred, about the dangers. In March 2010, a group of wealthy fans from the financial markets calling themselves the Red Knights—led by Jim O'Neill, then chairman of Goldman Sachs Asset Management and a highly influential figure in financial markets—launched an attempt to persuade the Glazers to sell the club to them. It was said at the time that the Glazers would have sold the club for $2.4 billion, though the Red Knights offered about half of this and negotiations never really got started.

However, also in 2010, the Glazers managed to refinance their debt. Together with the remarkable rise in revenues generated by the club—they had almost doubled in five years—it became clear that the club was not really at any long-term financial risk. All this happened during what became the most successful period in the club's history, winning five league titles and the Champions League under the leadership of Sir Alex Ferguson. By his retirement in 2013, the debt had fallen to roughly the same level as one year's revenue for the club, which even in a risky business must be considered sustainable.

The problems of succession at Manchester United after Ferguson's retirement are considerable, and the failure to qualify for the Champions League in 2013/14 caused concern. But by this time the Glazers had sold off 10 percent of the company on the New York Stock Exchange and at the time of writing (September 2014) the shares valued the company at $2.7 billion—which implies that the Glazers' investment is currently worth in the region of $2.1 billion—maybe five to ten times what the Glazers invested. Not a bad return over less than ten years!

Manchester United under the Glazers: Revenue, debt, and interest costs. (Source: Club financial accounts)

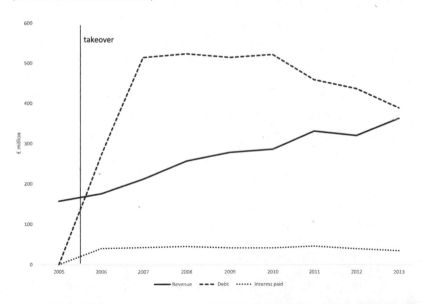

At any point in time any business usually owes money to different people. These debts are what accountants call liabilities. Liabilities include commercial debt lent by banks or other professional investors, but they also include much more. Liabilities are normally divided into short term and long term, which is one way to see if troubles are coming. A company that has problems meeting its long-term liabilities may ultimately become insolvent. This means that at some point in the future, if nothing changes, the company may fail, but there is still time to change. A company that cannot meet its short-term liabilities, meaning payments due within the next year, is likely to go to the wall very soon. About half of the liabilities of English soccer clubs are short-term, a fraction that seems to have diminished over time. In the past, soccer clubs were almost entirely dependent on short-term credit.

Two things have changed in recent years. First, TV contracts—which now account for one third to one half of revenue for the larger clubs—are signed over several years, and so there are now some lenders willing to advance money against these long-term contracts. Second, the significance of players as tradable assets has grown and so some lenders have been willing to match funding to the length of the player contract. This should have been good news for the financial stability of soccer clubs because longer term lending generally entails less risk.

UEFA's 2008 report included a breakdown of the liabilities of top division European clubs, which showed that two thirds of them were long term (see Table 5.1). In Europe as a whole commercial loans account for

TABLE 5.1 Liabilities of soccer clubs in Europe's top division in 2008

Bank & commercial loans	€5.5bn
Group & related parties	€2.2bn
Other long-term liabilities	€2.2bn
Taxes & social charges	€1.4bn
Transfers	€1.6bn
Other short term liabilities	€4.3bn
Liabilities: estimate clubs not in sample	€1.0bn
Total reported liabilities	€18.2bn

SOURCE: UEFA *Club Licensing Report* (2008)

around 30 percent of all liabilities, but as with the case of England, most of these loans were made to the "blue chip" clubs—the bigger clubs in the bigger leagues.

Almost 10 percent of liabilities relate to transfer fees—that is, money owed for players acquired. A significant part of "other short-term liabilities" is money owed to players in terms of wages, bonuses, and other financial commitments. The category of other short-term liabilities also includes services already delivered to a club (e.g., catering services), but not yet paid for. It might seem odd, but season-ticket payments are also included in this category. These represent cash coming into the business, but they are also a liability in the sense that while the money has been paid, the service (watching the next season's soccer matches) has not yet been delivered (and if it were not delivered, then the season-ticket holders would expect to get their money back).

One of the biggest problems for many clubs is paying their taxes and social charges. These appear as liabilities because these charges are paid in arrears. For example, clubs charge sales tax (called Value Added Tax, or VAT, in Europe) on tickets they sell. Later, the VAT collected has to be paid to the government. Practices differ by country, but it is not unusual for the payment deadline to be a month or so after the financial year in which the VAT was collected. For example, if a soccer club has a financial year that ends on June 30, VAT would be payable in the following August—which means that the VAT might have been paid to the club more than a year before it has to be handed over to the government. This is a free loan. The problem is that the club can invest the money, expecting to make a return, but if the investment goes wrong then the club may not have the money to pay the government when the due date arrives.

BOX 5.6: THE COLLAPSE OF RANGERS

The Scottish soccer club Rangers is one of the oldest in the world: founded in 1872. Always one of the two dominant clubs in the country alongside Celtic, the club had at least as many enemies as friends. About 15 years ago, the club started using a novel way

CONTINUES

to pay players—an Employee Benefit Trust—that seemed, to the tax authorities at least, to be a way of avoiding income tax, which also meant the players would look cheaper to the club.

The case went to court and became known as the Big Tax Case; if the tax authorities won, the amount of tax to be repaid by Rangers would be beyond the club's resources. Most experts believed that Rangers would lose the case. Around 2010, the long-time owner, Sir David Murray, who had invested a lot of his own money in maintaining the dominance of the club, decided he wanted to sell. Several potential bidders came and went until a maverick businessman named Craig Whyte showed an interest.

Whyte told Murray that he would be borrowing money from a reputable bank to fund player investment—Murray had indicated that he wanted the new owner to commit to investing in the club's long-term success. It appears that Murray and his advisers asked to know the identity of the bank, but Whyte refused to reveal it. Even so, the sale went through in May 2011.

It soon became apparent why Whyte had been so coy—the lender was not a bank but a company called Ticketus, which managed the ticketing business of soccer clubs and other organizations including Rangers. The money lent was to be repaid out of the securitized season-ticket income of the club itself.

The club went into administration in February 2012, largely because of an unpaid tax bill—which had nothing to do with either the Big Tax Case or the loans from Ticketus, but in a sense because of both. Rangers did not have the capacity to pay its taxes because a large part of its revenue was owed to Ticketus. It could not borrow against future income in part because of the uncertainty surrounding the Big Tax Case.

In the summer of 2012, the English businessman Charles Green acquired the club's Ibrox stadium and all the assets of the old club from the administrator, and placed them under the ownership of a new limited company he had created, initially called Sevco and then renamed "The Rangers Football Club Limited." Because the old club, which was liquidated, was the entity that played in the Scottish Premier League, the league did not allow the new Rangers to play in the following season, and it was required to enter the fourth tier of Scottish soccer, playing to crowds of 47,000 against teams whose average gate was less than 1,000.

Even more bizarrely, while Rangers fans are in no doubt that their club will survive in the guise of the new company, a very large fraction of Scottish fans who support other teams insist that the new club has nothing whatsoever to do with the club founded in 1872. Is a soccer club its community or the legal entity?

The ultimate irony is that Rangers ultimately won the Big Tax Case at the end of 2012. Had this been the expected outcome in 2010, the old company would have had a much better chance of surviving. Nonetheless, Whyte's strategy of borrowing against the club's future income in order to gain ownership clearly did little to enhance the financial health of the company. In September 2014, he was disqualified by a UK court from holding a company directorship in any company in the United Kingdom or connected to the UK for the next 15 years because of the harm he caused to Rangers.

UEFA's analysis spotlighted some particular countries and clubs whose tax liabilities were especially large. As UEFA put it, "The level of debts to authorities is of particular relevance as the political nature of these debts (compared to ordinary trade and commercial debts) can lead to problems building up."[5] There is certainly a problem for the soccer authorities if clubs are seen to be paying players extremely high salaries but then cannot pay their taxes. Many fans call for government intervention to control soccer clubs' spending. For their part, the people who run the clubs do not want government interference, and FIFA has fairly strict rules forbidding government influence over national associations. For example, when French President Nicolas Sarkozy indicated that he might intervene in the running of the French national team following the embarrassing players' strike during the 2010 World Cup, FIFA threatened to suspend France from all FIFA competition.

France in fact was identified as a country where unpaid tax liabilities were among the largest—accounting for one-third of all liabilities, and equal to more than one-quarter of annual club revenue. Spain is probably the highest profile case where tax liabilities to the government are seen as a problem. In a paper published in 2010, Ángel Barajas and Plácido Rodriguez examined the accounts of soccer clubs in the top two divisions of Spain.[6] Money owed to the tax authorities amounted to over 30 percent of annual revenue. Apart from Barcelona and Real Madrid, it is unlikely that the Spanish clubs will ever be able to repay these debts. Indeed, this type of crisis has been a common feature of Spanish soccer. The government had to restructure soccer club tax debts in 1985, 1991, and 1998. In 2012, matters came to a head—Spain's government was seeking support from the European Central Bank and its partners in the euro area to deal with the catastrophic national debt at the same time as it became apparent that soccer club tax debt was reaching new highs. Uli Hoeness, then president of Bayern Munich, commented, "This is unthinkable. We pay them hundreds of millions to get them out of shit and the clubs don't pay their debts." Ironically, two years later, Hoeness was sentenced to three years in prison for tax evasion.

BOX 5.7: THE DEBT OF SPANISH SOCCER CLUBS

In recent years, the debt of Spanish clubs has caused much comment in the press, with many clubs on the edge of bankruptcy. Undoubtedly these Spanish clubs are in severe financial difficulty, but people often make the mistake of thinking that this situation extends to the two big clubs, Real Madrid and Barcelona.

One of the best analysts of soccer finance is a blogger called Swiss Ramble who penned an excellent post on the subject in 2012: swissramble.blogspot.com/2012/04/truth-about -debt-at-barcelona-and-real.html. He assessed the size of debt of the big two after:

netting off the value of cash balances (that substantially reduces the headline figure);

taking into account the ability of the clubs to repay (looking both at their revenues and their profits);

taking into account the strength of the balance sheet (the assets that offset the value of the liabilities).

Based on this analysis he concluded that while many other clubs might be in deep difficulty, the big two are not really at risk at all.

All this suggests that while many liabilities of soccer clubs look like what we would normally call debt (such as money owed to the tax authorities), not all liabilities should be treated like debts. Season-ticket revenue, in particular, doesn't bear much resemblance to what we normally think of as a debt. One way to think of that is how easily the liability will be discharged. In the case of season tickets, we think it very likely that the club will be able to deliver. In the case of tax obligations we may not be so sure. The important issue when considering debt is the prospect that the debt will be repaid.

When debt is calculated in a narrow sense—commitments to repay sums of money to banks and other financial institutions—it is also normal to deduct the value of cash and other assets that can easily be turned into cash, in order to arrive at net debt. It might seem odd that a club holds onto money at the same time as having debts. After all, why hold a debt and the means to repay that debt at the same time? However, while almost all businesses borrow money, they also need cash in the short term to cover immediate payments and emergencies. People who own a house may have a large mortgage, which is a debt owed to a financial institution, but at the same time they may have cash in their bank account. One problem with accounts is that they give a snapshot of a business's state of affairs on a given day, which is the end of the soccer season for many clubs. But because this is the time of year when most clubs have just received a lot of cash in payment for next year's season tickets, the annual accounts can give an unrealistically healthy impression of the club's financial position. If accounts are drawn up in mid-season, the picture can look a lot different.[7]

But clubs have assets other than cash that can be used to repay debts and liabilities. These assets, whether in the form of player registrations, the stadium, or any number of other assets in which clubs invest in order to run their business, generate revenues in the ordinary course of business. They can also, at least in theory, be sold in the case of pressing need. According to the 2008 UEFA report, European top division clubs owned assets worth €20 billion ($25 billion), more than enough to pay off all their liabilities, if they were pooled together. Judged by normal financial standards, then, the European soccer business looks healthy. Moreover, the report also found that leagues in which the clubs had the largest liabilities were also those whose assets had the highest value in the financial accounts. Premier League clubs had by far the largest net debt of any league in Europe—nearly €4 billion (about $5 billion)—but they also had the largest assets measured by player registrations, stadium value, and other long-term assets: more than €4.5 billion ($5.6 billion). Only a few countries (notably Spain) had net debts that were significantly larger than their long-term assets.

But debt remains a problem for soccer clubs. First, thanks to the promotion and relegation system, the revenues of clubs can fluctuate wildly, and repayments are usually problematic when teams are relegated. Second, owning assets and being able to sell those assets easily for cash to repay debts is not a simple thing. If a club enters a fire sale of players then other clubs will start to negotiate a harder bargain. It is never good to be a forced seller, as the sad story of Leeds United testifies (see Box 5.8). Stadiums pose an even bigger problem—the stadium is an asset that may have considerable value, but without the stadium where is the club going to play? It is not straightforward to sell a stadium in order to repay club debts. The third problem is that the balance of assets and liabilities is not evenly spread across European soccer clubs. In the 2008 UEFA report, 35 percent of clubs had liabilities greater than their assets. These are the clubs that are in danger of not being able to pay their debts.

BOX 5.8: LEEDS UNITED AND THE VALUE OF PLAYERS

One of the most high-profile cases of financial failure of recent years was that of Leeds United, a team that has moved up and down the divisions over the years and last won the English League Championship in 1991/92. It is a team that has always enjoyed strong support, but in the late-1990s the club fell under the control of a group of ambitious directors that borrowed heavily to attract top stars.

Leeds United was a success story for the nineties. Its young team, under the stewardship of manager David O'Leary, performed strongly in the Premiership, finishing third in 2000, and in the Champions League, reaching the semifinals in 2001. Most soccer fans at the time agreed that Leeds would continue to progress and that this was just the start of something big.

The Leeds United board certainly thought so. The chairman, Peter Ridsdale, a businessman who tried to bring his commercial skills to the world of soccer, was keen to ensure the continued success of Leeds by buying more big-name players. The problem was that Leeds did not have the revenue to fund this and its other spending, so the club borrowed heavily. It had two main ways of doing so.

Player transfers, and the high-wage contracts that went with them, were paid for on a hire-purchase scheme. This entailed using REFF (Registered European Football Finance), a Guernsey-based investment vehicle, to buy top players and lease them back to Leeds. These players were owned by REFF and its institutional backers, including Barclays Bank. (A bank spokesman once quipped that "some of them might turn out for our five-a-side team.")

Leeds United had been spending significantly on players even before working with REFF and the club was in need of more cash for its expansion plans. It sold future gate receipts by issuing a bond for £50 million ($80 million)—a "securitization" scheme which was snapped up by investors such as M&G Investments, Teachers Assurance, and MetLife. At the time, the atmosphere at Leeds was buoyant, and Ridsdale spoke of Leeds United as "living the dream."

In 2001, Professor Bill Gerrard of Leeds University Business School placed a "sell-on" value of £198 million ($317 million) on the team's squad, a valuation that was then reported in the club's 2001 annual accounts, despite the fact that the book value of the squad was a mere £64 million ($102 million). Confident of the value of its investment, the club's management borrowed heavily to finance the payroll.

But everything went wrong for the club in that year. It had gambled on winning the European Champions League, but the team lost in the semifinal. This near-miss cost Leeds in the neighborhood of $16 million in lost broadcast fees, gate revenues, and merchandising. Moreover, the team also failed to qualify for the Champions League in the following season, denying it access to future prize money. Once it became clear that the club could not balance the books, creditors started calling in their loans and the club was forced to sell players. Its most famous player, defender Rio Ferdinand, whom they had acquired for a fee of £18 million ($29 million), was sold to Manchester United for £30 million ($48 million).

Soon after this, clubs began to realize that Leeds was a forced seller and the fees tumbled. According to press reports, Jonathan

CONTINUES

Woodgate was sold for $14 million, Robbie Keane for $11 million, Harry Kewell for $8 million, Olivier Dacourt for $5.6 million, and Lee Bowyer for $160,000. Several players were transferred for negligible fees or loaned to other teams. Given that at least 10 percent of these reported fees would have been paid to the player, and that the club continued to pay part of the salaries of some players after they had been sold, the revenue realized by the club would have been even lower than this figure. For example, when the club sold Robbie Fowler to Manchester City in 2003, it continued to pay $800,000 a year of the player's wages. Buying clubs knew how badly Leeds needed to sell players. By early 2004, almost all of the stars of 2001 had been sold, raising about $88 million (slightly less than the book value in 2001), and still leaving the club with large debts.

A downward spiral quickly developed as the manager fell out with the board because of the player sales. Results continued to worsen, the manager was sacked, and relegation became a very real possibility. Ridsdale was ousted in 2003 and a succession of chairmen—John McKenzie, Trevor Birch, Gerald Krasner—embarked on ever-deepening cost-cutting exercises. The culture of spending was halted and remarkable stories of misspending were unearthed. While the £240 (almost $400) that Ridsdale spent on goldfish for his office has become a symbol of this overspending, the almost $1 million a year spent on company cars and the $112,000 in one year on director's flights had more significance.

Revenue from the Champions League became a distant memory. Total revenue shrank as the debt mountain grew, and Leeds soon owed its creditors more than $160 million. Without stars, the club's performance on the field deteriorated, and it became clear by March 2004 that the club would be relegated. The club's stadium, Elland Road, and its training ground, Thorpe Arch, were sold and leased back to the club as the club fought to avoid going into administration and incurring the 10-point deduction. But in the end, administration proved unavoidable and finally came to pass in 2007.

Along the way the creditors took a big hit. The bondholders accepted $20 million for their $96 million debt, and REFF accepted $4 million of the $37 million it had provided. Leeds United survives but continues to struggle. Still, with its immensely loyal supporters, the club will no doubt rise to the Premier League again one day.

6

OWNERSHIP

So far, the analysis of soccer club finances has ignored the question of ownership and objectives. Talking about what soccer clubs do without discussing what they are for is a little bit like *Hamlet* without the prince. If you read a textbook on corporate finance, the purpose of the firm is usually discussed in chapter 1, and tied closely to this is a discussion of the ownership structure of the firm. By and large, professors of finance do not have great difficulty outlining the objectives of an enterprise. For them, it seems natural to think of the firm as a business organized to make money for its investors. The choice of organizational structure—sole trader, partnership, or limited liability company—is simply about selecting the one that best ensures that the investors' returns are maximized.

A soccer club cannot be said just to be the creature of its investors. Every club of any size represents a community. Almost everywhere, a city, a town, a suburb, or a village draws its identity from its team. In many cases, this civic pride is embodied in the stadium itself. In Europe, a majority of stadiums are built and/or owned by government— frequently the municipal authorities. Sports historian Richard Holt writes that the emergence of "professional football was essentially a big city phenomenon. There were thirty-six towns of over 100,000 in 1911 in Great Britain and almost all of them had professional teams."[1]

The move to the cities is one of the central tendencies in the development of modern life, and Holt argues that identity with a city's soccer club mattered: "These inhabitants of big cities needed a cultural expression of their urbanism that went beyond the immediate ties of kin and locality."

Much the same could be said for soccer clubs and cities across the world, and it remains true today. The city parade of the victorious team is one of the visual icons of modern life. It is notable that in many cases the strongest clubs actually divide loyalties within a city; examples include Manchester United and City; Inter Milan and AC Milan; and Galatasaray, Fenerbahce, and Besiktas in Istanbul. The notion of the "derby" game between two local rivals has long played an important role in England, and it seems plausible that the struggle for control of the city—a phenomenon that can be traced back to Roman chariot racing competition two thousand years ago—plays a powerful role in the psyche of fans.

Soccer clubs have also become powerful representations of regional identity. Perhaps above all stands Barcelona and its slogan "mas que un club" (more than a club). The team stands not only for the city, but also for the entire Catalan people, a large fraction of whom aspire to independence from Spain. Likewise, Athletic Bilbao is so closely tied to Basque identity that the club only recruits players who are either ethnic Basques or grew up in the region. (The Basque people live in northeast Spain and southwest France; their language is unusual in that it is unrelated to any other European language and remains something of a mystery. Though less than 1 million in total, their sense of identity is very strong.) Belgium is a nation deeply divided on linguistic lines—French and Flemish speaking—and Standard Liège has long been the symbol of the French-speaking Walloons. Another example, although without the same emphasis on separatism, is Bayern Munich, which is closely tied to the identity of Bavaria.

It is hard to think of any other financial activity (and I hope the analysis to this point has demonstrated that professional soccer is a financial activity, and an increasingly significant one) that achieves this level of emotional, social, and political commitment. People may be fond of particular products, and may even identify with them, but not usually to the point of fanaticism. Products are also usually not so restricted geographically. Bavarians may be fond of BMWs, but the car company would be far less successful if it sold only to Bavarians. Most companies try to expand their geographic reach—and so we even see companies play down their national identities (e.g., British Airways prefers to use the abbreviation BA).

Soccer clubs really supply a service rather than a product, and service businesses often have a local dimension and local loyalties—a local restaurant for example. However, we also often see service businesses try to replicate their success on a broader geographic scale (McDonald's must be the greatest example of the type) once they reach a certain size. However much they try to reach a global audience, soccer clubs by their nature and history cannot multiply locations, and are forever tied to their city and region.[2]

In the language of commerce, soccer clubs are in the entertainment business. However, that is almost as profane as saying that the Catholic Church is in the counseling business. It is probably going too far to say that fans would be prepared to lay down their lives for their teams, but it is important to recognize that while almost all businesses are just a means to an end, soccer clubs are more than that. A business is a means to an end in the sense that consumers do not care where the Coca-Cola they drink was made, or even the identity of the company that made it. They just want the product. I don't care much about who generated the electricity that supplies my house, just as long as the light comes on when I flick the switch. There are soccer clubs, players, and stadiums all over the world, but for a committed fan of Barcelona, clubs such as Schalke04, Rotherham United, or HB Tórshavn are not credible substitutes. In some sense, the club monopolizes its fans while still operating in one of the world's most competitive markets.

Now, this argument can be overstated. In *Soccernomics*, Simon Kuper and I argued that fan loyalty is not absolute—a fact demonstrated by the inevitable collapse in attendance when a club is relegated. Absolute loyalty would require the fans to keep attending regardless. Not only do many fans stop going to a club when it is relegated, but also, even if they may not admit it openly, some choose to start attending games at other clubs. This is the soccer equivalent of an extra-marital affair: it happens all the time but is seldom talked about. It's hard to say just how many fans are monogamous and how many are promiscuous, but even among those who are prepared to go and watch other teams, many no doubt would prefer it if their local team were thriving. Even people who do not go to watch their local club may still regard it as part of their identity.

The political dimension of a club's identity is further accentuated by the traditional association of soccer with the working class. In England, sports such as cricket and rugby are perceived largely as the preserve of the elites, while soccer became the game of the people—even if the rules had been laid down by the elites of English private schools and universities. Likewise, while the players who introduced soccer to most other countries hailed from the elite, soccer quickly came to be seen as the people's game.[3] Many on the left associate the creation of soccer as we know it with the sweat of the working man (a conception which gives rise to some significant controversy in gender politics).

The origins of almost every soccer club consists of a group of players coming together to form a team. In the early days, there were often supporters who contributed to creating the organization behind the club. And to this day, for many soccer fans when they talk of "our club," it carries a sense of ownership. However, this sense frequently collides with the strict legal definition of ownership. We saw in the last chapter how soccer clubs in England adopted the limited-liability structure only as a means to fund the construction of stadiums without the directors having to take on personal liability for the debt. The sports historian Derek Birley has argued that this was a disaster for the development of the game in England: "The money that came through the turnstiles might perhaps, in a different society, have gone towards creating something more like a genuine club atmosphere rather than in transfer fees and illegal payments, and much subsequent trouble would have been avoided. But in truth such an idealistic solution to the problems of emergent urban democracy was neither practical nor foremost in the thoughts of either the directors or their principal hirelings. Shareholding proved a singularly inappropriate method of determining control of League soccer."[4]

Historians have put considerable effort into identifying who the shareholders were in the early days. Wray Vamplew discusses at length the change in composition of club control following the transition from association to limited liability company and finds a growth in the influence of wealthier business people, often associated with the brewing trade. Meanwhile, the participation of ordinary working-class men declined, for the not surprising reason that they could not afford the shares.[5] Nonetheless, a certain sense of democracy still prevailed.

David Conn, whose popular book *The Football Business* stands as one of the most impassioned critiques of the way soccer clubs have evolved, put it like this: "In many ways [in the 1990s] soccer was easy business. The hard work had been done a century before. The early founders had set up clubs, carved out bits of land, formed companies only to protect themselves. People, ordinary people, had taken the game spectacularly to their hearts, propelled its astounding growth. Generations had supported their clubs, standing on the terraces, loyalty an article of faith, and the clubs, for all their faults, had never thought to overcharge them, the shareholders still, even in the late 1980s, not mostly in it to make money. The clubs were companies in structure, but clubs in style, and soccer was a game, not a means of making money."[6] In these early days, soccer clubs had many shareholders—hundreds of them, a large number considering that the clubs remained tiny organizations. In more recent times, ownership of English clubs has become concentrated in the hands of a few individuals. The same seems to be true elsewhere.

BOX 6.1: THE CHANGING OWNERSHIP PATTERNS IN THE PREMIER LEAGUE

The table below illustrates the changes in ownership structure for the fifteen clubs that were in the top division in 2014/15 and thirty years ago in 1984/85.

In 1984/85 most of the clubs were owned by a dispersed body of shareholders—usually in the region of one thousand, with no single

CONTINUES

Team	1984/85	2014/15
Arsenal	7,000 shares in issue, no single shareholder larger than 1,500 shares, the Board owned less than 3,000, 731 shareholders (dispersed)	Single owner (Stan Kroenke)
Aston Villa	Doug Ellis owned 32,309 out of 72,635 shares issued (44 percent)	Single owner (Randy Lerner)
Chelsea	Controlled by Ken Bates	Single owner (Roman Abramovich)
Everton	Sir John Moores owned 808 of 2,500 shares issued (32%)	Three directors own 68 percent
Leicester City	Directors controlled no more than 5,000 of 25,000 ordinary shares issued, dispersed	Single owner (Vichai Srivaddhanaprabha)
Liverpool	15,000 shares issued, Board of directors less than 1500 combined, dispersed	Fenway Sports Group (majority owner John W Henry)
Newcastle United	2,000 shares, total directors held less than 200, dispersed	Single owner (Mike Ashley)
Queens Park Rangers	James Gregory owned 386,000 out of 540,000 shares issued (71 percent)	The Mittal family and Tony Fernandes
Stoke City	Three directors controlled about 30,000 of 37,000 issued ordinary shares	Single owner (Peter Coates)
Tottenham Hotspur	Listed company, no shareholder larger than 5 percent	Joe Lewis and Daniel Levy 85 percent
West Ham United	Cearns family board members owned less than 1,000 shares out of 4,000 shares issues, dispersed	David Sullivan and David Gold 86 percent
Manchester United	Martin Edwards owned just over 50 percent of shares	Glazer family
Southampton	Directors controlled less than 20,000 out of 47,000 shares issued, dispersed	Single owner (Katharina Liebherr)
Sunderland	The five directors jointly owned over 50 percent of the 4,500 shares issued	Single owner (Ellis Short)
West Bromwich Albion	Directors held one share each out of 495 shares issued, dispersed	Jeremy Peace 78%

SOURCE Club financial accounts

individual owning more than 5 percent of the company. The exceptions were Aston Villa controlled by Doug Ellis, Chelsea controlled by Ken Bates, Stoke City controlled by the three directors of the club, Manchester United controlled by Martin Edwards, Sunderland controlled by its directors, and Everton, where Sir John Moores owned 32 percent of the club. Today all the clubs in this list are more closely controlled. Usually they are in the hands of a single individual, and at most a group of three or four people working in partnership.

In the rest of Europe, the members' association was the most common organizational model, and in the former Soviet bloc state ownership of soccer clubs was mandatory. In recent years, more and more clubs across Europe have become limited liability corporations. But, more importantly, the ownership of clubs has become concentrated in the hands of a small number of people. UEFA reported in 2008 that more than half of the teams in the top divisions of European leagues were controlled by a single person.[7]

A simple but compelling explanation of this trend is as follows. First, soccer clubs are not enterprises whose ultimate goal is to make money. They only exist for the pursuit of winning, and the only benefit to be derived from owning a soccer club is being a winner. Second, the pleasure of owning the winning club is greatest when the ownership is not shared, and only the wealthiest individuals have the money to invest on the scale necessary to win.

BOX 6.2: PROFIT MAXIMIZATION VERSUS WIN MAXIMIZATION

There has been a good deal of debate in theory about what the owners of soccer clubs really want. In 2009, Pedro Garcia del Barrio and I published a paper in which we used an economic test to see whether the choices of clubs are more consistent with win maximization or profit maximization.[1] There is a fairly reliable statistical relationship between wage expenditure and team

CONTINUES

performance in the league, and there is a fairly reliable statistical relationship between league performance and revenues. Profits are largely driven by the difference between revenues and wages. So it is possible to identify a level of profitability associated with every possible position in the league.

For each club, there is a league position that generates maximum profit, and positions higher than this can only be achieved at the expense of profits. There also exists a position, higher than the profit-maximizing position, at which profits are zero. Pedro and I tested whether the actual league position of clubs is closer to the profit-maximizing or the win-maximizing position.

We used data from the top two divisions of the English and Spanish leagues between 1993 and 2005. While each team varied, we found that the league position of clubs was generally closer to the position implied by win maximization. In the case of English clubs, the league position was a little lower than the win maximizing position, but for the Spanish clubs their actual league positions were statistically indistinguishable from the position they would have achieved under win maximization.

We concluded that in practice win maximization is a more plausible description of the behavior of English and Spanish clubs than profit maximization.

1. Garcia-del-Barrio, P., and Szymanski, S. (2009) "Goal! Profit maximization versus win maximization in soccer." *Review of Industrial Organization*, 34(1): 45–68.

The standard assumption about businesses is that they are organized to maximize the profits of the owners. Back in 1971, economist Peter Sloane observed that this did not make much sense when thinking about a soccer club.[8] He observed that the ninety-two professional English clubs had combined losses of £1 million per year (equivalent to about $19 million in today's money). He argued instead that clubs were "utility maximizers," which meant that their aim was to satisfy as far as possible some combination of the interests of the board of directors, the shareholders, the manager, the players, and the fans. In essence, he took this to mean that the clubs would "always strive to maximize their playing success"—although subject to the proviso that they should be able to survive financially.

An even simpler construction was suggested by the Belgian economist Stefan Késenne, who argued that the objective of a soccer club is simply to maximize the number of wins subject to a break-even constraint—that is, not to lose money.[9] Support for this hypothesis seems to be found everywhere in soccer. It is widely observed that soccer clubs fail to make profits. The 2011 UEFA *Club Licensing Benchmarking Report* shows that over the previous five years net losses at top division European clubs increased from $700,000 to $2.1 billion. In the financial year 2011, 63 percent of these clubs reported an operating loss, and 55 percent reported a net loss overall. The situation in lower divisions is almost certainly much worse. Clubs don't seem to be chasing profits; more likely, they are chasing wins.

At this point one needs to be careful about what one means by financial "losses." Mostly it means that there is very little cash flowing from the business into the pockets of the owners, but rather a lot of cash flowing from the owners to the business. This is required to pay creditors because the club is not generating enough cash to pay them out of operations. This in itself does not prove that the owners are win maximizers rather than profit maximizers, but it is suggestive.

Moreover, for some types of ownership, it is hard to conceive of any objective other than to win matches. Clubs that are run as membership associations have no shareholders and the members are mostly fans interested in the success of the team. It therefore seems inevitable that all available revenues will be spent on success. Clubs that have limited liability may also have restrictions on their ability to pay dividends to investors. This was the case in English soccer until 1982, and remains the case in countries such as France and Spain. And even among clubs with shareholders and the capacity to pay dividends, most do not. In England, Manchester United and Arsenal typically pay a dividend—but the other clubs do not. There are other ways for owners to take money out of their clubs, especially if the owner is a single individual. He can pay himself a salary to run the club, buy services from another business that he controls, and so on. But apart from a few exceptions it seems fairly clear that owners tend to put money in rather than take money out.

BOX 6.3: WHAT DOES IT MEAN WHEN WE SAY THAT A CLUB "LOSES MONEY"?

Essentially it means that expenditures exceeded revenues—which is not always such a bad thing. For example, a growing business might "lose money" if it is investing in creating future revenues. Generally though, investors disapprove of losses. They want to see profits, so that they can see a return on their investment and maybe even be paid out some of the profit in the form of a dividend.

All well and good, but should fans really care? Reading newspaper headlines, one could sometimes be forgiven for thinking that making money for the investors is the only purpose of a soccer club. Yet in reality many investors are prepared to accept *accounting* losses if these are compensated for by trophies. Fans should only care about losses to the extent that they might have longer-term consequences for the business (e.g., leading to insolvency or to investors withdrawing their support from the business). This happens often enough, but nowhere near as often as clubs declaring an accounting loss.

Between 1974 and 2010, English soccer clubs declared a profit in only 36 percent of cases where we have the accounting data. In reality the figure is probably closer to 25 percent, since in most of the cases where the data is missing it is because the club was in financial difficulties. Failing to make a profit is the norm in soccer. Losses are to soccer as methane is to dairy farming, a natural by-product.

It's often said that businessmen lose all sense of business acumen when they buy a soccer club. A good example is Simon Jordan, whose autobiography, *Be Careful What You Wish For*, is one of the most revealing and candid analyses of how ownership works. By his early-thirties he had built up a business in mobile phones using methods that were often questionable. In the book, he admits to using unlicensed software, bypassing credit checks, and passing off things he had read about as his own achievements. He also admits to bullying employees, exploiting family members, and generally riding roughshod over anyone he came into contact with. Then, in 2000, he sold the business for almost $130 million and bought Crystal Palace Football Club in southeast London. He had supported the team since childhood, and he proceeded to invest his fortune in making the club successful. In the following eight years, he and the Palace fans enjoyed a roller-coaster ride, getting promoted to and then relegated from the Premier League and finally going into administration in 2010. By the end, he had sunk at least $59 million of his wealth into the club. What is striking about his account is the contrast between how aggressive and brutal he had been in the process of making his fortune, and how self-pitying he became when managers, players, bankers, and would-be investors treated him in a similar fashion. The difference, perhaps, was that he cared about Crystal Palace.

In many cases, the owners of soccer clubs were fans long before they achieved control of the team. Perhaps the most famous example in England is Jack Walker, who made a fortune in steel in the 1980s and proceeded to spend most of it on propelling Blackburn Rovers to the Premier League title in 1995. Other clubs have been controlled by family dynasties—Andrea Agnelli, president of Juventus, is the great-grandson of Gianni Agnelli, who founded the Fiat motor company, and grandson of Edoardo Agnelli, who bought the soccer club for the family. But, increasingly, soccer club owners acquire their trophy assets despite having little or no long-term connection to the club. It is hard to believe that the young Roman Abramovich had even heard of Chelsea, or that the twelve-year-old Sheikh Mansour wept when Manchester City was relegated to the Second Division in 1983. Yet these two individuals have committed more money than any owner in history to the success of the soccer clubs they now own.

BOX 6.4: SUGAR DADDIES

The term "sugar daddy" means a man, typically an older man, who bankrolls the lifestyle of a younger woman in return for sexual favors. It has seedy connotations. In the last decade or so, it has come to be used to describe wealthy individuals who are

CONTINUES

willing to invest large sums of money in order the build a successful team. David Conn has argued that this is a relatively recent
phenomenon, unknown before the 1990s. This may be a rather
Anglocentric view—examples such as the Agnelli family involvement with Juventus, and, rather more blatantly, General Franco's
support for Real Madrid, suggest that powerful men using their
influence and/or money to ensure the success of their team is
a time-honored tradition. Even in England, such things were not
unknown. Sir Henry Norris was a successful London property de-
veloper who bought a controlling stake in Woolwich Arsenal in
1910, and oversaw the club's move to Highbury in North London,
and its subsequent rise to preeminence. In 1929, he was banned
by the FA from any involvement in soccer. Arsenal went on to win
four of the next six Football League championships.

The ban followed a libel case in which he sued the FA, having
been accused of breaking the rules concerning payments to players
(at that time there was a maximum weekly wage payable). In court,
it emerged that Norris had pumped in £15,000 (about $24,000) of
his own money into the club in order to achieve success. Does that
make him a sugar daddy? Allowing for inflation, £15,000 back then
is worth about £1 million (or $1.6 million) in today's money—far less
than the amount spent on clubs by the likes of Roman Abramovich.
But then wages were lower too thanks to the regulations, and the
average annual wage bill of a top-division team at the time was just
under $24,000—compared to more than $80 million today. It cost a
lot less to buy success in those days.

Norris brought the first celebrity manager, Herbert Chapman,
to the Arsenal and it was the bankrolling of the transfer of Charlie
Buchan—the first transfer fee in excess of £10,000—that paved
the way for the team's subsequent dominance. Perhaps he did
not operate exactly in the style of today's sugar daddies, but
Sir Henry Norris deserves to be talked of in the same breath as
Roman Abramovich and Sheikh Mansour.

No doubt, most owners love their club and take personal satisfaction
from its success. But the explanation for their investment must go beyond
this. The ownership of a successful team has become a means to display
social status—on a global scale. The idea that ownership and influence
over a soccer club conveys social status can be traced right back to the

origins of these clubs. As Derek Birley writes of the early investors: "It was more often civic pride, particularly in the smaller towns, and the desire to be someone in the community, that led people to take shares in a soccer club."[10] What has changed has been the globalization of the community, especially in the last thirty years or so. Already, by the 1950s, the investment in teams such as Juventus by Gianni Agnelli or Internazionale by Angelo Moratti (he made his money in the oil industry) presaged a new era in club ownership. While General Franco provided Real Madrid with political rather than economic patronage, industrialists in Madrid aimed to boost their own status through commercial support for the club. Until recently, the prestige of ownership was largely a local phenomenon. Now it is global. The owners of Manchester United and Manchester City are recognized across the planet.

Plutocrats can buy any product or service they want. After a point, cars, houses, and yachts fail to differentiate you from the merely rich. To really establish your status, you need to achieve something that other people cannot. That is where trophies come in. There can only be one Premier League champion each season, one winner of the Champions League. Winning these titles confers a status that is otherwise very hard to achieve. Not that soccer clubs are the only example. The economist Fred Hirsch coined the term "positional goods" to describe the concept.[11] One of the most famous examples is seen in the medieval town of San Gimignano in Tuscany, where wealthy citizens built ever-larger towers on their houses to demonstrate their status. The towers themselves served no particular purpose, but a family's status was demonstrated by the height of their tower relative to everyone else. What's important about this game is that there can only be one highest tower, and whenever one family increased its status by rising above someone else's tower, the act simultaneously diminished the status of at least one other family.

What's important about a positional good is that everyone agrees that ranking matters—that there is status derived from your position in the hierarchy. Soccer is perfect for this kind of competition, because it's the world's most popular sport, and the rankings are clear and unambiguous—the record books do not lie about who won and who lost. This form of competition has also been termed a "rat race," since more effort by the competitors cannot add to total satisfaction. Every increase in satisfaction for one competitor is exactly offset by a decrease in satisfaction for others. Clearly, this can be said of soccer competition. There are only so many places in the league. The number cannot increase no matter how much each team invests in players.

But this does not mean that the competition over positional goods is necessarily a bad thing—although some economists have tried to suggest that it is.[12] There are two clear benefits from this kind of competition over soccer rankings. First, and obviously, the winners of the race get to signal their position in society, which seems to bring them great satisfaction. But, much more importantly, this competition generates an enormous amount of investment in soccer—which is surely a good thing for those who care about the game. Some of the money goes to the players, some of the money goes to clubs in the form of transfer fees, some of the money is invested in improving facilities, and some in investing in training. And there are spillover effects: money invested in making one club more competitive can spur rival owners to invest in making their clubs more attractive. Of the roughly $3 billion invested by Abramovich and Mansour over the last decade, a significant fraction has ended up in the pockets of their rivals.

The combination of win-maximizing behavior, the logic of positional goods, and the globalization of soccer through technology has led inexorably to a concentration of ownership. As is often the case, the trend first became apparent in the United States. A paper published by Harold Demsetz and Kenneth Lehn in 1985 examined the pattern of ownership of American corporations.[13] They were interested in what could explain concentration of ownership—the fact that some companies seemed to be controlled by a small number of people. They found that concentration was especially noticeable in sports franchises—in baseball, football, soccer, basketball, and hockey. They compared more than a hundred sports clubs with 500 businesses that had similar ownership structures. They found that, on average, for every ten sports clubs there were twenty individuals who owned 10 percent or more of the business; on the other hand, for every ten comparable businesses there were only five individuals who owned more than 10 percent. In other words, it was far more likely that there would be concentrated ownership of a sports franchise. They argued that this result stemmed from the "amenity value" of owning a sports club—by which they meant the kinds of status benefits that we have been discussing here. They argued that individuals would not want to share these benefits, and hence sports clubs would likely generate more concentrated ownership (they also found a similar phenomenon in the media industry).

Concentration of ownership may be a trend, but there have been times when it seemed as if the direction of travel was being reversed. Louis Edwards acquired Manchester United in the early-1960s. According to the club accounts, he never took 100-percent ownership. At the end of the 1970s, he and his son Martin owned 58 percent of the club. After Louis's death in 1980, Martin became chairman. He was closely involved with many of the changes in soccer over the following decade, which led ultimately to the creation of the Premier League in 1992. During this period he owned just over 50 percent of the shares in the company (although it is possible he had control of more through his family). By the end of the 1980s, having seen the value of his inheritance grow, he decided he wanted to take his money out.

Martin Edwards has always been something of a hate figure in English soccer. He profited royally from his ownership of the club and was a key figure in the growing commercialism of the club, and English soccer in general; there have been newspaper allegations that he paid for prostitutes while on club business, and he was cautioned by the police for peeping under a women's toilet door. But one thing that Manchester United fans will always be grateful to him for is not sacking Alex Ferguson at the end of 1989 when he had been in the job for three years, trophy-less and floundering in mid-table. Few managers since have received such extended tolerance, and at the time, Edwards was almost alone in retaining confidence in the great Scot.

Edwards reduced his stake from 50.1 to 28 percent in 1991 by floating the company on the stock exchange through an Initial Public Offering (IPO). While he remained as chief executive until 2000, he gradually sold more shares on the market, so that when he stood down his stake had fallen to 6.5 percent. He remained as a non-executive director of the club for another two years, but when he resigned in 2002 he sold off the remainder of his shares. In the decade following the 1991 IPO, the stock-market valuation of the club had risen from just under $80 million to a peak of more than $1.6 billion. He is said to have made over $200 million from his share sales.

As Edwards reduced his share in the club, its ownership became more diverse. Undoubtedly, a few fans bought shares just to be able to say they owned a piece of the club that they loved. However, the major investors were professional institutions—pension funds, insurance companies, and the like—businesses that look after the money that people save. Smaller scale professional investors also have bought shares, and so the total number of shareholders in the club increased dramatically after 1991.

More importantly, the success of Manchester United on the stock exchange made professional investors willing to put money into soccer clubs. In the two-year period between October 1995 and October 1997, sixteen English clubs raised a total of about $240 million in capital on the stock exchange. (Table 6.1 lists the clubs that came to the stock exchange during this period.) In many cases, the sale of shares enabled owners to take some money out of the business, to raise some money for investment (especially in new stadiums after the Taylor Report into the Hillsborough disaster), and to raise the profile of the club with investors.

It quickly became apparent that Manchester United had very little in common with most soccer clubs. The reason that United's share price had risen was not because the club won trophies, but because the club generated profits and used those profits to pay its shareholders a dividend, giving them a return on their investment. The sixteen clubs that floated after them failed to do this. Failing to pay a dividend will not necessarily prevent a company's share price from rising, but investors do have to believe that there will be profits one day, and that these profits will grow, signaling that they own something which has an increasing value. Apart from Manchester United, clubs seemed incapable of generating a profit. Indeed, they seemed to continue to spend every penny that came into the club on trying to buy success and pay no attention to generating a return for their shareholders.

As the share prices crashed, the professional investors who put their money into the stocks quickly decided that professional clubs were not for them—and so this avenue to increased investment was effectively

TABLE 6.1 English soccer club flotations, 1995–1997

Club	Float date	Method	% offered/ placed
Preston North End	October 95	Placing/offer	86
Chelsea	March 96	Introduction	0 [a]
Leeds United	August 96	Takeover and placing/offer	60
Queens Park Rangers	October 96	Placing/offer	44
Sunderland	December 96	Placing/offer	26
Sheffield United	January 97	Takeover and placing/offer	42
Southampton	January 97	Reverse takeover	100
West Bromwich Albion	January 97	Placing	100
Birmingham City	March 97	Placing	30
Charlton Athletic	March 97	Placing/offer	35
Bolton Wanderers	April 97	Reverse takeover	100
Newcastle United	April 97	Offer	28
Aston Villa	May 97	Placing/offer	16
Swansea City	August 97	Takeover	0 [b]
Leicester City	October 97	Introduction	0 [c]
Nottingham Forest	October 97	Offer	11

[a] Chelsea FC was owned by Chelsea Village PLC in which the directors and three other interests jointly held 83.5 percent of the equity at the company's introduction.

[b] Swansea City FC was purchased by Silver Shield PLC, a car windscreen replacement company. Although located in Wales, Swansea plays in the English Football League and hence is treated as an English club.

[c] Leicester City FC was acquired by Soccer Investments PLC.

SOURCE: Stephanie Leach and Stefan Szymanski (2015). "Making Money Out of Football," *Scottish Journal of Political Economy,* vol 62, no 1.

shut off. New clubs were unable to enter the market—Bradford City and Watford are the only clubs to have obtained a listing since 1997, Bradford in 1998 and Watford in 2001. Moreover, before long, the clubs that had floated withdrew from the stock exchange. Effectively, they returned to private ownership, often in the hands of one person. West Bromwich Albion was a listed company when Jeremy Peace, a successful investment banker, became chairman in 2002; but he took the company off the stock exchange in 2005, and by 2013 he owned 100 percent of the club. By 2012, all the English clubs that had ever listed on the stock exchange had de-listed, mostly to fall under closer control than they had been before their IPO.

Some clubs in the rest of Europe have also entered the stock exchange. The practice had some popularity in Italy (Roma, Lazio, and Juventus), Portugal (Porto, Benfica, and Sporting), Turkey (Galatasaray, Fenerbahce, and Trabzonspor), Scotland (Celtic, Rangers, Aberdeen, and Hearts), and Denmark (Aalborg, AGF, Akademisk, FC Copenhagen, Brondby, and Silkeborg). Borussia Dortmund and Ajax are two other famous clubs that have been through an IPO, but these are rare cases. A study in 2010 by Michel Aglietta, Wladimir Andreff, and Bastien Drut found that only forty-nine European soccer clubs had ever floated shares on a stock exchange.[14] This is only 2 to 3 percent of the two thousand or more professional clubs across Europe. According to UEFA, just nineteen of the 235 clubs (8 percent) competing in its competitions in 2012/13 had a stock exchange listing.[15]

The lack of profitability in soccer has tended to make it unattractive to investors on the stock exchange. Meanwhile the lure of trophies has meant that wealthy individuals have been willing to pump their private fortunes into making clubs successful. In the 1990s, many critics argued that individuals were taking over clubs only to make a fortune by selling them to the market. It seems likely that some owners did have this in mind, but few, if any, made money on anything like the scale that Martin Edwards did. The average amount of money raised by stock market flotations in England in the mid-1990s was about $24 million. Of this probably 10 to 20 percent went on administrative fees and 50 percent or so went to investment in the club, leaving only the odd few million for the owners. Now, this is not a small sum of money by any means, but also a drop in the bucket compared to the more than $4 billion per year that the Premier League clubs generate in revenues nowadays. The $240 million or so raised on the stock exchange in the mid-1990s in total pales in comparison with the estimated $3 billion or so invested by Roman Abramovich and Sheikh Mansour.

Soccer is not the only commercial activity that has turned out to have a bad fit with the stock exchange. Indeed, research by Rafael La Porta, Florencio Lopez-de-Silanes, Andrei Shleifer, and Robert Vishny suggests that in most of the world outside of Britain and the United States concentrated ownership, often in the form of families, is the norm in much of business.[16] Richard Branson famously floated part of his Virgin business empire in 1986, and then bought it back two years later complaining that professional investors did not understand his business. One would be hard put to argue that he has done badly since. For different reasons, soccer clubs too, seem to be better off in private hands.

The 1990s were a period of dramatic change in soccer. Money flooded in from broadcasting contracts, and thanks to the increased public exposure there also came increased interest in sponsorship. As well as share flotations and increased interest from wealthy people in controlling trophy clubs, there also came interest from the broadcasters in owning soccer clubs.

Silvio Berlusconi started in business in the 1960s, and in 1973 he set up a small cable company in Milan. Over the following decade he created a national network out of local companies. In soccer crazy Italy it was easy to see that the sport would drive subscriptions, and his acquisition of AC Milan gave him the bargaining power to secure control of the market. AC Milan was bankrupt when he bought it in 1986; he proceeded to invest millions in turning it into a dominant European power by the early-1990s. Others media moguls followed: Rupert Murdoch and Sky in Britain, and Leo Kirch in Germany, used soccer rights to drive pay TV subscriptions. League soccer came to be seen as "must have" content. The very success of this strategy provoked the threat of competition from other media companies, and in the late-1990s Murdoch decided that control of Manchester United was a logical step. In 1998, he launched a bid that valued the club at £624 million—over $1 billion. That was more than any sports franchise in North America, when only a decade earlier Martin Edwards had been willing to sell the club for just £20 million ($32 million). Immediately, all of the other broadcasters in the UK market acquired stakes in soccer clubs. A national cable broadcaster, NTL, bought 6 percent of Newcastle United, and Granada bought 10 percent of Liverpool. In France, the pay TV broadcaster Canal+ bought Paris Saint-Germain. It seemed as if the broadcasters who most needed the content supplied by the clubs would end up owning the clubs too. In the end, the broadcasters retreated.

Murdoch's bid was blocked by the UK competition authority, and Canal+ eventually sold PSG. As cable and satellite TV became an established part of the broadcast landscape, the value of soccer as driver of content did not disappear, but perhaps became less critical.

The big four leagues in Europe are in England, Germany, Italy, and Spain. England and Italy have clearly been at the forefront of the commercial changes in soccer—changing ownership structures, the development of broadcasting, financial innovation, and, to a large degree, financial chaos. Germany and Spain, by contrast, have been far more conservative, most notably when it comes to ownership.

In 1990, almost all of the top division clubs in Germany and Spain were controlled by member associations. Unlike their English and Italian counterparts, these organizations had never adopted limited liability status. In the German case, the legal system protects the directors of membership associations (clubs) from personal liability in a way that English law does not. Spain had only recently emerged from the era of the Franco dictatorship. The Spanish economy lagged behind the rest of Europe under Franco, but its soccer clubs, led by Real Madrid, dominated the field. When Franco died in 1975, the Spanish economy quickly blossomed and living standards rose toward those of the rest of Europe. But the soccer clubs soon got into financial trouble. With each club electing a president, and with each president eager to please the members, spending got out of hand, and by the 1980s many of the teams were bankrupt. At this point, the Spanish government stepped in and forced the clubs to convert to limited liability status, on the theory that this would make the clubs act in a more responsible manner (financially speaking). However, at the last minute, four clubs successfully lobbied to retain their democratic structures: Real Madrid, Barcelona, Athletic Bilbao, and Osasuna. But, even then, the clubs that converted to limited liability were given a special legal status—companies with a sporting objective, not businesses that could make profits for their owners.

In Germany, modern soccer developed slowly. In the postwar era, the national soccer team became the dominant source of national pride following the "Miracle of Bern"—West Germany's unexpected 1954 World Cup victory in Switzerland. Club soccer was seemingly organized to ensure the national team's success. League soccer attracted limited interest, and there was no national league until 1963, when the Bundesliga was created. It was also only at this point that professionalism was officially recognized. A few of the clubs were company owned, notably Bayer Leverkusen, owned by the Bayer chemical corporation, and VfL Wolfsburg, owned by Volkswagen. Otherwise they were member associations (*Eintrager verein*, or e.v., in German). The Bundesliga did not go through a bankruptcy crisis of the kind that forced the Spanish clubs to change their ownership structure. Instead, it was the creation of the Premier League, and its apparent success at generating revenue, that caused the German clubs to consider reforms in the late 1990s. The revival of interest in soccer in England and the increasing strength of its clubs in international competition led some German club directors to believe that adopting a corporate structure and floating on the stock exchange like English clubs was the right way forward.

Furthermore, the clubs in the Bundesliga, which until that time had been controlled by the national federation (the Deutsche Fussball Bund, DFB), wanted to control the competition themselves. To this end, they created the Deutsche Fussball Liga (DFL), representing the thirty-six teams in the top two divisions. While the majority of clubs accepted that it should be possible to adopt a capital structure to raise money from equity investors, they also wanted to preserve the membership system. In 1998, the DFB adopted the 50+1 rule. This allows the club to become a commercially run entity (such as a limited liability company) and distribute profits to its investors. At the same time 50 percent plus one of the voting shares of the soccer club must remain in the hands of the e.v., so that ultimately the members' association retains ultimate control.

BOX 6.5: IS FAN POWER EFFECTIVE?

Many people admire the German model of soccer governance. The "50+1" rule, which preserves ownership in the hands of the ordinary membership of the soccer club, is especially praised. However, the following quote from a paper by eminent sports economists Helmut Dietl and Egon Franck suggests that matters are not so simple:

CONTINUES

Legally, all the power is with the members, usually the fans of the club. At the surface, the consequence of this peculiar governance structure seems to be that in German football, priority is given to the fans as members of the club over other stakeholders, such as investors. The voice is with the fans and not with the providers of capital. However, if we look a bit deeper, the picture becomes more blurred. There are thousands of fans in every club. Their interests are fairly heterogeneous (wanting a responsible voice in how their club is run, lower ticket prices, the purchase or sale of players, etc.).

There is no cheap and reliable mechanism to aggregate the preferences of a heterogeneous and large group of people such as the fans. Obviously, therefore, the members–club structure suffers from significant transaction costs to make the voice of the fans effective. The outcome is a governance vacuum. Coupled with dysfunctional incentives, this governance vacuum results in a situation that invites the elected representatives to seize control of German football clubs to derive personal utility from the fame and publicity associated with sporting success, without, at the same time, being personally liable for financial losses of the club, as it would be the case with genuine owners. In particular, given their age, these representatives sometimes heavily discount future liabilities of the club and tend to support strategies of investing the club's future income to increase current playing strength to gain fame.

Schalke 04 provides a typical example for this combination of dysfunctional incentives and a governance vacuum in a membership club. The club's representatives heavily borrowed against the club's future. In 2003, for example, Schalke raised more than €80 million by securitizing future ticket revenues for the next 23 years. Although the deal helped to transform short-term into long-term liabilities, it is a heavy burden for Schalke's financial future. At the end of 2004, Schalke's liabilities surpassed €110 million. Nevertheless, the club continued to heavily invest in new players. The manager of Bayern Munich, Uli Hoeness, openly expressed his concerns that his colleague at Schalke seemed to prepare his big retirement "show" by investing in prestigious titles at the end of his career and therefore taking excessive risks. Indeed, the manager of Schalke, considered a regional celebrity in the Ruhr area, hired older players and gave them long-term contracts. Unfortunately, Schalke was less successful than expected and did not qualify for the 2006/2007 season of the Champions League. Despite having heavily borrowed against the club's future, the team and its manager did not win the expected titles. Forced to correct down expected future revenue streams, the club could no longer hide its dramatic financial situation. The club's manager, who was recently urged to resign, seems to have preserved his celebrity status despite the financial distress of the club. He attracts the bulk of publicity when he attends the home games of Schalke as a "normal" fan.

SOURCE Dietl, Helmut M., and Egon Franck. "Governance failure and financial crisis in German football." *Journal of Sports Economics* (2007) 8(6), p. 665. Reprinted by permission of Sage Publications. Egon Franck now sits on UEFA's Club Financial Control Body tasked with enforcing the rules of Financial Fair Play.

For many fans, these models are ideally suited to representing their interests. The success of clubs such as Barcelona and Bayern Munich seem to suggest that systems giving a voice to the ordinary supporter can at the same time work both commercially and on the field. From the 1990s onwards there was a rise in fan activism, most notably in England, driven by disenchantment with the growing commercialism of soccer.

At the beginning of 1992, Northampton Town, then in the fourth tier of English professional soccer, became insolvent. A small but passionate body of fans wanted to be involved in keeping the club alive, but somewhat obtusely the directors of the club wanted nothing to do with them. The supporters, led by Brian Lomax, a theology graduate and charity worker, formed the first Supporter Trust in England. The Trust raised money to help bring the club out of insolvency, and was rewarded with two seats on the club's board of directors. The Trust ensured that from then on there would be a regular dialogue between those who run the club and its fans. The Trust also helped to ensure political support from the local government for stadium development.

Greater fan involvement has been a consistent demand of supporter groups and activists in England, but in reality they are usually only listened to when a club is in financial difficulties. Lomax used his experience at Northampton to encourage the creation of new Supporter Trusts, at clubs such as Middlesbrough, Plymouth Argyle, and AFC Bournemouth. In 2000, the UK government funded the creation of Supporters Direct, an organization dedicated to enhancing the role of fans in the running of soccer clubs that they support. There are now more than 170 Supporter Trusts in the United Kingdom. Not all of them have representation on the board of the club, but their influence and power is growing.

BOX 6.6: SWANSEA'S SEVEN SECRETS OF SUCCESSFUL SUPPORTER TRUSTS

Swansea City is the new poster child for a well-run club. In a decade, it has moved from the brink of liquidation and in danger of relegation from the fourth tier of English soccer to the Premier League and solvency. The club celebrated its centenary in 2012 by finishing eleventh in the Premier League, and it has maintained a comfortable mid-table position since. In the first game of the 2014/15 season, Swansea defeated Manchester United 2-0 at Old Trafford stadium.

The club almost folded in the 1980s but was saved by the support of a local builder, Doug Sharpe, who bankrolled the team for the next decade with little success or gratitude from the fans. In the mid-1990s, he sold out, and the club fell into the hands of a sequence of increasingly incompetent investors. The last of these, a chancer called Tony Petty, sold the club to a consortium of investors at the end of 2001. The new owners were smarter and richer, and they wanted to involve the fans by giving the Supporter Trust a seat on the board. So began one of the most remarkable revivals in the history of the game.

Here are the key lessons:

1. *Get rid of your debts.* Even with Petty gone, the club was still on the brink of collapse, with debts of around $3 million and no obvious way of paying them. The new owners took advantage of the insolvency laws. Lending money to a soccer club is always a risky business, but lending to a club like Swansea is particularly hazardous since, unlike many clubs, it doesn't own its stadium. Creditors can try to get the courts to close down the business and sell off the assets. And for most clubs, the stadium is the one big asset; the creditors seldom get to sell off the players, since insolvency usually

dissolves contracts with the league, leaving the players as free agents. The result was that Swansea played hardball with its creditors, and offered to pay a mere 5 percent of what was owed in exchange for canceling the debts, knowing that the realistic alternative for the creditors was nothing. This kind of deal goes by the name of "Company Voluntary Arrangement," though in reality it's about as voluntary as agreeing to hand over your wallet with a gun pointing at your head. The creditors were not big multinationals that wouldn't miss the money. For the most part, they were small local businesses: local hotels, local outfitters, or local doctors, who had provided services to the players. Only the Inland Revenue and the football creditors (of whom more later) had to be paid in full. When the creditors reluctantly agreed on March 25, 2002, the debt was effectively reduced to just under $800,000, and Swansea finished the season five places from the bottom of the fourth tier. Had the present rules been in place, which deduct points from teams that take advantage of the insolvency laws to get rid of debt, they would have lost their place in the Football League.

2. *Surround yourself with smart business people who are also fans of the club.* Swansea was blessed with a number of shrewd individuals who knew about running a business: Huw Jenkins, a building contractor (12.5-percent stake); David Morgan, who worked in insurance (5 percent); Robert Davies, who had been treasurer under a previous owner of the club (10 percent); Mel Nurse, a former player and businessman (5 percent); and Leigh Dineen, who ran a vending-machine business (5 percent). All of these men were keen supporters of the club who had been working not just to oust Petty but to change the culture of the club and give the fans a say; and so they agreed to endow the Supporters' Trust with a 20-percent stake. Finally, two financial heavy hitters were persuaded to join the venture: Martin Morgan, a wealthy local businessmen with interests in hotels, agreed to take a 22.5-percent stake, and Brian Katzen, a South–African-born entrepreneur whose main interest is in turning around failing companies, bought 20 percent.

3. *Get the owners to put real money into the club.* Most new owners of soccer clubs, like Petty, promise that they will put

CONTINUES

in their own cash, but often the promise is not kept. The owners of the new company (Swansea [2002]) put about half a million pounds ($800,000) of their own money in at the beginning to help clear club debts, and until it reached the promised land of the Premier League they put in a further million and a half ($2.4 million).

4. *If you don't have a stadium, get the local government administration to build one for you.* Swansea sold its stadium, Vetch Field, to the council in 1974 for £50,000 when the club was short of cash. Vetch Field was doomed by the 1990 Taylor Report, but throughout the 1990s the local government hemmed and hawed about building a replacement. Schemes came and went as the club sank deeper in the mire, and only in 2002 did the local government finally settle the plans that would finance a new stadium. Construction started in 2003 and Swansea was able to play its first game in the new home in 2005.

5. *Choose great managers.* A series of inspirational managers marched them up from the bottom of the leagues. In 2003, Brian Flynn's team flirted with relegation until the last day of the season when a win over Hull City kept the team in the Football League. In 2006, Kenny Jackett led Swansea to promotion to League One, and, in 2008, Roberto Martinez took Swansea to first place in the Football League Championship. Paulo Sousa then led Swansea to its highest yet position in English soccer: seventh in the Championship table in 2010. As if all this were not enough, Brendan Rodgers took the club into the Premier League in 2011—and then proved almost everyone wrong by keeping it there with a credible eleventh-place finish. Flynn and Jackett were not bad, but Martinez, Sousa, and Rodgers are top-drawer managers, and all three went on to secure major positions after they left the club. Even if Swansea didn't expect to hold onto them for too long, it knew that these men could change the culture of the team, making it attractive for the players and ensuring a high quality of soccer for the fans. Moreover, it's good for smaller clubs to have friends in the bigger clubs.

6. *Get the fans out.* In the previous decade, the club had flipped between the third and fourth tiers with an average gate of just over 4,000, more or less in line with the average crowds for teams in these divisions. Over the next six years, while

remaining in the bottom two divisions, the average crowd rose to over 10,000—nearly 60 percent above the league average for the period. Clearly, the Supporter Trust model can take a lot of the credit for this performance, informing and reassuring the fans that the club was taking their interests into account. Whether you call them fans or customers, people are more likely to buy what you are selling if you show them that you care.

7. *Reach the Premier League.* For all the good work that was done between 2002 and 2011, the club was still a financial wreck. Reported losses amounted to $16 million, and this didn't even include two years when the club was not obliged to report its profits (or, more likely, losses). In 2002, wages amounted to an unsustainable 90 percent of revenue; in 2010, they were 82 percent of revenue, still unsustainable. Promotion to the Premier League changed all that. Revenue rose from $19 million to $104 million, mostly thanks to the PL broadcast money. An $18 million loss became a $29 million profit.

Competitive businesses are almost never successfully operated on democratic principles. In certain times and places workers' cooperatives have had some success, but they have usually been ousted by capitalist business models. The reason for this is not complicated. Democracy has a value that we identify with fairness—it is right that people should have a say in the decisions that affect their lives—but democracy has little or nothing to do with efficiency. Success in competition requires ruthless efficiency, and the single-minded pursuit of a competitive edge. The more competition there is, the more ruthless you have to be. Just as professional athletes have to be narrowly focused on doing whatever it takes to win, companies have to be narrowly focused on decisions that will improve their chances to attract customers and beat the competition. It's not that democracy is necessarily incompatible with this objective. It is just irrelevant to it.

Fan democracy at Barcelona and Bayern Munich is to a significant extent illusory. The control of power in these clubs has usually rested in the hands of ruthless individuals determined to do what is necessary to win. In 1999, Joan Laporta, a lawyer and politician, coauthored an article explaining how the then president of Barcelona FC, Josep Núñez, a businessman from the construction industry, abused the system to maintain an iron grip on power.[17] Three years later, Laporta took over as president and was soon being accused of exactly the same behavior. But in reality hardly anyone cared so long as the ruthless individuals delivered success. Helmut Dietl and Egon Franck, two German economists who have written extensively about soccer in their country, have characterized the e.v. system as one in which the fans nominally have control, but in reality the club is controlled by powerful individuals, often former star players, who have limited accountability and take no responsibility for the consequences of their actions (see Box 6.5). Financial mismanagement is a huge problem in English and Italian soccer, but is also a huge problem in more democratic Spanish and German soccer.

BOX 6.7: NOTTS COUNTY SUPPORTERS TRUST

Notts County, founded in 1862, claims to be the oldest surviving soccer club in the world. Juventus, founded in 1897, plays in the Notts County team colors. When the new Juventus stadium opened in 2011, Notts County was invited to play the opening game. But County's glory days came before World War One when there were only two English divisions and it was mostly in the first—its best-ever finish was third in 1891 and 1901.

The club first fell into real financial difficulties in the 1960s—almost collapsing in 1965—but then enjoyed a recovery and even made it to the top division in the 1980s. However, this revival coincided with the reign of Brian Clough as the manager of local rival Nottingham Forest (1975-93). Under his leadership, Forest won the league and the European Cup twice, and so it became the dominant team in the city.

By the 2000s, County was owned by a local businessman, Derek Pavis, who ran the club on a sound basis, ensuring that there was investment in the stadium, but he did little to satisfy the ambition of the fans. When Pavis decided to sell in 2000, the club was bought by Albert Scardino, an American journalist, whose wife, Marjorie Scardino, was a highly successful business-woman. Scardino proved less adept, and by June 2002 the club had fallen into administration, pushed over the edge by the loss of promised revenue from the ITV Digital deal.

At this point, the club seemed genuinely threatened with extinction, so a group of supporters came together to work for its survival. This culminated in the creation of the Notts County Supporters Trust. Eighteen months later, the club emerged from administration thanks in part to £300,000 ($480,000) raised by the 1,500 Trust members to buy a 30-percent share in the club. The deal also saw the creditors write off a large part of the club's debt.

Even more important than the trust was the investment of £3 million ($4.8 million) by Haydn Green, a lifelong fan who bought the stadium and then leased it back to the club for 150 years for a small rent. Green also acquired 50-percent ownership of the club. A man with no ego, he asked for no recognition, did not take a seat on the board of either the club or the trust, and news of his contribution did not leak out for some time. In 2006, he went further and gave most of his shares to the Supporters Trust, giving it complete control of the club. Sadly, he died suddenly only a few months later.

It was quickly evident that trust's ownership was not easy. While the club had been saved, it struggled to maintain itself in the fourth tier, supporters failed to renew their membership, and disputes erupted among board members. There were resignations, accusations of a lack of transparency, and suspensions of board members for misconduct. The view became widespread that the club needed an investor since the trust would never be able to raise the money to meet the ambitions of the fans.

In 2008, the board announced that it was in secret negotiations with an investor, and in May 2009 it was revealed that Munto Finance, a Middle Eastern investment vehicle, was interested in injecting capital into the club. Everyone was very excited—Manchester City had been acquired by Sheikh Mansour in 2008, and fans persuaded themselves that another oil sheikh would like to do the same thing for the "world's oldest football club." The board of the trust proposed to gift all of its shares to Munto Finance and, for good measure, to waive the debt owed to the trust. Notts County Football Club was handed over to Munto Finance for nothing. No documentation was provided, the negotiations were

CONTINUES

conducted in secret, and the supporters were asked to trust their board—which claimed that it had seen enough evidence to be confident that the new owner would invest substantially in the club. It was put to a vote of the trust members (now fallen to around 1,000) and 93 percent voted in June 2009 to give their club away to Munto Finance.

Munto Finance turned out to be unable to invest anything. Even today, it is not clear who exactly stood behind Munto Finance, but investigations have been undertaken by the police and the Serious Fraud Office. Without the injection of cash the club came close to collapse and was eventually taken over by Ray Trew, a rather less glamorous figure, but at least a real person with real financial backing.

The problems with Munto Finance emerged only three months after the supporters' vote. It still seems hard to believe that the trust could fail so badly. This debacle led many to question whether fan ownership is really appropriate for soccer clubs.

However, a degree of democratic input, even if limited, may improve efficiency. If the democratic process can at least enable the fans to dismiss a failing management team, something that cannot be done if the management team also owns the club, then there is some benefit to democratic oversight. A more significant problem for fan power is the scale of the capital investment required, and the difficulty of raising this capital without a sugar daddy. Apart from Barcelona, Real Madrid, and Bayern Munich, there are few membership clubs in the world that have been able to compete consistently with their more capitalist rivals. In all three cases, the gap between these clubs and their domestic league rivals has grown scarily large—it seems almost as if they can only succeed by monopolizing domestic support. This isn't a model for success that is replicable on a large scale. At the same time, there seems to be a constant stream of sugar daddies willing to sink their own money into building successful clubs.

Within the model of soccer that we have, the position of the members' association seems increasingly anachronistic while the model of the wealthy owner willing to sink his fortune into running a successful team seems to be more and more the norm. To which some critics respond, "Then we should change the model."

7

STRATEGY

As the experience of soccer clubs on the stock exchange seems to suggest—with the notable exception of Manchester United—winning and making money do not seem to go together in soccer. In practice, clubs seem to spend up to the limit of what they can afford in the pursuit of success. So many clubs now rely on wealthy individuals to bankroll the team because in this way they can buy more success.

This raises the issue of strategy in achieving this success. Properly speaking, strategy is the study of the choices available within the context of what is feasible. In a competitive context such as sport, strategy must focus on those choices in the light of actions available to competitors. Competition in soccer puts distinct limits on possible actions.

These limits are summarized in Figure 7.1. It shows the relationship between league position, wages, and revenues—based on financial data for the English Premier League over its first twenty-one seasons. Outcomes are defined relative to the average of all the clubs in the division. How much you spend on the team doesn't matter in an absolute sense when it comes to winning. What matters is that you spent more than your rivals.

In 1994, Manchester United paid out £11 million ($18 million) in wages and won the Premier League championship; in 2013, it paid out £183 million ($293 million) to achieve the same feat. In both cases, the club spent just over twice the average of the wage bill of a Premier League club, but over twenty years the average wage bill had risen from

174

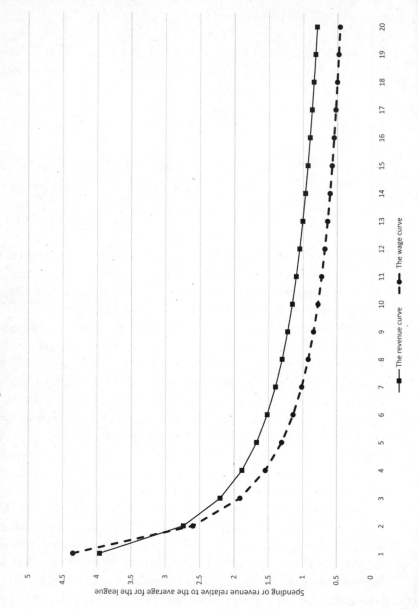

FIGURE 7.1 League position, the wage curve, and the revenue curve based on English Premier League, 1993–2013. (Source: Author analysis using club financial accounts)

£5.3 million ($8.5 million) to £89.4 million ($143 million). Likewise, teams generate revenues in proportion to their success. Higher league positions mean more revenue compared to the average team, but also average revenues have been increasing over time (as discussed in chapter 4).

The two curves in Figure 7.1 describe these relationships. The wage curve (dashed line) shows how, on average, wage spending has translated into league position in the Premier League since its foundation. It suggests a club would need to spend:

- over four times the average to win the league
- two and a half times the average to come second
- just under double to come third
- about 50 percent over the average to come fourth (which would guarantee Champions League competition in the following season).

The wage curve also suggests that spending exactly the average would mean reaching seventh position, while anything below 50 percent of the league average would imply relegation.

Now, these are just averages. In reality, the most that any team spent in this period was just below three times the average (Chelsea, when they won the title in 2005). Arsenal spent almost double the average while only coming fourth in 2006. In 1999, Blackburn Rovers spent 15-percent more on wages than the league average and still got relegated. These are averages, not certainties. You can beat the averages by luck—which often happens—or you can try to beat the averages by strategy, which as we will see, is much more difficult.

The revenue curve (the solid line in Figure 7.1) shows how league position affects revenue relative to the average. Higher league positions are associated with much higher revenues, lower league positions with lower revenues. When the Premier League started in the 1992/93 season, a club with average revenues would spend just under half those revenues on wages; by 2012/13 the wage bill had reached 70 percent of revenues. When thinking about the strategic possibilities of the clubs, we should think about revenues relative to wage spending.

Figure 7.1 shows that the team finishing last in the league would have a wage spend equal to 50 percent of the average (from the wage curve) and revenue equal to about 80 percent of the average wage spend. From what is left, the club would have to finance not only its other operating expenses (mostly match-day expenses at the stadium) but also capital investments to acquire players in the transfer market and maintain/develop the stadium.

For the bottom half of the league the ratio is roughly constant: wage expenditure accounts for between 60 and 70 percent of revenues. These figures are consistent with reporting accounting losses—which is what most clubs do—after taking into account all of the other expenditures required to run a soccer club. However, in the highest league positions, the ratio of wages to revenues rises sharply. At the top of the league, the implied wage expenditure is actually higher than the expected revenue. In other words, at the upper end of the league, clubs need to spend much more than they earn in terms of revenues.

This is largely the effect of Roman Abramovich and Sheikh Mansour on the Premier League. Chelsea and Manchester City have in fact spent more than they have generated in revenues in order to achieve success, while Manchester United and Arsenal have consistently reported profits. The chart reflects an average of these clubs, with the effect of the big spenders outweighing the effect of the profitable clubs.

The problem for clubs like Arsenal and Manchester United has been that the spending of Chelsea and Manchester City has driven up the cost of acquiring and holding on to talented players, and so has undermined their profitability. Much the same thing is happening at the bottom of the league. A mid-table position does not generate a profit on average. If the clubs below spent less, then it might be possible to target mid-table with relatively modest spending. That would be more attractive to some owners than trying to win the Champions League. But teams at the bottom are spending almost as much as the teams in mid-table, and it is not that difficult for a mid-table team to drop into the relegation zone. So the smaller teams have to spend heavily just to have a chance of hanging onto a Premier League place.

These relationships are not set in stone. They ultimately depend on the behavior of those who run the clubs, but as we have seen, there has been a trend toward concentrated ownership funding ever-bigger spending, even as the revenues of the leagues have grown. The difference in spending between clubs has grown, not just in absolute but also in relative terms. Between 1960 and 1980, all except three league champions spent less than 66 percent above the average for the top division. Three actually spent less than the average: Burnley in 1960, Ipswich Town in 1962, and Everton in 1970. Since the start of the Premier League, all but three league champions have spent more than 66 percent above the league average. Moreover, the difference in revenues between winning and losing is much larger than it was in the past.

The wage curve and revenue curve for the English top division between 1960 and 1980 are shown in Figure 7.2. The revenue curve is almost flat, while the wage curve rises steeply at the highest league positions. In those days the market for players was less competitive, so it was harder to buy success. Back in 1960, the league operated a maximum wage—fixed at £20 ($32) per week—roughly the earnings of a semi-skilled manual worker at the time. Those were the days when players still traveled with the fans on the train to away games because most players did not own a car.

The maximum wage was abolished in 1961, but competition in the market for players developed only slowly. There were no foreign players in English soccer until 1978, and clubs were known to engage in pacts to keep wages down. The transfer system also tied a player to his club, and until 1963 he could not move without its permission. While players won more freedom of movement in the 1970s, restricted mobility still meant less competition and lower salaries than today.

The steepness of the wage curve at high league positions is actually a reflection of how little wages explain during this period. Today, league position is more sensitive to wage spending than it was in the past, and so back then much larger increases in wage spending would have been needed to get to the top of the league. By the same token, teams getting relegated would not be spending much less on average than those in mid-table. That the sensitivity is higher today is shown by the fact that wage spending accounts for 56 percent of the variation of league position among clubs in the top division in the Premier League era, but it accounts for only 13 percent of the variation between 1960 and 1980.[1]

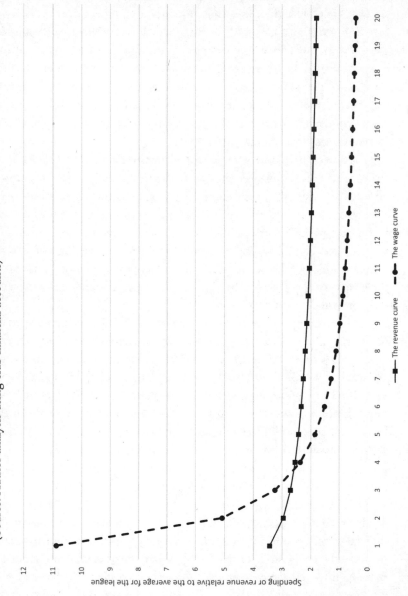

FIGURE 7.2 League position, the wage curve, and the revenue curve based on English First Division, 1960–1980. (Source: Author analysis using club financial accounts)

Figure 7.1 suggests that clubs are likely to struggle to make a profit at any level in the Premier League nowadays, and the problem actually gets worse as you rise higher in the league. If, as I have argued, the purpose of a soccer club is to win, then the implication is that the only way to win for most clubs is to have a sugar daddy who will fund the enterprise. That certainly seems to be the case if a club wishes to ascend from the bottom to the top. Improving performance means signing better players, which means investment now, in the hope of a return in the future. Even if the strategy is successful, the club can only expect that its revenues will grow to match expenditure when it reaches the top. While it is in the process of ascent, revenues will remain low, so there is a financial bridge that someone needs to build, without any expectation of ever getting the money back. And, of course, luck always plays a role, so there is every possibility that the strategy fails and the club is left with a top-end wage bill and a middling ranking. This story is true in the English Premier League, and it also seems to hold true in every other league. Some financial data is available for French, Italian, and Spanish clubs, and this tends to confirm the story told by the Premier League data: profits are hard to come by, and it is harder to be profitable at the top than it is at the bottom.

According to this logic, a club is fenced in on every side. Markets determine how much success it can achieve and how much revenue it can generate, history determines where the club is today, and the future is determined by the breadth of the owner's ego, and the depth of his pockets. But what if the market can be beaten by something more than luck? Can skills be brought to bear in order to outperform the market?

THE MANAGER

The role of the soccer manager has grown significantly over time, and nowadays he tends to be seen as a kind of Messiah, a man of extraordinary capabilities who can turn straw into gold—at least when things go well. In the early days of soccer, clubs hired coaches to keep the players fit, and the board of directors picked the team. The coach/manager would also search for players to acquire in the market, but once again the board would take the final decision. In general, this is not a bad way to approach a problem where judgment is called for—big decisions require careful consideration, and sharing responsibility among several people can help to avoid costly mistakes.

Herbert Chapman, who first led Huddersfield Town to two league championships, in 1924 and 1925, and repeated the trick at Arsenal in 1931 and 1933,[2] laid the foundations for the cult of the manager. It became well and truly established by Sir Matt Busby at Manchester United in the 1950s and 1960s. By the 1970s it sometimes seemed as if the manager was in charge of the entire club, rather than an employee responsible to the board of directors. In the case of Brian Clough, one of the greatest managers ever produced by English soccer, this was almost the case. He rose to prominence at Derby County by simultaneously cajoling and bullying the club's board into spending money on players that he (and his managerial partner, Peter Taylor) deemed valuable when almost no one else did. The duo then moved to Nottingham Forest, the last member's association club in English professional soccer (the club did not become a limited liability company until 1982), where once again Clough played the autocrat. He and Taylor were largely tolerated because they were remarkably successful on a limited budget. In terms of the regression charts in chapter 2, the club consistently sat well above the regression line under their leadership.

But there was a darker side. In the 1990s, Alan Sugar, then owner of Tottenham Hotspur, stated in court that his manager (Terry Venables) had told him that "Clough likes a bung"—meaning an illegal payment in cash to himself on the transfer of player. Such practices may have worked in the days when player transfers of $160,000 were considered significant and the average annual turnover of a top division club was about $8 million, but by the 1990s the sums were reaching a scale where turning a blind eye was no longer possible. Directors of clubs everywhere started to insist that financial practices were brought up to date. Inevitably, this reduced the power of managers and exposed their conduct to even more scrutiny.

Nowadays, the role of the soccer manager usually combines the functions of the head coach (responsible for training, player selection, tactics on the field) and the general manager (responsible for contract negotiations and signing new players). Recruitment of new talent is clearly an important part of the job, be it through the scouting network or through the youth academy. The manager needs to establish a training regime for the players and an atmosphere in which the players can thrive. This means creating a coaching staff and a medical staff—on hand at the club, and also for medical treatment required following injury. The manager needs to make sure that the players are fit mentally as well as physically, which really requires a subtle appreciation of the psychology of personal motivation. The press tends to focus on the role of the manager on the sideline at a game, barking orders, and giving half-time talks. But in the context of the broader requirements this seems rather like the conductor of the orchestra waving the baton. No doubt it has some significance, but the real work of the conductor is creating the context in which beautiful music can be played.

Given all these tasks, a modern manager is clearly a delegator. He must rely on skilled lieutenants who will implement his grand strategy. Modern leadership theory largely focuses on team building and capacity to bring about change in organizations. The most important task is to move people away from doing things that don't work toward doing things that do work, and, when people are unwilling to change, to manage the process of replacing them. Of course, this presupposes that the manager is able to identify those things that will work. In the past, this was a little easier.

In the days when players drank huge quantities of beer on a regular basis, it was easy to see that reducing alcohol consumption would improve performance. The managers who led the way in changing this ethic (for example, Arsène Wenger at Arsenal) reaped a reward. Improved fitness regimes in general have had a positive impact on team performance. The problem is that improvements such as these are quickly copied if they work. It is possible both to be an innovative manager and have almost no measurable impact on performance. The only way to avoid this is to introduce successful innovations that cannot be copied.

This fact is also what makes most of the management literature unreadable. In any business, a manager who is successful wants to cash in on his or her success by explaining how their inspirational methods caused their success. But, first, unless the manager has retired, he or she is unlikely to want to share the real secrets. Second, if there are thousands of managers and success is purely determined by chance, then dumb luck will still produce a few managers with glittering careers—so how are we to tell skill from luck?

We can think of asset-management companies as being like soccer managers. Both put together teams of individuals whose job is to find the best stocks (or players), and put them together in a successful portfolio (or team). True, by and large, the asset manager cannot directly improve the performance of the stock in the way that the soccer manager might hope to improve the performance of the player. But as we saw in chapter 2, the decision making of club managers is dominated to a large degree by picking which players to put on the field for the next game, which really is just like picking stocks.

There is a large literature trying to measure the skill of asset managers. Most of it finds no visible evidence of skill at work. The performance of asset managers is measured by the percentage rate of return on their stock portfolio. That percentage can be modeled using a small number of easily measured factors, most important of which is the riskiness of the stocks. You can always get a higher rate of return on average if you are prepared to accept larger swings (up or down) from year to year. It also appears that you can get higher returns by investing in smaller, fast-growing companies. It is easy to use a computer program to construct a portfolio with these characteristics. Research tends to show that asset managers cannot beat such benchmarks on average. For example, a recent paper by Nobel Prize–winning economist Eugene Fama and Kenneth French found the returns of asset managers were very tightly distributed around a mean of zero after allowing for the fees that the managers charge. They conclude that there are very few asset managers who could truly deliver above-average performance through skill rather than luck.[3]

We can ask a similar question about soccer managers: can they deliver above-average performance consistently, rather than just by luck? Thomas Peeters of Erasmus University in Rotterdam and I have been examining the career records of managers in English soccer going back to 1974. Over this period, there have been more than one thousand managers in charge of clubs, but many of those have only held office for a short period. We therefore focused on the 528 managers who were in charge for thirty games or more. We then estimated the effect of the manager on individual games—our sample included more than 100,000 games—as well as allowing for the wage bills of the two clubs and home advantage. In our sample, we found around two hundred managers who had a *positive* impact on their club that was statistically significant (i.e., unlikely to be due purely to luck). That is about 20 percent of the population of one thousand–plus managers. Only fifteen (about 1.5 percent) had a statistically significant negative impact.

Now, if soccer management was only about luck, then we would expect to see about 2.5 percent of managers who were significantly positive and 2.5 percent who were significantly negative—there will always be a few big winners and big losers on the roulette wheel. But our results suggest that there are noticeably more winners, and noticeably fewer losers, than mere chance would predict—which implies that there is some skill involved in soccer management. The worst managers are quickly dropped, and the best managers add substantially—the top twenty or so managers produce an extra half to three-quarters of a point per game. Because the average points per game is about 1.4 (given three points for a win and one for a tie), these people are adding about 30 to 50 percent to performance on a consistent basis. So we conclude that most managers make little difference, while a few have a significant impact.

BOX 7.1: THE RELOCATION OF WIMBLEDON FOOTBALL CLUB

Wimbledon Football Club, based in the southwest London suburb famous for its iconic tennis tournament, The Championships, was founded in 1889. It was a semiprofessional team playing in the Southern League until it was admitted to the fourth tier of the Football League in 1977. It then rose rapidly to reach the top division by 1986 and beat Liverpool in the FA Cup Final of 1988.

Despite success on the field, the club was dogged by problems relating to its stadium, which was inadequate for playing top-level soccer. Disputes with the local council blocked agreement on construction of a new stadium, and in 1992 the club was obliged to enter a stadium-sharing agreement with Crystal

CONTINUES

Palace, six and a half miles away. The club managed to survive in the Premier League but struggled financially.

Because no agreement could be reached with the local council in Wimbledon, the club started to float the idea of relocation. One proposal was to move to Dublin in Ireland, but this was vetoed by the Irish Football Association. In 2000 the club, which was by then owned by two Norwegians, was approached by a consortium offering to provide them with a stadium in Milton Keynes, a satellite town of London about 60 miles away.

The club announced the deal in 2001 and provoked immense opposition, not only from Wimbledon fans but also from fans across the country, many of whom feared that this would set a precedent. Initially, the FA vetoed the move, but then was obliged to reopen the case after a court found they had not acted fairly. The second review led to approval and Wimbledon, previously known as The Dons, became the MK Dons.

Outside of Milton Keynes the club remains one of the most hated teams in England. Many fans refuse to acknowledge the team even exists; others refer to it disparagingly as "the franchise club." Lots of fans simply support anyone they play against. Peter Winkelman, who formed the consortium that brought the club to Milton Keynes, has said he now regrets doing it.

Fans of the old team formed a new club, AFC Wimbledon, owned by a Supporter Trust. It started from the bottom tier of English soccer (the ninth) and worked its way to the fourth tier by 2011. It still doesn't have a stadium in Wimbledon and plays in the nearby town of Kingston-upon-Thames—but in 2007 the MK Dons agreed to hand over all memorabilia and trademarks related to the old club to AFC Wimbledon.

It is possible that the two teams could meet in the same league division one day. They have already played against each other in Cup competition—the FA Cup in 2012, the League Cup and the Football League Trophy, both in 2014—all three times in Milton Keynes. MK Dons won the first two encounters, and AFC Wimbledon savored victory at the third attempt. It seems unlikely that relocation will ever be permitted again.

Saying that some managers can make a difference is not the same as saying that you can base a strategy around hiring a better manager.

Some aspects of management seem fairly obvious. One part of *Soccernomics* that generated a lot of comment was a list of simple rules to follow when operating in the transfer market. Mostly, these recommendations were about ways of avoiding mistakes that result from cognitive biases—systematic and avoidable errors in judgment. For example, don't buy players at inflated prices after a few good games at the World Cup. World Cup stars grab our attention, but performance over four or five games is not a good basis for judgment. Also, your performance for your national team isn't necessarily a good indicator of how you will play for your club. This is basic stuff, even if some managers never seem to learn.

In *Soccernomics*, we also argued that most managers do not make a difference, consistent with the data reported here. Chris Anderson and David Sally, in their book *The Numbers Game*, argued that we were wrong about this. They said that while the wage performance line can explain a lot, it is still possible to make a difference by design, thereby preserving a significant role for managers. Like Simon Kuper and I, they have suggested some simple heuristics for improving performance. For example, they suggest that managers should pay more attention to the performance of the "weakest link." The worst player on the team is more likely to make the mistake that leads to defeat than the strongest player is to create a goal out of nothing and win the game.

Judging the reliability of these kinds of prescriptions is itself problematic. But one thing we can be sure of is that if they work, they will be copied. I think one of the proudest moments of my career came in the summer of 2012 when Roberto di Matteo, then manager of Chelsea, who had just pulled off the near miracle of beating odds-on favorite Bayern Munich in the Champions League final played at Bayern's home stadium, was spotted buying a copy of *Soccernomics*. It's flattering to think that someone that successful might think it worthwhile to read; it's worrisome to think that he was fired in November that year—I hope it wasn't anything we suggested that turned out not to work.

One of the most striking features of professional soccer has been the declining tenure of managers—the amount of time employed as manager at a given club. Averages can be misleading. Because there are only twenty managers in the English top division at any one time, if one manager has been in the job for a long time the average becomes inflated. Sir Alex Ferguson was in charge at Manchester United for twenty-six years until he retired in 2013 (itself an unusual way for a manager to leave his job). A better measure of average tenure is the median—the tenure of the tenth- or eleventh-place manager who has spent the most/least time in the job. In the 1980s, the median tenure of a manager in the top division in England was almost three and a half years. In the last decade, it has fallen to less than one and a half years. This pattern is mirrored across Europe. UEFA's analysis of managers at 624 top division clubs as of November 2013 showed that average tenure was seventeen months. Northern Ireland and Finland were outliers at eighty-six months and fifty-four months respectively, but in twenty out of the forty-seven UEFA member nations surveyed, club managers had average tenure of less than one year. In lower divisions, tenure can be even shorter. In the fourth tier of English soccer, the median tenure of the manager was less than fifteen months back in the 1980s. By the last decade it had fallen to 271 days, barely the length of the season. But given that a manager is almost never hired on the first day of the season, this implies that the typical manager does not get to run the team for an entire season before moving on. (Not all managers are fired; some get better jobs.)

Even three and a half years is not a very long time for a manager to get on top of running a business and producing some success. In the business world, senior managers spend much longer in the job. A recent study shows that the average tenure of the chief executive officer in large US companies is six years.[4] Moreover, most CEOs have spent a large fraction of their career at the company that they eventually run. This is perhaps not so surprising. In most businesses, the skills required are quite specific to that company. Making ball bearings in Norway, for example, is a very different proposition from exporting fresh fruit from Spain. There are skills that are specific to both the product itself and to the region in which the business operates. You would not expect managers to move very often between either businesses or location. In the same way, you would not expect to find a successful soccer manager taking over the coaching of a National Basketball Association team.[5] But the skills required to manage a team in a given professional sport will work at different clubs and seem to be transferrable internationally. Herbert

Chapman successfully transplanted his skills from Huddersfield Town to Arsenal in the 1920s, and for more than a century managers have been moving abroad for employment. Nowadays there seems to be an elite group of coaches who travel the world coaching both the biggest clubs and national teams.

But the fact that soccer managers get so little time in the job, and that the amount of time has diminished so rapidly in recent years, requires explanation. In American professional sports, managerial tenure tends to be longer than it is in the soccer world. In the National Football League and Major League Baseball, current median tenure is around three years, while it is more than four years in the National Hockey League. Only in the NBA is the median tenure comparable to soccer at just over one year. In this respect at least Major League Soccer resembles the game world-wide, and managers last little longer than one year in the job. Of all the major sports, American college football probably has the longest tenure. When Joe Paterno, the coach of the Penn State football team, was fired in 2011 (for failing to take sufficient action after being shown evidence that his assistant coach was involved in child abuse), he had been in the job for forty-five years.

The obvious explanation for short tenure in soccer is that it doesn't take long to find out if a manager has what it takes to create a successful team. In this sense the relationship between manager and club is rather like the relationship of a couple. When a relationship starts you usually know something about the person involved. You have an idea that they are your "type," but you can't be sure how well things will go once you interact over time. Hiring a manager is like moving in together after a couple of dates: it is an inherently risky business. Time together helps you learn about the person, but if too many clashes occur you start to question if the relationship has a future. Eventually, if things don't improve, you decide to cut your losses and break it off. Eventually, most people go back into the dating market and try again. For a soccer club, living alone is like having a caretaker manager, a temporary fix but not the long-term solution.

Most dismissals usually occur after a run of poor results (there is a large literature on the timing of dismissals). The longer the bad run, the lower the probability that the manager will eventually turn out to be effective. The club can expect that the average replacement will be no better or worse than average—that is what the statistics tell us—but there is also a possibility that the next manager might be "the one." There is very little risk, according to the data, that the replacement will be so bad that things will actually get worse. Perhaps a better analogy for the managerial-hiring process would be a lottery. Each number gives you a chance to win; if your number doesn't come up on the present ticket then you should buy another. Overall, the probability of winning the lottery is small, but if you do get lucky then the rewards are huge. Playing the lottery is not a way to get rich, but people who do it find it enjoyable.

BOX 7.2: FIRING THE MANAGER

The table below shows what happens when you fire the manager. It is based on 103 managerial changes in the Premier League between 2001 and 2010.

The manager's...	Played	Won	Draw	Loss	Points
Last three games	252	48	45	159	189
Last game	83	14	16	53	58
First game	83	29	16	38	103
First three games	249	82	67	100	313

Firing the manager seems to work—the number of points won in the first game after firing the manager is almost double the number of points won in the last game before firing. Over three games, the improvement is around 50 percent in terms of points won, which still looks like a dramatic improvement.

So why not fire the manager even more often? Well, the problem is that what we see could just be the operation of chance and not skill. Because it's hard to measure managerial skill and because results are all that matter, managers tend to get fired when results are poor. Suppose that results are really only determined by chance but the board of directors thinks that results depend on managerial skill. There will be (randomly) runs of bad results—and these will cause the manager to be fired. It's less likely that the run of bad luck will continue, and so firing the manager will appear, on average, to improve results. This is a phenomenon known as "regression to the mean," which is a serious problem when trying to analyze cause and effect in lots of situations.

A recent paper by Maria De Paola and Vincenzo Scoppa examined the firing of managers in Italy's Serie A between 2003 and 2008 and found that there was no measurable effect of changing the manager.[1] The improvement in performance after firing the manager could be entirely attributed to regression to the mean.

Economists tend to think that, consciously or unconsciously, decision makers will usually grasp the implications of anything that can be revealed by statistical analysis. So why do managers get fired so often when there is a dip in team performance that is not really their fault? One answer is that managers are being scapegoated by the directors of the club. Another theory might be that even if the dip is not the manager's fault, nonetheless the performance reveals that the manager is not likely to be among the 20 percent-or-so of managers whose performance is significantly above average. In this sense, managers are like lottery tickets—you never know if your next one will win you the jackpot.

1. De Paola, M., and Scoppa, V. (2011) "The effects of managerial turnover: evidence from coach dismissals in Italian soccer teams." *Journal of Sports Economics.*

But why, then, should tenure be getting shorter over time? The answer almost certainly lies in the market for players. Recall that back in 1960 there still existed a maximum wage. This meant that there was very little scope for variation in pay among players, especially when the maximum was so low. The ratio of the salaries at the top and bottom of the top division in 1958 was less than 3:1. By 2013 it had reached more than 5:1. Moreover, back in the 1950s and 1960s, top division clubs competed with clubs in the second, and even third tier to attract the best players. In 1958, the clubs in the top half of the second tier paid more in wages than the clubs in the bottom half of the first tier, and the club that paid the highest wages in the third tier (Brighton and Hove Albion) paid more than eight clubs in the top division. In 2013, the highest paying club in the second tier had a wage bill that was 82 percent of the lowest paying club in the Premier League, and the highest wage bill in the third tier was only 31 percent of that level. Back in the day, managers earned their corn by finding ways to attract players, legally or otherwise. Many managers in the past got into trouble for breaking the rules on player recruitment. Herbert Chapman was banned from soccer in 1919 for his alleged involvement in using illegal methods (the ban was later overturned).

Nowadays the difference in what clubs can pay at different levels has become sharply differentiated, so it is not hard to get the right player if he has the talent, so long as you are prepared to pay his price. Arguably, this has taken some skill out of the job of being a manager. In the past, the manager might be able to find players that no one else had heard of; nowadays kids playing videogames like "FIFA Soccer" and "Football Manager" have almost as much information in hand as the real managers. In 2014, it was announced that the owners of "Football Manager" would partner with the data analysts Prozone to offer recruitment services to Premier League clubs. But if some of the functions of the manager are being commoditized, then clubs have weaker incentives to hold onto managers who do not appear to be doing well in the short term. This does not mean that managers are less skillful overall than they were in the past. It's just that the job description of a manager has changed.

In April 2014, it was announced that Sir Alex Ferguson would take up a contract with Harvard Business School to teach executives about management—the implication being that managers in other businesses can learn lessons from his skills in human-resource management. It was not until the 1930s that the FA introduced even basic training skills for managers. In fact, by the 1950s, England was falling badly behind in terms of management practice. Clubs in Italy, Spain, Germany, and the Netherlands long ago started to treat soccer management as a serious business, and this was reflected in the technical quality of the soccer players and teams produced in those countries.

But despite the increase in skill levels in management, skill may make less of a difference than in the past. This argument was advanced by Stephen Jay Gould to explain the fact that no player has achieved a batting average above .400 in Major League Baseball since 1941, whereas twenty-eight players hit that mark between 1876 and 1941. Gould argued that this was a result of what is sometimes called talent compression—as talent is drawn from a larger pool of people, then the difference between the best and worst gets smaller, and so the chances of any one person's performance being significantly above average falls.[6] This results in what Michael Mauboussin, a portfolio manager who has used his financial market skills to analyze sports, calls the paradox of skill.[7] On average, people can get better at their job, while at the same time luck can appear to be more important, just because in this larger pool there are fewer standouts.

BOX 7.3: MEASURING THE CONTRIBUTION OF MANAGERS: THE CASE OF PAUL STURROCK

When we were writing *Soccernomics* I generated a simple league table of managers based on league performance allowing for the wage bill. When we examined the list of best managers, some were the familiar names—Alex Ferguson, Bob Paisley, Arsène Wenger, Kenny Dalglish—but some were less familiar. One such is Paul Sturrock, so my coauthor, Simon Kuper, went and interviewed him and wrote an extended article about him in the *Financial Times*. This is a summary of what he wrote:

Generally speaking, the people who matter most in soccer aren't managers but players. The club that pays the highest wages typically comes out on top; the club that paid least finished last. The correlation between players' wages and league position is very high. As Sturrock says, "Money talks, and money decides where you finish up in the leagues."

If players' wages determine results, it follows that everything else—including the manager—is just noise. Most managers are not very relevant. In the long run, they will achieve almost exactly the league positions that their players' wages would predict. But just a few are able to do significantly better than that. Some of

CONTINUES

these managers are the famous ones everyone has heard of—
Wenger, Mourinho, and company. Others, like Paul Sturrock,
achieve the same feat but at a lower level of competition.

Sturrock's achievements:

Plymouth Argyle: Promoted from League Two to League
One (2001/02), promoted from League One to Championship and League Champions (2003/04, although Sturrock
left for Southampton six weeks before the promotion was
confirmed)

Sheffield Wednesday: Promoted from League One to
Championship (2004/05)

Swindon Town: Promoted from League Two to League One
(2006/07)

It's hard to explain what good managers do right, because if
it were obvious everyone would simply copy them, but people
working around him identify the following traits:

1. Unusually for an ex-player, Sturrock cares about statistics. He
    employs his own "stats guy" who provides advice. He has
    concluded from the stats that "long-ball football done in a
    clever way" wins matches in the lower divisions. [Long-ball
    football involves getting the ball into the last third of the field
    as quickly as possible on the theory that if the ball is in this
    area it is more likely to end up in the opponent's net. In the
    simplest version, a goalkeeper or full back just kicks the ball
    from one end of the field to the other to start the attack—
    hence "long" ball.] Sturrock hasn't used the long-ball game
    his entire career, and presumably he would work differently if
    he had better players. He says that it's not just blindly punting
    balls long: "There's a way of doing it. I think you've got to be
    accurately playing balls up to your front men. And supporting
    them." Playing clever long-ball football is a craft.
2. During a game he can instantly see what is going wrong and
    change it.
3. Soccer's besetting plague is panicked decisions, but he re-
    sists that; he never gets rushed into decisions. Instead, Stur-
    rock arrives at verdicts through clever deliberation.
4. He's very consultative, but he's not interested in consen-
    sus. He'll be interested in more or less everybody's view.

But he's very happy to make his own decision. And afterward Sturrock can analyze his own decision. Sometimes he'll say, "I f***ed up."

So why hasn't Paul Sturrock been working in the EPL his entire career? The problem for men like him is that it's hard to judge managers on their results. After all, results are mostly down to players' wages: that's why Plymouth Argyle, say, finishes lower than Chelsea. Nobody, as far as we know, has ever systematically investigated which managers overachieve relative to their clubs' wage bills.

It's also hard for outsiders to judge managers on their day-to-day work. Most of the biggest managerial decisions are made in private, and the outcome of those decisions (e.g., signing a certain player) might only become apparent much later. This difficulty of assessment also bedevils judgments about corporate chief executives. That's why a man can appear on a magazine cover as savior of his company one month and appear in the dock the next.

One day, the market in managers might finally become efficient. But it will probably be too late for Sturrock.

Now, some managers can still outperform the giants of history. Sir Alex Ferguson is easily the greatest manager in English soccer history measured by league championships (and no doubt in many other ways too). Only ten other managers have won more than two league titles in England's top division. Ferguson won thirteen. The next best manager won six (George Ramsay between 1894 and 1910). Ferguson deserves to go down in history as one of the great statistical outliers; no one else is even close. But Ferguson also started in a different era. His first three seasons at United did not produce success and he came close to being sacked. It is unlikely today that any manager would be given an equivalent period of time.[8] His successor in the job, David Moyes, did not last a full season. So is it possible that clubs are foregoing the opportunity to secure the next Alex Ferguson, or has the nature of the game now changed to the point where money really is the only thing?

THE BRAND

So far, we have focused solely on the manager as a source of a club's competitive advantage. This amounts to finding more ways to be successful without spending more money on players. The alternative is to find ways to generate more revenues from a given level of success than your rivals. Attendance is closely related to league position; nonetheless, some clubs can achieve higher attendance at a given league position. Or, if a club has limited capacity, it may be able to charge a higher price for the same level of attendance and league position. One example might be Arsenal. Because of its location close to the center of the capital city, the club is able to charge higher ticket prices than most, while still selling out.

Location is important, and in North America many owners of professional franchises have increased their profits by moving the club from a location with relatively few fans to areas where there is more enthusiasm. This option is not available in professional soccer, at least not in most of the big markets. In England, Arsenal moved from Woolwich to Highbury in 1910, but since that date there is only one significant example of a relocation, which turned out to be extremely unpopular (see Box 7.1). It is fairly clear that neither soccer fans nor the soccer authorities will tolerate relocation—even by relatively minor clubs. This may not be true in every country, but it is probably the case for all of the big leagues except in the United States. As a result, location in soccer should be thought of as the luck of the draw, an inheritance that cannot be tampered with. The idea behind the concept of a brand is that there is something about the name and image of the business that has a value in its own right. Take Coca-Cola as an example. People will buy Coke wherever they see the name and the image; if asked what soft drink they would like, they are more likely to say "Coke" than anything else. It is a name with near universal recognition. It does not matter where it is made, and it does not matter who owns it. If the Pepsi taste tests are to be believed, it may not even matter much what it tastes like. Consequently, the right to use the name Coca-Cola is hugely valuable—even without the capacity to make it. If you owned the brand name, you could pay someone else to produce the drink, bottle and distribute it, and still be left with a healthy profit. That profit is brand value.

Do soccer clubs have brand value? Well, we've already established that they are not mobile. The ownership can change, but the location of the club is more or less fixed. But the real question is: are you left with a profit once you have paid the people you need to pay in order to operate as a soccer club? We have seen that clubs typically don't make money. All, or almost all, the money goes to the players in wages. If you don't invest in the team, then performance declines, and fans stop coming. This suggests that most clubs really don't have brand value. The one clear exception to this in England is Manchester United, which has a history of generating substantial profits for its owners over thirty years now. Other examples are harder to find. Clubs such as Barcelona, Real Madrid, and Bayern Munich also probably fall into this class, but because they are membership associations and cannot distribute profits in the same way as Manchester United it's hard to tell. Nonetheless, these clubs can genuinely claim to have brand value. Few others can.

What is notable about clubs like Real Madrid, Manchester United, and Bayern Munich is that they have all been dominant in leagues that themselves are dominant. What could a club do that would succeed in raising it to the level of these few exceptions? Clearly, some clubs have an extraordinary history behind them: One would have expected to see the names of Italian giants such as Juventus, Inter, and AC Milan in this list, but the financial problems of the league as a whole are so great that these clubs increasingly struggle to be profitable. Clubs such as Ajax, Porto, and Celtic, while being giants in the history of the game, are held back by the small national markets within which they are confined.

Other clubs might find ways to increase their revenues, but the problem of competition is never far away. Replica soccer jerseys were rarities thirty years ago; nowadays, every respectable fan must have at least one. This marketing ploy has raised revenue, but it has worked in the same way for all clubs. The clubs that have been able to generate the most revenue from replica jerseys have been the most successful clubs. And almost all of the extra revenue generated, either by big or small clubs, has been paid out to the players as part of the competition to attract talent.

BOX 7.4: BRAND VALUE IN SOCCER

One definition of a brand is that it consists of the value of intangible assets such as trademarks and related intellectual property rights. In the case of soccer, imagine a club that possessed a stadium and playing staff similar to that of Manchester United, but did not have the right to use that name—how much would it be worth paying to use the name? The answer to that question would be the brand value. Manchester City, whose recent history until the takeover by Sheikh Mansour was dire, might well qualify as a suitable comparison—City won the EPL in 2012 and 2014, United in 2011 and 2013. City looks like United without the brand name. In 2011/12, City's revenue was $370 million, in 2012/13 United's was $581 million—the difference might be deemed the annualized value of the United brand: $211 million.

Now this differential will not be permanent if United is not as successful as it was in the past (its brand value will depreciate) and City continues to be successful (its brand value will appreciate). Put simply, the brand value in soccer represents the greater earning potential of a club when it has a history of success that enables it to do more business and charge higher prices when doing that business. If one were to try to sell the United name to someone else then it might be worth four or five times the difference, implying that the difference added by the United name alone lasts only for a period of five years or so. After that either the success of the club would create its own brand value, or the lack of success would erode the value of the United name.

This method of valuing a brand is known as the Royalty Relief Method—what you would be willing to pay to acquire the trademarks of the business. It is of course entirely hypothetical in soccer, since another club would never be allowed to acquire Manchester United trademarks, any more than Manchester United would be allowed to relocate to London or New York. But it is a useful way of thinking about how much the Manchester United business would be worth if it were sold. The total value of the club might be thought as the sum of the value of the stadium, the player contracts, and the trademarks.

The fact that established, successful teams have brand value helps them to sustain their dominance. Manchester United can simply invest the excess revenue it generates and so ensure that it continues to dominate in the future without becoming insolvent. Manchester City can only achieve this by a continued and substantial subsidy from its owners. Once City has done this for a few years, it too will start to have brand value and be self-sustaining. Teams might join the dominant group even if they don't have money simply by being extremely good or extremely lucky over a period of years, and clubs might drop out of the dominant group by being extremely bad or extremely unlucky, but such events are rare. Mostly, the dominant group is stable and the only way to join the dominant group is by substantial investment in developing a brand. This is simply another way of restating Sutton's endogenous sunk-cost theory as it applies to soccer.

The brand value of most clubs is negligible, even when they have a long and illustrious history. For example, Rangers Football Club, founded in 1872 and a dominant power in Scotland for more than a century, went into administration in 2012. The administrator sold the business, history, and assets of the club for $8.8 million to an investor. This included Ibrox Stadium, a 51,000-seat venue of great historical significance that would cost well in excess of $160 million to rebuild from scratch. Seemingly, the brand name was worth nothing.

The Rangers case is extreme, but when it comes to brand value most clubs are more like Rangers than Manchester United. Despite their great histories, significance to their communities, and instant name recognition, most soccer club brand values are close to zero.

It seems paradoxical that soccer clubs can be so recognizable and yet have so few opportunities to profit from their visibility. The point is that in most cases what we really mean by a brand is that we recognize it. We instantly recognize names such as Ajax, or Paris Saint-Germain, or Lazio—but this does not invest these names with brand value. That is only true if people value the name on its own, and nothing else that goes with it. In reality, fans want their club to win trophies and so glorify its name. Without the success, the name of the club is diminished. Given that the players on the field are the only ones who can deliver what the fans want, in an unrestricted market like soccer, they tend to receive almost all of the rewards.

8

INSOLVENCY

DOMINANCE AND DISTRESS IN SOCCER ARE TWO SIDES OF THE SAME coin—the extremes of success and failure. Big teams with real brand value are dominant because they can sustain investment in players and generate more revenue from success than a typical team. Every other club aspires to join their ranks, and spends everything it earns in pursuit of success. When things don't work out, as is often the case, financial distress ensues. Financial distress is a term of art in the business world that refers to the situation where it is becoming apparent that a company is struggling to meet its obligations to creditors—it cannot pay its debts. Once the directors of a company believe that the financial distress cannot be relieved (by, for example, an upturn in the business environment) then the company is insolvent and the duty of the directors shifts from an obligation to run the business successfully for the owners, to protecting the interests of the creditors. Insolvency is the endgame of financial distress.

Insolvency has been part of soccer since the game began, but it has become a growing part of the media discourse on soccer in recent years. The exact meaning of insolvency depends upon the law of the land—and each nation's laws differ quite substantially. However, there is a common history behind the way the insolvency laws have evolved across the world, and there is growing international standardization.

The word "bankruptcy" refers to the situation in which an individual cannot pay his or her debts. For centuries, bankruptcy was always treated very severely under the law. Bankrupts were usually sent to prison and often permanently disgraced. The inability to pay your debts was a crime. Attitudes started to change in the nineteenth century as the world of business became more sophisticated. The growing recognition that all business involves risk, and that any kind of innovation requires taking risks, led to a more tolerant attitude toward those who failed. Nowadays, it is often said that every successful innovator has ten failed businesses behind them.

By the end of the nineteenth century bankrupts were no longer sent to jail, although sanctions remained severe (e.g., prohibiting bankrupts from starting new businesses). The development of limited liability companies required a new approach. What happened to a company, rather than a real person, when it could not pay its debts? This is the situation we refer to as insolvency. In English law, real people can go *bankrupt*, but companies (which are also persons, albeit fictional) are described as *insolvent* when they cannot pay their debts. In US law the term bankruptcy is applied to companies as well, but here I will use the word insolvency, so as to be clear that we are not talking about real people who cannot pay their debts, but only companies.

The whole idea of limited liability is that the company directors or shareholders should not have their personal assets seized to pay the company debts. Instead, the law prescribes a process by which all of the assets of an insolvent company can be sold, usually under the supervision of a court or someone appointed by the court. This is called the liquidation of the company. Once this is completed the company is "dead." Of course, if a company is insolvent, then those owed money, the creditors, will only get back a fraction of what they were owed. Moreover, not all creditors are equal. Some have a higher priority for repayment than others, and so some will get more out of an insolvency and liquidation.

If a debt is due for repayment today and there is no money to pay it, then clearly the company is insolvent. But, in practice, it is usually foreseeable well in advance that this day will arrive, and a company is technically insolvent once it is clear to the directors that repayment will not be possible. At that moment, the directors of a company have a duty to declare the company insolvent and cease commercial operations. Continuing to operate the business after this point can lead to significant penalties, even imprisonment, for the directors. However, deciding the point of insolvency is normally a matter of judgment, and directors are likely to be optimistic, so creditors also have a right to petition the courts for insolvency proceedings to start. This is the usual course of events.

In the context of soccer clubs, it is important to note that, legally speaking, insolvency is a matter to be decided by the courts, not the soccer authorities (e.g., the Football League or Football Association). However, the soccer authorities can sanction a club if they believe that its finances are too precarious. The Italian clubs that were excluded from competition in 2010 had failed to meet the standards set by the Italian federation, not the standards of insolvency law. It was only after the exclusion of the clubs that they became insolvent under Italian law—because they could no longer expect to generate revenues from such things as ticket sales and broadcast rights. The Spanish *Ley Deporte* ("Sports Law") of 1990, which forced most clubs to become limited liability companies, was not passed because of the technical insolvency of the Spanish clubs, but they were clearly in severe financial difficulties and unlikely to be able to repay their debts.

Until the 1970s, in most Western countries, insolvency almost always led to liquidation. Companies could negotiate with creditors to accept an alternative to insolvency proceedings (such as voluntarily writing off some of their debts, usually requiring unanimity of all creditors), but once insolvency proceedings started there was normally only one end. Change began in the United States where the Bankruptcy Reform Act of 1978 introduced a new procedure described in Chapter XI of the bankruptcy code. Chapter XI gives the directors of a company the right to suspend the process of liquidating the company and enter negotiations with creditors to write off some debt while at the same time enabling the company to survive. Moreover, Chapter XI no longer required unanimity among creditors, and so it made it much more likely that a deal could be reached. This approach, it was hoped, would be more efficient, reducing legal costs and limiting job losses.

Many European nations have since adopted their own version of Chapter XI. England reformed its insolvency law in 1985 and 1986, and introduced the process known as "administration." This has much the same effect as Chapter XI. Usually, after a creditor applies to have the company liquidated in order to recover what it is owed, the company directors ask the court to put the business into administration. The court appoints an administrator, a registered professional capable of managing the business, who then tries to raise as much money as possible to repay the creditors, while at the same time keeping the business alive. The administrator proposes a settlement with the creditors, who then vote on it. If a majority agrees then the scheme is implemented. Once the main commitments of the agreement have been fulfilled, the business can exit administration. The *Ley Concursal* (described in chapter 1) is similar and was introduced in 2003. Italy adopted major reforms with similar effects in 2005; so did Germany, in 2012.

As a result of these legal changes, the balance of power has swung away from creditors toward debtors. No doubt this has reduced some abuses that took place in the past. It used to be too easy for vindictive or careless creditors to destroy businesses with a viable future. But giving more power to the debtor, providing them with a route to the survival of the company, comes at a cost. The potential now exists for a different kind of abuse. In many cases, debtors can now more or less force the creditors to write off their debt and allow the company to continue as if nothing had happened. Some critics argue that current laws no longer encourage sensible risk-taking by managers, but instead encourage excessive risk-taking. Managers and shareholders know that they will profit if things go well, while the creditors will bear the costs when things go wrong. The "too big to fail" problem, which lay at the heart of the 2008 global financial crisis, is not just relevant to the banking industry.

In soccer, the cause of insolvency seems simple: clubs spend more than they can afford, they get into debt, they can't pay their debts, and so they become insolvent. There are many variations on this story. Sometimes the story told is that people who run the clubs just aren't very smart, and this is what causes insolvency. The case of Simon Jordan at Crystal Palace might seem to fit this version very well. In other cases, the story told involves murkier conspiracies. Portsmouth FC is a case in point. Its ownership changed hands so many times in the 2000s that it got to be like a game of hot potato. Serb businessman Milan Mandaric sold the club in 2006 to the French and Israeli businessman Alexandre Gaydamak, who then sold it in 2009 to the Emirati businessman Sulaiman Al-Fahim, who quickly lost control to Ali Al-Faraj—allegedly a Saudi businessman, who was never seen at the club and who may not even exist. Then the club fell into the hands of Balram Chainrai, a Nepali businessman who claimed he had lent money to Al-Faraj. At this point the club was insolvent and went into administration. Along the way, Gaydamak had separated property assets adjacent to the stadium, and Chainrai instigated a fire sale of players to pay off money owed to him. Assets, which would have been the basis for future revenue, were stripped out of the club by some or all of these characters. The precise cause of the club's first insolvency in 2010 was the lack of funds to repay loans to Chainrai, but the club was sliding into insolvency long before that.

Such stories are not uncommon in the world of soccer, but most owners are not asset strippers—they really are interested in turning the club into a success. In any case, squeezing money out of clubs is a difficult business as the experience of stock exchange flotations has shown. The far more common story told in the media is that clubs have overinvested in chasing success, flown too close to the sun, and come crashing down when the strategy of buying success fails. Leeds United is frequently mentioned as an example. The club invested heavily in the late-1990s and was forced to sell off a galaxy of star players at knockdown prices after failing to qualify for the Champions League in 2002.

But how typical is this story? Once again we have to rely on financial data from England, where there have been lots of cases of insolvency and where we can inspect the accounts of the clubs. It turns out that the true story of club insolvency is rather different from the one we are usually told.

My analysis is based on the experience of forty-eight clubs that went into legal insolvency proceedings for the first time between 1982 and 2010. The exact date at which the insolvency of a company was legally registered can be found on the Companies House website (companieshouse.gov.uk). The data of Figure 8.1 shows the league rank of the clubs that went into insolvency for a period of 29 years. This includes the 22

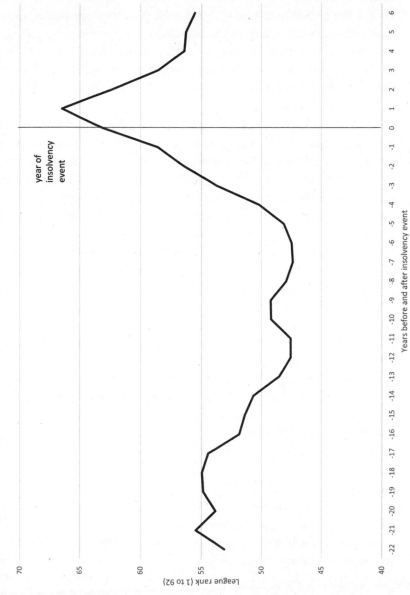

FIGURE 8.1 League rank of English soccer clubs before and after insolvency. (Source: Companies House)

years before the insolvency event, the year itself, and then six years after. League rank runs from 1 to 92 for the clubs in the data (for example, since 1995 rank 1 is champion of the Premier League, rank 20 is the bottom of the Premier League, rank 21 is champion of the Football League Championship, rank 44 is bottom, rank 45 is champion of Football League One, and so on).[1]

The average rank twenty-two years before insolvency of the sample clubs is about 55, which corresponds to mid-table in the third tier (there have been some small changes to the number of teams in each division over the years, but the third tier usually covers the range of ranks 45–68). In other words, it is not the big clubs that are succumbing to insolvency. There was, on average, a slight upturn in the performance of these clubs somewhere between twenty and seven years before insolvency. This amounts to an average rise of eight places, which is less than half a division. What is striking in the chart is the collapse in performance in the six years leading up to insolvency—an average decline of sixteen league places, a fall that would almost inevitably entail relegation. (Note that a higher rank number means a worse position in the league—e.g., 20th is worse than 1st.) Clubs that become insolvent do not have a recent history of rising up the league but a recent history of falling down the league.

Figure 8.2 shows what happens to attendance and revenues in the run up to insolvency. Average attendance at league games for these clubs is between 9,000 and 11,000 up to five years before the insolvency event, and then drops by 27 percent until insolvency occurs. This decline has, of course, more to do with the fact that the performance of the club on the field is deteriorating rather than the belief that the club will become insolvent. The dashed line in Figure 8.2 shows the revenues of the clubs relative to the average of clubs in the four divisions. Until four years before insolvency these clubs have revenue equal to about 80 percent of the league average, reflecting their middling position in the system. Then, as performance and attendance declines, revenues slip to about 50 percent of the league average. The decline in relative revenues lags one year behind the fall in attendance, probably because season ticket sales fall after a bad season rather than before it.

FIGURE 8.2 Attendance and revenues (relative to the average) of insolvent English soccer clubs. (Source: Club financial accounts and Sky Sports *Football Yearbook*)

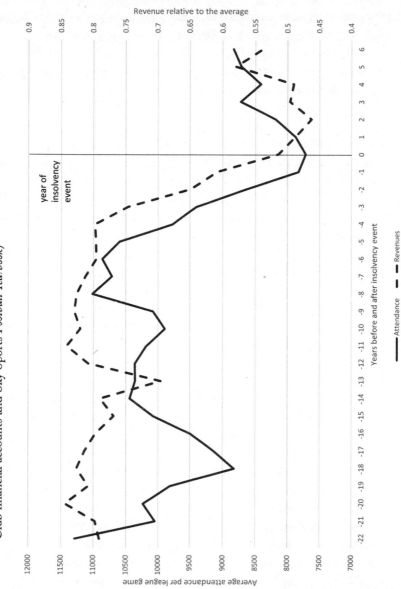

This precipitous decline in revenues in turn feeds back in to the performance of the club, as can be seen from Figure 8.3. As clubs approach insolvency, their wage-to-revenue ratio rises—from a typical value of about 65 percent to 90 percent at the point of insolvency. Indeed, this fact alone makes it clear that these clubs are insolvent, because with almost all the money going toward wages there is little to cover any of the other expenses of the business.

However, the clubs were doing their best to avoid insolvency. They were trying to adjust their budgets to account for lower revenues. The dashed line in Figure 8.3 shows the wage spending of the insolvent clubs relative to the average of the league. It falls significantly in the run up to insolvency, from above 70 percent on average to below 40 percent. The chart suggests that the directors typically tried to keep the club solvent, but falling revenues outpaced the fall in wages. It's hard to see how this could have been avoided given that players have contracts, and contractual commitments have to be honored.

Clubs are often criticized for not putting clauses into contracts that allow them to dispose of players quickly when the club gets into trouble—for example, following relegation. This ignores the fact that players are hired in a competitive market. If you want to hire good players you will have to meet their terms, or else they will go to a competitor. No player (or his agent) will willingly sign a contract that says he won't get paid if things go wrong at the club. After all, that is the responsibility of the club's directors. On the other hand, players will sign clauses that let them leave the club if it is relegated, a deal that tends to work well for both sides. Sometimes, a club overpays for a player and it turns out that the player cannot be released without a substantial loss. But equally clubs sometimes get more out of a player than expected and end up with a windfall gain. Given the number of players that pass through a club's books, the likelihood is that the ups and downs even out over the long run. The problem of insolvency, based on the data examined here, is that in the short term there is no necessity that events even out. By the law of large numbers you will have as much good luck as bad luck—eventually. But in the short term it is perfectly possible to suffer from a long sequence of bad luck. And that, it appears, can lead even the unambitious to insolvency.

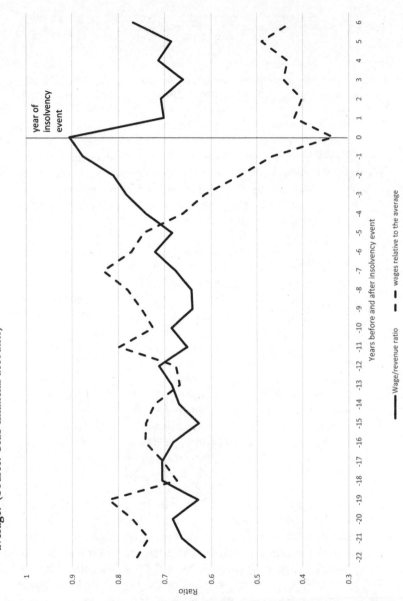

FIGURE 8.3 Insolvent English soccer clubs: Wage/revenue ratio and wage spending relative to the league average. (Source: Club financial accounts)

BOX 8.1: THE FOOTBALL CREDITOR RULE

The liquidation of Bristol City Football Club in 1982 was the first time in the modern era that an English club became insolvent while still participating in league competition. All clubs are share-holders in the league in which they play (today the twenty clubs in the Premier League each own one share in the Premier League Limited, and the seventy-two clubs in the Football League each own one share in the Football League Limited; teams promoted to the Premier League swap their share with a relegated team). Bristol City was saved by creating a new company that was given the old company's share, but only after most of the players em-ployed by the old club agreed to waive their contracts in order to make the new company viable. This deal was brokered by the players' union, the Professional Footballers' Association (PFA), under considerable pressure from the fans.

In order to avoid a repetition of these circumstances, the union negotiated with the Football League to enforce a rule saying that before an insolvent club could be saved, all debts owed to players must be honored; clubs insisted that transfer payments owed also had to be settled. This is the Football Creditor Rule (FCR).

Until recently, insolvency law in England specified that the tax authorities were preferential creditors—meaning that they should always be paid ahead of everyone else. In 2004, the UK tax authori-ties challenged the FCR on the basis that it ranked the football cred-itors ahead of the government; they lost in court. The tax authorities challenged the FCR again in 2012 on the grounds that it gave football creditors an unfair advantage against *all* creditors; again they lost.

Many people feel the FCR is deeply unfair. Not only do millionaire players get paid in full while taxes end up being written off, but small creditors such as St. John Ambulance, a charity that provides first aid to fans at stadiums, also end up not getting paid their expenses.

The courts have sympathized with this point of view, but have refused to strike down the FCR. Instead, the courts have accepted that the FCR is a reasonable guarantee to other clubs in the coop-erative venture of a league that financial promises will be honored. Payment to the soccer creditors is made by whichever business takes over the club from the insolvent company, and creditors of the failed company have no rights over that new business. Alternatively, if the creditors agree to accept payment of their debts in part while keeping the existing company alive (this is called a Company Voluntary Arrangement), then they do this on the understanding that the FCR was in place and that these creditors will have to be paid in full as a condition for continuing membership of the league.

In chapter 2, we looked at the relationship between wage spending and league performance. Figures 2.1 to 2.6 showed the pay-performance line based on long periods of time for many clubs. The pay-performance line can change, but it seems to be fairly stable in the short term. Another way of saying this is that clubs can have a reasonable expectation of achieving a particular place in the league for the amount of money they spend. This relationship is never exact. The outcome will always deviate somewhat from what could have been expected. Generally the deviations will be small but occasionally they can be quite large. Large deviations can make a big difference to a club. Any deviation is as likely to be above the pay-performance line as below because good and bad luck are equally likely. The luck you get this year is also independent of the luck you had last year. The data on which this analysis is based can be shown to be consistent with these assumptions.[2] Economists call these events "shocks"—whether they're due to good or bad fortune. It is possible to suffer a series of positive or negative shocks, persistent bad luck, or persistent good luck.

Persistent bad luck, as measured by these negative shocks—the shortfall between the pay-performance line and the actual position achieved—often leads to insolvency. Negative shocks cause an increase in the wage-to-revenue ratio. That is because wage contracts entail commitments that clubs cannot easily escape. The wage-to-revenue ratio rises as underperformance leads to a fall in attendance, which in turn leads to a fall in revenue. A rising wage-revenue ratio makes it harder for the club to meet its expenses from its revenue. That makes it more likely that the club will need to borrow, and make it more difficult to pay off any debts that are due. All these factors make insolvency more likely. Indeed, it turns out that not only are deviations from the pay-performance line likely to lead to insolvency, but also deviations from the revenue-performance line (see Figure 4.5 and 4.6 in chapter 4).

Insolvency, the perennial problem of soccer around the world, appears on this evidence to be mostly just a consequence of bad luck. A commercial enterprise like a club is risky. You pay out for players in advance and then hope that league performance, the fans, and the revenues will follow. On average they do, but sometimes they don't—and in that case a club is likely to become insolvent. This seems to contradict the standard narrative of soccer, which is that clubs fail because of bad management, not just bad luck.

Bad luck is not the only factor in insolvency. There's no doubt that management involves skill as well as luck, and poor skills can also make failure more likely. It could be, for example, that poor management made some clubs more likely to become insolvent as a result of negative shocks. Another possibility is that clubs can just be in the wrong place. Some clubs fail because the local population is in decline and fewer people want to go to matches, or because alternative sports are more interesting (in Wales, for example, where rugby union has always been popular and many soccer clubs have struggled to survive). This is a kind of long-term bad luck, especially given that relocation is taboo in soccer.

Another factor that seems important is a history of failure. Of the forty-eight English clubs that experienced an insolvency event between 1982 and 2010, thirteen were repeat offenders. Five clubs—Rotherham United, Halifax Town, Luton Town, Bradford City, and Darlington—went through three separate sets of insolvency proceedings during this period.

BOX 8.2: WHICH DIVISION WERE TEAMS IN BEFORE ENTERING INSOLVENCY?

When English clubs become insolvent it is usually the case that they have been underperforming for some time, not because they have been spending money to operate at a higher level than they can sustain. Table A shows the ten-year history of clubs entering insolvency in England for the first time between 1982 and 2010. In all cases, the team entering insolvency for the first time was in the second, third, or fourth tier at the time—never in the top tier (Portsmouth is the one club ever to enter insolvency while in the Premier League, but that was its second insolvency).

In almost all cases, clubs entering insolvency had spent most of the previous ten seasons either in the same division or a higher division, so that at the time of insolvency they were in decline. For example, the clubs that were in the third tier when entering insolvency had spent one third of the previous decade in the third tier, 30 percent in the second tier, 10 percent in the top tier, 24 percent in the fourth tier, and 4 percent in the fifth or lower tier. Thus, only 28 percent of the previous decade was spent in a lower tier, 33 percent in the same tier, and 40 percent in a higher tier.

PANEL A: **10-year history of teams before year of entering their first insolvency**

Division at date of insolvency	Percentage of club years in division over previous decade					
	1	2	3	4	lower	n
1	0%	0%	0%	0%	0%	0
2	47%	48%	5%	0%	0%	120
3	10%	30%	33%	24%	4%	210
4	0%	5%	32%	59%	5%	150

SOURCE: Companies House and *Sky Sports Football Yearbook*

Panel B shows the ten-year divisional history for all English clubs in 2010. This shows that in the ten years prior to 2010, if a club was not in the same division as it was in 2010, then it was equally likely to have been in a higher division or a lower division. For example, teams in the third tier in 2010 had spent only 28 percent of the previous decade in higher tiers, and slightly more time (29 percent) in lower tiers. This shows that the ten-year experience of clubs entering insolvency was significantly worse than the ten-year experience of a typical club.

PANEL B: **10-year history of all clubs in the four divisions in 2010**

Division in 2010	Percentage of club years in division over previous decade					
	1	2	3	4	lower	n
1	68%	26%	5%	3%	0%	200
2	18%	49%	23%	8%	2%	240
3	8%	20%	43%	23%	6%	240
4	1%	8%	23%	46%	23%	240

SOURCE: Companies House and *Sky Sports Football Yearbook*

It is useful to compare what happens in soccer to the rest of the business world, where companies are constantly being closed down (dissolved). There are more than three million registered companies in the United Kingdom. Nowadays, about half a million new ones are created every year and some 300,000 are dissolved.[3] Many of these dissolutions occur because the company has been hit by hard times, which might be no more than a series of negative shocks, like achieving a lower league position than you could reasonably expect given what you spent.

The difference with soccer is that most dissolutions do not involve insolvency proceedings. Instead, the company directors agree to shut down the business before it becomes insolvent. Less than 10 percent of dissolutions involve insolvency,[4] meaning that just one half a percent of all companies go into insolvency proceedings each year. But we have seen that out of just under one hundred professional soccer clubs in the four English divisions, insolvencies have been running at an average of more than two per year, or 2 percent—a far higher rate than for businesses in general. In the last twenty years, according to figures published by Deloitte, the rate is closer to 3 percent.

Insolvency of soccer clubs is common, far more common than it is in other commercial activities. Yet the disappearance of clubs is much less common than the disappearance of businesses in general. In *Soccernomics* we pointed out that almost every single one of the eighty-eight clubs that belonged to the English Football League in 1923 was still with us in 2012: 97 percent still existed and 91 percent still played in the top four divisions. Likewise, of the seventy-four clubs playing in the top divisions of England, France, Italy, and Spain in 1949/50, seventy-two still existed in 2013, and 80 percent still played in the top two divisions of their country. Only two of the seventy-four clubs had disappeared in nearly two thirds of a century.[5] There is a remarkable history of stability, especially at the higher levels of soccer. Of the forty-eight English clubs that underwent insolvency proceedings between 1982 and 2010, all have survived. In most cases the club has remained intact, but in some cases it has been refounded. For example, in March 1992 Aldershot FC was shut down, and later in the spring refounded as Aldershot Town FC.

Soccer clubs survive despite frequent insolvency because they are not typical businesses; they embody communities. There is always a way to keep a club alive even if the commercial operation has failed. One of the most striking examples of failure and survival is the case of Rangers Football Club. When the Rangers Football Club Limited went into liquidation in 2012 it was a member of the twelve-team Scottish Premier League (SPL), and the club owned one share in the SPL giving it the right to play. Once the company was liquidated the share reverted to the SPL.

In the summer of 2012, British businessman Charles Green bought all of Rangers' assets from the liquidator, including the stadium, existing player contracts, and all intellectual property (e.g., crests) for $8.8 million. He then applied to acquire the old Rangers SPL share, but the other members voted 10-1 not to give it to him. As a result, the new company, called Sevco, applied to join the bottom tier of the next league down—the Scottish Football League (SFL). Clubs in SFL3 typically play to a crowd of five hundred souls, compared to Rangers' average attendance of around 50,000.

In the following season, an average of 45,587 fans turned up to watch a club owned by Sevco play the minnows of SFL3. What was that club? Ask any Scottish soccer fan who supports a team other than Rangers and they will probably tell you that those people support a completely new club. The old Rangers, they assert, no longer exist. Of course, Rangers fans say that the new club is a continuation of the old Rangers, playing at the same stadium, with the same shirt and crest, and with the same name.

Unless you are involved in the fervid atmosphere of Scottish soccer, all this may be a little hard to comprehend. But it goes to show that clubs are more than businesses. The non-Rangers fans would be right if clubs were just businesses rather than a community of interests. But they aren't just businesses, and they do embody communities. Emotionally, the Rangers fans are right: Rangers is still Rangers. The problem is that soccer clubs also involve substantial commercial transactions nowadays, and the requirement for a commercial/legal structure to be in place, in order to conduct business matters in an orderly fashion, conflicts with the emotional ties that bind communities together.

Following the 2008 global financial crisis, triggered by subprime lending in the United States, we learned that the major banks, however badly run they might be, were too big to fail. The reason for this was contagion. Because banks lend to each other, the failure of one bank (meaning insolvency and the failure to repay debts owed to other banks) would almost certainly lead to the failure of all. The banking system is like a house of cards—it is hard to withdraw even a single bank from the structure without bringing the whole thing crashing down. The problem of contagion and mutual interdependence is not a problem in most businesses. If Burger King were to be liquidated, it would not harm McDonald's; in fact, it would probably help them. Few businesses have the kind of mutual interlinkages that we see in the banking system, but sports leagues do. Teams in a league need rivals to play, and the withdrawal of one can hurt the others. Most leagues are based on the home-and-away system. Each club plays one game against a rival at their home stadium and keeps the money from selling tickets, while the rival team obtains a reciprocal benefit at the corresponding away game. If one team fails, all the other teams stand to lose the revenue from a home game. In theory this could cause all of them to fail.

But, in reality, this interdependence is not the cause of the "too big to fail" problem in soccer. When Rangers no longer played in the SPL the clubs saw a slight fall in attendance (about 5 percent on average), but it did not push any of them to get into severe financial difficulties.[6] The reason that soccer clubs are too big to fail is that the fans insist that they be kept alive. This demand manifests itself in different ways. Local politicians must keep an eye on what is done to their club, or else they may find themselves losing the next election. Tax authorities trying to collect back taxes find themselves receiving phone calls from Members of Parliament suggesting that they find more important work to do. Local businessmen are often willing to step in and use their own personal fortunes and become (at least for a short while) a local hero. For an insolvent soccer club the most important asset is the stadium. If the club owns the stadium then it could potentially be sold off to repay creditors—most likely to build new houses or a supermarket. However, local planning authorities will almost never allow this. Usually, the only use permitted is to play soccer, and so the only route to making money from the property again (at least in theory) is reestablishing the club. If the stadium is owned by the local government then there is usually no question of allowing an alternative use.

BOX 8.3: THE MEANING OF MORAL HAZARD

Following the banking crisis of 2008, "moral hazard" has become a term that is widely used in the media but pundits seldom explain exactly what it is and why it arises. Moral hazard is at root a problem about knowledge; in particular, it arises when someone who is acting on your behalf knows more about what is really going on than you do.

Banking and finance are obvious situations where moral hazard arises because financial transactions often require specialized and technical knowledge that most of us don't have. Likewise, the doctor-patient relationship creates the potential for moral hazard, as indeed does my own profession of teaching. Moral hazard is a problem in business precisely because the shareholders appoint managers to run the firm on their behalf.

The potential for moral hazard is realized when a manager does something that he or she knows shareholders would not want to happen, and does it out of the manager's self-interest. Obvious examples include buying a larger company car than is necessary, or taking time off on the golf course while claiming to entertain clients. It can also involve illegal activities like defrauding the business of money. The first thing to note is that not everyone does this. Some people are honest, and it is called "moral hazard" because a moral person will not in fact succumb. Cynics think that everyone is on the make, but in reality society would probably grind to a halt if that were true. Most of us can be tempted, but often we resist temptation as well.

The kind of moral hazard we are talking about in soccer is really hard to measure. The argument is that the directors take excessive risk, more than would be advisable, in pursuit of their personal glory. However, it is hard to define "excessive," and many fans actually want the directors to take the risk. Moreover, because

---

CONTINUES

soccer is such a competitive business, failing to take risks can lead to disaster as well. Many well-run and solvent teams still sink to the bottom of the leagues and fade into obscurity.

Financial failure usually has real consequences for directors. They may lose their job, they may have their reputation tarnished, and they will certainly have to endure a lot of stress. So it is not as if the actions of directors are without consequences. The real problem is the lack of consequences for the club. The limited liability company that owns the club may fail and be liquidated, but not the club itself.

Moral hazard can be overcome if the consequences of failure are harsh enough. But in the case of soccer the harsh punishment would have to fall on the clubs themselves, not the directors of the businesses that own the clubs. If financial failure could really lead to liquidation of a soccer club—never to play again—then management of soccer clubs would overnight become far more prudent.

As we have seen, clubs seldom die, and there are good reasons why insolvent clubs do not expire but are reborn. The crest of the reborn Aldershot Town FC pictures a phoenix—this ought to be a badge used by all such clubs. But this creates the same problem (called the moral hazard problem) that is found in banking. "Too big to fail" is a problem because the managers and directors of the business know this in advance. Normally, managers balance risk and reward, but the inevitable survival of the soccer club means that the risks are limited. If things go horribly wrong, the club will still survive. Moreover, if the objective of the club is to win, rather than make money, then taking risks means spending up to and beyond your means in the hope that you get lucky. This incentive to spend any money that the club can get hold of is the real root of insolvency in soccer. And the insolvency laws have made things worse. There were no insolvencies in the four divisions of English soccer between 1946 and 1982. Yet during these thirty-six years English soccer experienced secular decline. Total attendance at league games halved—to 20 million from 40 million. Between 1982 and 2010, a period of twenty-eight years, there were sixty-seven insolvency events involving teams in the top four divisions. Yet this was a period of economic recovery. Attendance rose by 50 percent to 30 million in the 2009/10 season, and revenues rose far faster. The general economic climate seems to have little to do with the likelihood of insolvency.

As we have seen, English law shifted power away from creditors and toward debtors thanks to the reforms of 1985 and 1986, which developed the administration procedure. Almost all of the insolvencies have taken place since then. In 2002, the British government made administration even easier to manage, and the league authorities came to believe that directors of some clubs were deliberately going into administration to write off their debts and then emerge from it stronger than rival clubs. As a result, in 2004, the Football League agreed to introduce a points penalty for clubs going into administration. Fans often wonder why a club that is in financial difficulties receives a penalty in addition, but the reason is to deter directors from taking their club into administration in the first place.

The same thing seems to have happened in Spain. As soon as the *Ley Concursal* made administration an option, twenty-two Spanish clubs opted for it. Actually, the reform of insolvency laws is not generally seen to have been a great success in the business world. Relatively few cases of administration end up in the survival of the business. Only in the case of soccer—where the commitment to the survival of the club is embedded in the community and there are so few alternative uses for the main asset involved (i.e., the stadium)—has the law of insolvency been effective. It saves the clubs while encouraging them to overspend. Perhaps that isn't what the legislators intended.

BOX 8.4: STATE AID AND SOCCER

A part of the "too big to fail" problem in soccer is that insolvent clubs will, like banks, turn to the government for a bail out. Under European law state aid to a commercial undertaking is prohibited if it will create a distortion in the European market, unfairly giving advantage to some businesses over others.

Because governments, both national and regional, have always been closely involved in supporting soccer clubs, especially in the

CONTINUES

construction of stadiums, it was inevitable that one day the issue of illegal state aid would be raised. In 2013, the European Commission, responsible for administering the law, formally started investigations of a number of cases involving Spanish and Dutch clubs. The Spanish cases involved loans on non-commercial terms from the local government to Valencia; the corporation tax rate differential between member-owned clubs (Real Madrid, Barcelona, Athletic Bilbao, and Osasuna) and the remaining limited liability clubs; and land transfer between the city of Madrid and Real Madrid. The Dutch cases related to subsidies concerning stadiums of near-insolvent clubs.

Given the cultural significance of soccer clubs, national governments have stressed their intention to resist any sanctions under these rules, and the investigations could still result in the granting of an exemption for the clubs. There are grounds for exemptions under the law when the subsidy serves some clearly defined social purpose—which could include the provision of facilities and ensuring that clubs do not disappear. However, these rules are rather strict and require the nature of the support and the benefit to be clearly defined. There is some doubt whether soccer clubs would pass muster.

An example of the granting of an exemption is the roughly €1 billion of subsidies being provided by French national and local governments for stadium construction and renovation associated with hosting Euro 2016. It is thought that the French government will need to guarantee that these facilities, which will mostly remain under the ownership of the local governments, will be rented out to the clubs at commercial rates.

Another possibility for those clubs under investigation is that they are penalized, possibly by UEFA, with bans on transfers or squad limits as a way to compensate their competitors for the unfair advantage they have received.

Settlement of these cases will be politically controversial and it may be that national governments will resist enforcing any penalties that are handed down by the European Commission. However, the mere fact that these high-profile investigations are taking place suggests that the government subsidies for soccer clubs in the future will be more tightly regulated, limiting at least to some extent the moral hazard problem which lies at the heart of the "too big to fail" dilemma.

Insolvency is a cause of great distress to fans, who often fear that their club will disappear. Without wanting to minimize their suffering, this should have made clear that in practice this fear is almost completely without foundation. Only in the case of very small clubs (with maybe a few hundred fans) is there a risk that a club will be liquidated and no successor club will be created. Even then, such cases are relatively rare.

It has long been said that there are too many professional soccer clubs in England. As long ago as 1960, a British Member of Parliament described the English League system as "inefficiently organized, semi-bankrupt."[7] A government-sponsored report in 1968 recommended merging some clubs,[8] and in the 1970s, 1980s, and 1990s it was commonly suggested that the number of professional clubs should be reduced. Often English commentators pointed to the smaller number of national divisions in countries like Germany, Italy, and Spain. However, in recent years, these countries have tended to add more teams playing at the national level. The amount of professional soccer seems to be expanding.

"Too many" is a judgment that itself is based on the financial difficulties that clubs find themselves in. If clubs could cover their costs then it would not be seen as a problem. In the United States, there are just thirty-two teams in the National Football League and thirty teams each in Major League Baseball, the National Basketball Association, and the National Hockey League. These are nationally based leagues, although they also have a regional dimension to their playing schedules. The equivalent for European soccer would be to turn the thirty-two-team Champions League into the main professional league of Europe.

9

AMERICA

Every year, *Forbes* magazine publishes a valuation of sports teams. Initially, *Forbes* only gave valuations of North American teams in major league sports—the NFL, NBA, and Major League Baseball. But in recent years the magazine has also tried to put a value on the top twenty soccer clubs. Back in the day, soccer clubs were worth very little compared to major league franchises, but by 1998 Manchester United had risen to become the most highly valued sports club/franchise in the world. Today there are three soccer teams that *Forbes* believes to be more valuable than any American sports team: Real Madrid, Barcelona, and, still, Manchester United—which now happens to be owned by Americans.

Figure 9.1 charts the valuations of the major league teams against those of the top twenty European soccer clubs. It shows that while the three most valuable teams are European, the typical American major league franchise is worth far more than the typical European soccer club. Arsenal is judged the fifth-most-valuable soccer club, but there are eleven major league teams deemed more valuable. The twentieth-most-valuable soccer team, Napoli, is valued at $296 million, less than the estimated value of the ninety-second American team (the Milwaukee Bucks of the NBA, valued at $405 million).

Although *Forbes* does not provide a valuation for the twenty-first- to ninety-second-most-valuable European soccer clubs, we can extrapolate a value based on the data given, which is shown as the thin dotted line

FIGURE 9.1 *Forbes* valuation of American major league franchises (MLB, NBA, and NFL) and European soccer clubs 2013–2014. (SOURCE: *Forbes*)

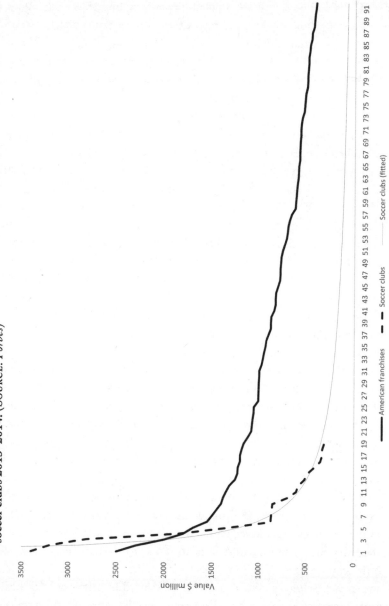

on the chart. The logic of the extrapolation is that the next seventy soccer clubs will be worth less than the twentieth and that their values will decline progressively at the same rate as they do from first to twentieth. From the extrapolation, the ninety-second soccer club would be worth about $77 million, less than 20 percent of the value of the Milwaukee Bucks. The *Forbes* data gives a collective value to the three major leagues of $81 billion, while the extrapolation for the soccer clubs gives a total value of $32 billion, about 40 percent of the value of the major league teams collectively.

Given that European soccer is every bit as popular in Europe as American sports are in America, this gap in valuation requires some explanation. The simplest explanation is that American teams generate more revenue. The total revenue generated by the ninety-two American teams is $20.8 billion (according to *Forbes*), while according to Deloitte the combined revenue of the ninety-eight clubs in the five biggest European leagues in 2013 was about $13 billion—some 63% of the level of major league revenues. While most of the big soccer clubs are in the big five leagues, there are also some large clubs in other countries (e.g., Ajax in the Netherland, Porto in Portugal, Galatasaray in Turkey, or Celtic in Scotland). If we took the ninety-two largest clubs in Europe by revenue, the ratio of European to American revenues would probably exceed two thirds. Basing the valuation of an asset on the revenues that it generates, however, also requires some evaluation of growth prospects. The revenues of European soccer *as a whole* have been growing faster than the revenues of American sports for some time now, and that is only likely to continue as the Europeans expand into global markets that are difficult for American sports to penetrate. Being the most popular game in the world must be worth something.

Whichever way you look at it the valuation gap cannot be entirely explained by revenues. If European soccer clubs can generate two thirds of the revenues of American franchises, why don't they have two thirds of the value, instead of only 40 percent? To put it another way, every dollar of revenue generated by major league franchises equates to $4 of value to the owner, while every euro of value generated by European clubs translates into less than 2.5 euros of value for the owners. Why are euros earned by soccer clubs worth less than dollars earned by US franchises?

The value of an asset (such as a franchise or a club) is usually determined in one of three ways: its cost (either the cost of creating it, or the cost of replacing it), its income (how much profit it will generate over its lifetime), or its market value (what someone is prepared to bid for it). In theory, these values should all be related to one another, but in practice they often do not look very similar.

Forbes uses revenues as the basis for valuing teams. The correlation coefficient between the *Forbes* value of the ninety-two American teams and their revenues is +0.9—meaning they are very closely correlated with one another.[1] This is rather like the way high-tech companies tend to be valued; often they make little or no profit today, but as their revenue grows so they can be expected to generate profits, and the larger the revenues the higher the value. One reason that this might be a reasonable way to value sports teams is that their attractiveness is related to their success, which in turn tends to be reflected in their revenues.

Forbes estimates that the revenues of the four biggest soccer clubs (Real Madrid, Barcelona, Manchester United, and Bayern Munich) amount to $2.4 billion, while the revenues of the four biggest American teams— Dallas Cowboys, New York Yankees, New England Patriots, and Washington Redskins—were only $1.8 billion. But as one goes down the list, the revenue of the American team with the equivalent rank of the soccer club soon becomes larger. Ultimately, the aggregate value of American sports teams' revenue exceeds that of the aggregate soccer club revenue. But this still does not explain why *each* dollar of revenue in *Forbes* translates into a higher-dollar franchise value for the major leagues than is the case for European soccer clubs.

Given that *Forbes* seems to be valuing the teams on the basis of their revenues, shouldn't the team valuations be closer? Bringing European clubs up to the same valuation as a percentage of revenue (i.e., 4 euros of value for every euro of revenue) would increase their worth by a staggering $20 billion (from $32 billion to $52 billion)—more than 60 percent above the *Forbes* valuation.

The explanation has to do with what people in financial markets call "multiples." One of the most commonly used indicators of financial value is the price/earnings (P/E) ratio. This is the ratio of the value placed on a company measured by its share price divided by the profits that each share earned in the last financial year. That's really what *Forbes* is doing, but instead of using a multiple of profits it is using a multiple of revenues (some financial analysts might consider the substitution of revenues for profits dubious, but let that pass for the moment).

The point is that high multiples imply a high valuation of the company, and are usually associated with a perception that earnings will grow rapidly and reliably in the future, while a low multiple reflects a low valuation and low or unreliable growth expectations. When a company is valued at four times its current earnings it is being treated as a better prospect financially than a business valued at only two and half times its earnings. In the *Forbes* data the multiple for the larger teams is generally higher—reflecting the fact that these are believed to be more attractive teams to potential buyers because their revenues are likely to grow and entail lower risk.

Forbes uses a much lower multiple for European soccer clubs. Only three of the twenty soccer clubs were given a valuation multiple higher than three-times-revenue, but seventy-six of the major league franchises had a multiple larger than three. Even big teams like Bayern Munich and Arsenal are given multiples that are no better than some of the smaller US teams. The average multiple for soccer clubs ranked from eleventh to twentieth in the *Forbes* list is below two, lower than the multiple applied to any of the US teams. Clearly, in the estimation of *Forbes*, the growth prospects of all but a handful of soccer clubs are perceived to be risky.

The higher valuation multiple applied to the earnings of American teams reflects greater certainty that these same teams can continue to generate the same (or more) revenues in the years to come. If you buy one of these teams, you are buying this stream of revenues stretching out into the future. With most soccer clubs you can have no such confidence. The main reason that soccer club revenues are riskier is the promotion-and-relegation system, which is absent from American major league sports. For example, over the decade 2004–2013 only nine teams participated in the English Premier League every season. The other eleven slots were taken by teams that were promoted or relegated at least once during this period. Over the last half-century, only three teams (Arsenal, Everton, and Liverpool) have been ever-present in the top division. For most of the last half-century these have also been among the dominant teams (Manchester United and, to some extent, Tottenham were also dominant in this period, and each of these spent only one year in a lower division). Of these five teams all except Everton appear in the *Forbes* top twenty. Dominance ensures stability, which means both higher revenues and a higher multiple, and hence a much higher valuation.

BOX 9.1: COMPARING THE POPULARITY OF US MAJOR LEAGUES AND EUROPEAN SOCCER

In Europe, no sport approaches soccer in popularity. In the United States, football is deemed the most popular sport, but baseball and basketball also command large followings. My argument is that the hundred biggest major league teams are roughly comparable to the hundred biggest European soccer teams (Europe dominates the world of soccer—there are a few teams in Brazil and Argentina that might compete to get into the top one hundred, so, overwhelmingly, the list would be made up of European clubs).

The three big American leagues (ninety-two teams) together sell in total 108 million tickets in a season consisting of 3,670 games. The top divisions of the five biggest European countries (ninety-eight teams) sell 54 million tickets but play only 1,823 games. The average attendance is almost identical at around 30,000. The ten largest leagues in Europe by attendance, as reported in UEFA's 2012 club licensing report are, in addition to the big five, the UEFA Champions League, the UEFA Europa League, the Dutch league, and the second-tier leagues of England and Germany. The total attendance of the ten largest leagues, playing a season of 3,681 games, was 88 million, giving an average of 24,000.

On these dimensions, then, the big three US leagues seem roughly comparable in terms of popularity to the top European soccer leagues. Of course, there are other leagues one could also include in the comparison, such as the National Hockey League and Major League Soccer in North America. In the 2014 Wikipedia list of attendance for professional sports leagues in

CONTINUES

the United States and Canada, total attendance is 192 million, compared to a total of 160 million for attendance at all European leagues reported by UEFA. But this omits college sports in America, where the players are not paid but the level of interest matches that of professional teams. Men's football and basketball at the college level attracts a combined total of about 80 million. Even high school football in the United States is a major spectator event.

American leagues have never had a promotion and relegation system; even when Major League Soccer was established in 1996 the founders chose to adopt the American model, which is based on a closed system. In a closed system there is competition to become the champion just as there is in the open system of promotion and relegation. The difference is that there is no penalty, at least in sporting terms, for finishing at the bottom of the league. This gives teams considerable security. People who are used to only one system of league organization, either open or closed, tend to think that the system with which they are unfamiliar cannot work well. Of course, much depends on what you mean by "well," but by the standards of popularity with fans the open system of European soccer and the closed system of the American major leagues both work very well indeed. They both have more than a century of history behind them. Baseball's National League, founded in 1876, is the oldest surviving sports league, while the English Football League is the second oldest, having been founded in 1888. But if the closed and open (promotion-and-relegation) systems are both durable and successful, they still produce very different types of results.

BOX 9.2: WHY DID THE UNITED STATES OPT FOR THE CLOSED SYSTEM WHEN ALMOST EVERYONE ELSE CHOSE THE OPEN SYSTEM?

In the book *National Pastime* written with Andy Zimbalist, we looked at the origins of the two systems. The American closed model derives from baseball's National League founded in 1876—all other American leagues have largely copied its structure (while adding some innovations), and the open system is based on English soccer, which established a mechanism for linking the first division (the founder of the Football League in 1888) and the teams in the second division (created in 1892). Almost all other nations, and many other sports, followed the English administrative system of which promotion and relegation is just a part.

In our view, the choice of system did not reflect any specific ideological preferences, simply the circumstances that surrounded the foundation of the leagues. The first known sports league was the National Association of Professional Base Ball Players, founded in 1871, but this collapsed four years later because of problems with gambling, players jumping in mid-season from one team to another, and teams not turning up to play games. The founder of the National League, William Hulbert, believed that the only way to create a stable league was to enforce a set of agreements based on the rights and responsibilities of the teams. In return for the commitment to play games and maintain discipline over players, franchises would be guaranteed security through an exclusive territory. Creating instability through a mechanism such as promotion and relegation would have been unthinkable.

The Football League was founded under different circumstances. A successful competition, the FA Cup, already existed and was the highlight of the playing calendar even for teams in the league. While the league was successful, it did not want to fall out with significant clubs that had not joined the league as founding members. As the league grew more popular, it seemed sensible to offer those clubs the chance to participate and the opportunity to reach the highest level of league competition one day. Exclusion would most likely have spawned competitive, rival leagues. In due course, the system turned out to be very popular and significantly enhanced interest in competition at all levels. Within fifty years, it had become the natural order.

I have argued in this chapter that the promotion and relegation system undermines the economic value of almost all teams in the league. Perhaps the surprising thing is that it ever got established in the first place. It is unimaginable that any of the American major leagues would adopt it today. By contrast, it is easily imaginable

CONTINUES

that the big clubs in Europe might one day seek to start a Superleague of their own without promotion and relegation. It has
been talked about for years; it may never happen, but the financial
incentives are clear.

In a closed system the ultimate authority rests with the league itself,
and each team owner has a vote in establishing the rules of the league.
Whereas most soccer leagues are ultimately answerable to a governing
body (national association) that claims jurisdiction over the game wherever it is played in the country, major leagues are subject to no such controls. The most obvious consequence of this is in the release of players
to play in national representative teams. Soccer clubs must release their
players for the national team without compensation. Clubs that refuse
can be expelled from league competition. The bigger clubs generally do
not like this arrangement because their stars players, whose wages they
pay, sometimes get injured while on international duty, creating a potentially significant loss. But there is little they can do.

Major league clubs have autonomy and can refuse to release their
players. National Olympic committees are very eager for star players
from major league basketball and hockey teams to be released for the
Olympics. But player release is not automatic and subject to negotiation
between the teams, the leagues, and the Olympic authorities.

A closed league system encourages a different kind of relationship
among the teams compared with the open system. Open systems are
hyper-competitive because the price of failure is a loss of status, which,
as we have seen, can often enough end up in insolvency. The costs of
failing in competition can be very high. The closed league system places
a limit on what a team can lose from losing. It is still true in a closed
system that higher revenues tend to be associated with higher placings
in the league, and so, equally, lower placings mean lower revenues. But
the losing team is still guaranteed to compete in the major league in the
following season, and so in effect can plan for a fresh start. Knowing
that the consequences of failure are not so severe, there is more willingness among teams in the major leagues to cooperate with each other
as businesses.

In 1995, Rodney Fort and James Quirk, two leading American econo-mists, wrote: "Professional team sports leagues are classic, even textbook, examples of business cartels."[2] Cartels are agreements between companies in the same line of business that are aimed at restricting competition and increasing profitability. When firms compete against each other they try to attract customers by offering prices lower than their competitors, or by offering a better product than their competitors for the same price, or in some other way offer something that is better value than their rivals' offer. If one firm is far better than its rivals, then the other firms will go out of business and the one dominant firm will gain a monopoly and be able to charge whatever it wants. More likely, though, is that a significant number of firms can survive competition so that both prices and profit-ability will stay low.

A cartel is, from the point of view of the companies, a way around this problem—it is an agreement among businesses to refrain from competi-tion, an agreement to restrain trade. For example, the agreement can be *not* to reduce price below a certain level, or *not* to compete on each other's ter-ritories, or *not* to hire each other's employees. It must be an agreement not to do something that would increase competition. The cartel aims to in-crease profitability, primarily by restricting choice for consumers (although it can equally restrain the choices of employees). That makes a cartel a very attractive proposition, at least for the companies that belong to it.

There are three problems for those wanting to form a cartel. First, the cartel will only work if everyone joins it. Imagine half the firms in an indus-try have an agreement not to cut prices but the other half does not. In that case competition among those who do not belong to the cartel will undercut the cartel price, the cartel members will lose customers, and ultimately they may go out of business. OPEC, the international oil price cartel, has strug-gled to maintain high prices largely because not all oil producers belong to OPEC. Consequently, oil prices have tended to rise only when there have been significant breakdowns in supply due to various conflicts (e.g., the sec-ond Gulf War in the mid-2000s that cut off the supply from Iraq).

Second, even if everyone belongs to the cartel, it is often hard to get the members to keep to the agreement. Again, OPEC is a good example. OPEC first came to prominence in the 1970s when there were two oil supply crises—one in 1973 caused by an Arab embargo on supplies to

Europe and the United States following the Yom Kippur War, and the second in 1979 caused by the toppling of the Shah's regime in Iran and his replacement by a fundamentalist Islamic state. Oil prices peaked in 1980, but then declined more or less continuously for twenty years as OPEC proved incapable of disciplining its members. Through OPEC, the main oil-producing countries agreed to hold back supply so that the price of oil would be high, but the problem was that most of the member countries breached their own agreement—oversupplying the market and so pushing prices down. This kind of cheating on an agreement is very attractive if you believe that everyone else will stick to the agreement. It is self-defeating if everyone acts on this belief, but it's often very difficult for cartel members to maintain their discipline.[3] The best way around this problem is to have a legal agreement among cartel members imposing strict penalties on anyone found guilty of cheating.

The third problem with cartels is that they are generally illegal. This also helps to explain why they fail—because it is impossible to write a legal agreement to punish the cheats. Prohibition of cartel-like behavior has a long history. In 386 BC, grain merchants in ancient Athens were prosecuted for seeking to control the price in the market. However, the modern legal position follows the Sherman Act of 1890 in the United States, which made "conspiracies in restraint of trade" illegal. This legislation came at a time when various industries, most notably the oil industry led by John D. Rockefeller, was increasingly organized into business groups to control supply and prices. These groups were known as trusts, and hence the use of the word "antitrust" to describe the legislation. By this time American legislators were convinced of Adam Smith's famous dictum: "People of the same trade seldom meet together, even for merriment and diversion, but the conversation ends in a conspiracy against the public, or in some contrivance to raise prices."[4] The law established that any agreement among businesses that harmed the interests of consumers by limiting competition was illegal.

The American model of antitrust eventually became standard throughout the world. The Americans imposed similar rules on Japan after World War Two. The Treaty of Rome, which founded what is now the European Union in 1956, also adopted a text modeled closely on the American law. The World Trade Organization, founded in 1995, encourages the adoption of competition law across the world.

The punishments for participating in cartels can be severe. Not only can the companies be forced to pay enormous fines, but also the executives involved in negotiating a cartel agreement often go to prison. Many people think that collusion among competitors is the norm. Most economists who research this issue believe that while it can happen, it is considerably more rare than the majority of people think.

In the United States, teams in the major leagues make lots of agreements among themselves. Historically, the most famous agreement is the reserve clause, an agreement made by the baseball teams of the National League not to hire each other's players without consent. This agreement was adopted in 1879, three years after the league's foundation. Later it was made all the more powerful as the league made agreements with the minor leagues also to respect the reserve clause. That gave birth to what was known as "Organized Baseball." This system unquestionably kept player wages down and helped to make the teams more profitable.

In modern times, it is the draft system that has come to seem more important in the organization of American sports. The draft was introduced by the NFL back in the 1920s as a way of recruiting players. Whereas the big teams in professional baseball tended to find their players in minor leagues, with players working their way up after leaving school, much like soccer in the rest of the world, the main recruits to professional American football came from college teams where the so-called student-athletes are amateurs. (Until the last fifty years or so, college football was far more popular than professional football.)

Because these student-athletes enter the professional league when they graduate from college, they have a common entry point and it is relatively easy to organize the recruitment process (draft) by identifying all of those players interested. The draft system allocates the right to recruit a player to a single team instead of letting them all compete. Each team gets to pick a player from the pool, with the order of picks being fixed by the rules of the league. Once a player is picked, he must negotiate his contract exclusively with the team that chose him. And so instead of a situation where potentially a player could be playing off one team against another in competition for his services, he is obliged to do a deal with one, and only one, team. The draft was subsequently adopted by the other major league sports, eventually even by baseball, which not only drafts college players but also players coming out of high school.

BOX 9.3: COLLEGE FOOTBALL

The major league sports in the United States are very different, but college football has some interesting similarities with the structure of soccer in the rest of the world. Although the players are students and not paid, the top two hundred or so college teams generate over $8 billion per year according to figures estimated by *USA Today*, and there are about another 800 smaller football programs across the United States. They are controlled by a governing body, the National Collegiate Athletic Association (NCAA), which sets the rules and imposes discipline, just like UEFA and FIFA. As with those organizations, there is tension between the interests of a small number of big programs (e.g., my own University of Michigan generates more than $150 million a year, has a 110,000-seat stadium, and participates in national TV contracts), and those of the small programs that form the majority (the hundredth-largest program has a revenue of only $25 million, the two hundredth just $10 million).

The colleges are organized in divisions, but these define the level of resources required to be eligible to compete. To be in the highest division, the Football Bowl Subdivision (FBS), which makes you eligible to participate in a prestigious end-of-season bowl game, you have to offer a minimum number of scholarships for students to play football, ensure a minimum level of attendance at games, and participate in a number of other competitive collegiate sports. The one hundred twenty or so teams in the FBS are organized into conferences. These are voluntary groupings that began more than a century ago as regional competitions.

Since participation is voluntary, there has been a great deal of conference "jumping" as colleges re-align themselves to make the most attractive competition. This has been encouraged by growth of football coverage on TV (most NFL games are played on Sundays, but Saturday is reserved for the college game, ensuring that the two forms of entertainment do not compete head-to-head). Michigan is part of the Big 10 conference, which is the oldest, founded in 1896, but currently has 14 members. It was traditionally a midwestern conference but has now accepted teams on the East Coast, which will help to grow audiences in the country's largest TV markets.

Given that teams play fewer than 10 conference games per season plus a handful of invitational games, there has been a longstanding problem about deciding which is the best team in the country. Originally, the biggest bowl games were played between the champions of specific conferences (e.g., the Rose Bowl, the oldest and most prestigious, was played between the winner of the Big 10 and the Pac-10 conferences). In the 1990s, an agreement was made that made it more likely that the two best teams could meet in a Bowl Game. Deciding eligibility is complex, depending not only on team records ranked by computers, but also on the votes of journalists. Not surprisingly, there is huge controversy over bias in voting. In January 2009, then President-elect Barack Obama weighed in and said that there should be a play-off system for the best teams—and play-offs were inaugurated for the 2014/15 season.

Many of these issues are reminiscent of the organizational problems in European soccer. There are regional leagues (albeit with fixed borders) with vastly different economic strengths; and there is conflict between the big teams and small teams about the structure of competition, which has been adjusted several times in recent decades. There have been many proposals for cross-border leagues in Europe in order to gain better access to TV markets, and in 2012 UEFA finally agreed to the creation of the BeNe Leagues, a women's league for teams from Belgium and the Netherlands.

The long-term problems for college football and European soccer are essentially the same:

- how to ensure that the best teams play each other, since these are usually the most attractive games, while preserving the traditions that many people love; and
- how to ensure the financial viability of the smaller teams when the biggest teams perpetuate their dominance because they generate the lion's share of all the revenues.

Neither system has yet found a satisfactory solution.

Another form of agreement among American teams is that of exclusive territories. Unlike European soccer, where teams tend to stay put, American teams may move to another city if the owner so wishes. And when another city offers to build a new stadium to house the team, owners often do so wish. In this world, it is useful to have protection against a rival team moving too close and competing for fans. Generally, the league grants exclusive territorial rights within seventy-five miles of the home stadium. In the larger cities, two teams are often allowed (e.g., in New York, Los Angeles, and Chicago). By contrast, in the 2014/15 season, there were six Premier League teams in London alone (and in earlier seasons there have been as many as eight). The competition for fans in European soccer is much more intense.

American major league teams also enter into direct economic agreements. The most notable of these is the salary cap. This sets the maximum that any team can spend on player salaries and is based on an average of league-wide revenues. In 2014, the salary cap in the NFL was set at $124 million per team, in the NBA at $63 million, and in the NHL at $69 million. MLB does not have a cap, but imposes a luxury tax, which means that if teams spend over a given limit then they also have to pay a tax, proportional to their overspending, which is redistributed to the other teams in the league. The use of salary caps in the major leagues is relatively recent—the NBA cap was the first to be introduced in 1984—and their administration is complicated. The NFL operates a "hard cap," meaning that that teams in a given season cannot breach the limit. By contrast the NBA operates a "soft cap," which allows teams to go beyond the limit under certain conditions, generally relating to players who have been with the team a long time. Salary caps are a particularly effective way to limit the wages of star players because paying them their market rate (based on what other teams would be willing to pay in an auction) would usually breach the cap.

Collective selling is another cartel-like agreement that has been long established in American professional sports. Sports broadcasting started to generate significant revenues for baseball during the radio era in the 1920s and 1930s. Each team negotiated its own local contract for radio broadcast because, generally, only people in the local area of the team wanted to follow the games. The teams viewed the radio broadcast as an extension of going to the stadium. The television era changed all that, and the NFL in particular saw TV as a way to broaden the appeal of their league to a national audience. To this end, it negotiated a single contract to cover league games with the national network broadcasters. That naturally got the teams a better price for their rights because the networks could not play off one team against another in negotiations. Other leagues learned from the NFL, and indeed most soccer leagues have adopted a similar practice (Spain being a notable exception). However, the American leagues have taken this further by developing the collective selling of merchandising. In the soccer world, teams keep the revenue generated by selling replica jerseys, scarves, and so on; in the major leagues, all of the revenue is divided equally. Given that some teams are far more popular than others, this represents a significant amount of redistribution.

These are just the main examples of collective agreements in the US professional leagues, where the teams negotiate almost everything collectively, exactly as a cartel would. But how can this be the case when there is antitrust law prohibiting cartels?

The answer lies in the special nature of professional sports as a form of competition. Teams competing against each other in a league are clearly sporting competitors, but are they economic competitors? Economic competitors try to compete for the best resources (e.g., players) and they can compete for customers (e.g., fans)—but there is an important sense in which they do not compete economically. If a team is to play games and sell tickets to watch those games, then it needs an opponent. Commercial sport is unique in that it is the only product or service supplied in the market that cannot be produced without the cooperation of a rival. And one can go further: arguably, a team needs its rivals to be strong enough to make the game interesting. When the major leagues have been challenged in court, this is the argument that they have advanced to justify the restraints on economic competition that they have agreed upon. We might call it the competitive-balance defense.

There is a large literature in economics devoted to this topic, seeking to define what is meant by competitive balance, to measure it, and to see what effect it has on demand for a given league.[5] In the original formulation, the suggestion is that fans will not go to watch a game if the outcome is known in advance—uncertainty of outcome is a defining characteristic of attractive sporting competition. While this is true, it does not tell us how balanced a competition has to be in order to provide enough uncertainty of outcome. A contest between David and Goliath, where Goliath is the heavy favorite, can be attractive precisely because David wins, even if only very occasionally.

The need for uncertainty of outcome could apply to an individual game, a season taken as whole, or a sequence of seasons. The NFL has always seemed to embrace the idea that every game should be highly uncertain, with its slogan "on any given Sunday any team in the league can win." But most games are attended by home team fans who much prefer the home team to win. These fans may not want the game to be very balanced (although they might prefer the season as a whole to be balanced). We also know that record breaking is attractive, and so a team that goes an entire season unbeaten can do as much to enhance interest in the league as a league table in which there is almost no gap between the top and the bottom. Even in the longer term, dominance can be attractive. The New York Yankees are as important to baseball for the enormous number of fans who are dying to see them lose as for the huge number of fans who want them to win.

Statistical research attempting to isolate this kind of uncertainty and the demand associated with it has been surprisingly inconclusive. It is simply not clear that fans want a balanced competition. This in itself is a challenge to the competitive-balance defense. The extreme inequality and dominance in European soccer—while being acknowledged as the world's most popular sport—is another. Nonetheless, up until now, sports leagues in the United States have had considerable success in using the competitive-balance defense to justify economic restraints.[6]

Whether or not the competitive-balance defense is valid in legal and economic theory, the restraints imposed by the major leagues, by limiting economic competition, have helped both to make the member teams profitable, and to ensure that the profits are relatively evenly distributed. And it is this that explains the data in Figure 9.1. The American model restrains competition and means that teams can keep more of the revenue they generate as profit, and at the same time ensures that the differences between teams do not grow too great.

It seems paradoxical because we normally think of Europe as leaning toward socialism and social democracy, while the United States seems organized on principles of laissez-faire capitalism, but in the world of professional team sports the situation seems to be the reverse. If anything, the major leagues look socialist in that they hold property in common, limit competition, and redistribute resources from the successful to the less successful—whereas the soccer leagues of Europe (and the rest of the world) operate mostly on the basis of "dog eat dog" with only limited redistribution and economic cooperation.

BOX 9.4: WILL MLS EVER BECOME A TRUE MAJOR LEAGUE?

Major League Soccer (MLS) started in 1996 with ten teams and by 2014 it had expanded to 19 teams with four new franchises due to open, including a New York City team owned by Manchester City, and a Miami team part owned by David Beckham. In 2013, the league average attendance was over 18,000 per game, ranking it ninth in terms of soccer league attendance globally.

The organizers of MLS set out to avoid the mistakes of the North American Soccer League (NASL), which enjoyed some success in the 1970s by bringing in aging superstars from around the world (including Pelé, Johan Cruyff, Franz Beckenbauer, and George Best), but then collapsed because of financial problems in the 1980s. MLS is modeled on the American system, with no promotion and relegation, a salary cap, and a commissioner with wide powers that include the right to move players from strong teams to weak teams even in the middle of the season.

Despite the high attendance levels, MLS owners still say they are not profitable. The salary cap is set at around $4 million per team, with the potential for an exemption for bringing top stars into the league. The Dutch league, with only slightly higher average attendance than MLS, pays average salaries per team of more than $21 million. According to the UEFA club licensing benchmarking reports,

CONTINUES

there are twenty leagues in Europe that pay higher average salaries than MLS, including the Romanian league. Globally there are probably more than thirty professional soccer leagues that pay more.

Given that there is now a global market for soccer talent, this makes a difference. MLS is shown on network TV in North America; so is the Champions League and the EPL. In the EPL, the average salary bill per team in 2013 was more than $125 million per team. The quality difference is especially visible on TV. NBC shows live MLS and EPL games alongside each other, and EPL games tend to attract audiences almost double the size. The EPL broadcast contract in the United States is currently worth about three times the MLS contract.

The problem, as the sports economist Todd Jewell has pointed out,[1] is that MLS still makes 90 percent of its income at the gate, whereas the biggest leagues in the world make more than half of their money from sponsorship, merchandising, and broadcasting. MLS would need to raise the quality of play to bring in more money from those sources, but that would mean paying much higher salaries in what is a highly competitive market.

Fans of MLS argue that it has adopted a "softly, softly" strategy, building an audience first, and will increase spending on players as revenues increase. The problem with this is that in the global market other leagues will not stand still and wait for MLS to overtake them. Salaries are being pushed up by global competition, which is only likely to increase in the future. Competition is already intense among the top European and South American leagues, while emerging markets in the Gulf and China will add to price pressures. Given the scarcity of talent, it is likely to get much more expensive in the future.

The fact is that the American organization model works well when there is limited competition from elsewhere (as in football, baseball, and basketball), but it's not designed for a competitive market. MLS has built up a niche audience in some parts of the country—among Hispanics in various regions, and in the Pacific Northwest for example, among people who enjoy going to watch live soccer—but the struggle to become a mainstream sport in the United States is much harder. Unless their business model changes, MLS may always be minor league soccer.

1. Jewell T. (2014) "Major league soccer in the USA," in Goddard, J., and Sloane, P. (eds.). *Handbook on the Economics of Professional Football.* Cheltenham: Edward Elgar.

There are many things that soccer clubs have learned from the American major leagues in recent decades. To name just as few: the benefits of collective selling, the need to market the game and develop merchandising opportunities, and the potential of sponsorship. Some might argue that the adoption of commercial practices from the United States has diminished the beautiful game, but Americans can also point out that they do not allow sponsors to put their names on team jerseys, as the Europeans do—that is sacrilege. No doubt, though, ideas will continue to flow from American sports to the rest of the world.

In recent years, Americans with a background in major league sports have bought European—primarily English—soccer clubs. The Glazer family at Manchester United (and the NFL's Tampa Bay Buccaneers), Stan Kroenke at Arsenal (NFL St Louis Rams and NBA Denver Nuggets), Randy Lerner at Aston Villa (once owned the NFL Cleveland Browns), and John Henry at Liverpool (and MLB's Boston Red Sox) are just the most prominent investors in recent years.[7] This raises both the question of what attracted them in the first place, and also whether they want to change soccer's organizational structure. The answer to the first question seems to be that they are lured by the global prominence of the game. Twenty-five years ago, the annual revenue of European soccer was about $1 billion—less than any of the three major league sports taken on their own. Now it generates more revenue than the three of them combined ($27 billion against $23 billion). This astonishing growth, in an era when the major leagues themselves enjoyed huge increases in revenues, made a lot of Americans sit up and take notice. American owners also believe, with good reason, that this revenue growth has not ended and is likely to continue for some time to come.

The problem that they see, that is plain for all to see, is that no matter how fast revenues increase, soccer clubs hardly ever produce a profit. American investors must wonder how to change this. After all, as we have seen, most of the major league teams are profitable, and carry a considerably higher market value than most European soccer clubs. They must, surely, have reached the conclusion that the promotion-and-relegation system promotes excessive competition. Furthermore, they might reasonably have concluded that a closed-league structure would not only put an end to this, but also enable them to adopt the socialist measures that have helped make so much money for owners in the United States. For example, the Champions League could be transformed into a closed transnational competition, or the Premier League, already far and away the dominant soccer league in global economic terms, could go it alone and shut out the smaller clubs forever.

Yet the promotion-and-relegation system is one of the few things that people believe is sacrosanct about the structure of soccer. No lesser authority than the European Commission, the executive branch of the European Union, has stated that it is an integral part of the European sports model and that attempts to abolish it would meet with political resistance. Indeed, it may be that the promise of promotion is the glue that holds the soccer system together. Smaller clubs and their fans will fight on forever whatever the financial cost just in the hope that one day they might compete at the highest level, regardless of how improbable this might be. Hope is, after all, one of the most powerful motivators known to humans. Certainly if it were put to most soccer fans that a solution to the problems of insolvency that beset the clubs would be to abolish the promotion-and-relegation system, there would be few takers.

Yet soccer fans often are attracted by measures that are applied in the closed American system and argue that they could be copied in the open European system. For example, it is often claimed that some kind of salary cap could be adopted, in order to hold down salaries and keep clubs solvent. But in fact this wouldn't work: at the highest level, the biggest teams play simultaneously in a domestic league, where their spending overwhelms the smaller team, and in the Champions League, where their rivals are similar in size. A salary cap designed to equalize competition in the Champions League would have no effect on domestic imbalance, while one that equalized domestic competition would render the big teams from that league uncompetitive in the Champions League. That change would actually disadvantage the smaller domestic clubs because UEFA pays out money to share domestically based on the success of clubs from each country in its competitions.

But, more fundamentally, a cap would tend to equalize resources, which would only make it more likely that the dominant teams might one day be relegated. We saw that this almost never happens in the current system. We also know that relegation can lead to financial disaster—so why would the big teams ever vote to put themselves at that kind of risk? If pressed by the smaller clubs (which are, after all, more numerous and could therefore outvote them), the big clubs could threaten to form their own breakaway league—a by-no-means unrealistic proposition in those circumstances. More generally, any redistributive or equality-enhancing measure such as those adopted by the American closed leagues would expose dominant teams to the threat of losing their dominance, which they are unwilling to contemplate.

Not that there is no sharing at all in soccer. The leagues do usually have collective-selling agreements for broadcast rights, and these are to some extent redistributive. However, the effects are usually limited. The American major leagues agree to strictly equal sharing, but in most soccer leagues there is also a performance-based element, which ensures that the dominant teams get a larger share of broadcast revenue.

One aspect that might seem appealing about the major league system is that insolvency is almost unknown. However, like the German example cited in chapter 1 (many people think German clubs are better run than English ones, but in fact insolvency seems just as common in the lower divisions), this is potentially quite misleading. In sports such as football and basketball there are no minor leagues, only college teams that invest in player development. College football is a vast entertainment complex, with many attractions, and as many problems, but in any case it is not a model that the rest of the world is well positioned to emulate.

In baseball, there are minor leagues that are comparable to the lower divisions of the soccer world, although they never operated a promotion-and-relegation system. There were hundreds of minor leagues in the past that served the local population, and new leagues could be created almost at will. They also folded regularly. Dozens of minor leagues have expired—a process accelerated by television and wider access to watching major league competition. These leagues, and the teams that played in them, seldom commanded the kinds of local loyalties enjoyed by soccer clubs in Europe, and so once they became insolvent they just shut themselves down. The fate of the minor league system was to become simply an adjunct of the major leagues. The majors entered into agreement with the minors to supply them with players as development leagues; in exchange, the majors paid the players' salaries. As a result, the minors lost all control over the players on their teams, and minor league competition became meaningless, with major league teams switching players throughout the season to suit their interests. Today's minor league club is little more than a park-keeper taking admission money. This, surely, is not a system that anyone in Europe would willingly adopt.

It does not look likely that the problems of insolvency in soccer can be addressed by copying the American model, or at least not without abandoning some of the things that people love most about soccer. This means that if soccer wants to resolve its financial problems, its only choice is to regulate itself more strictly.

10

REGULATION

PERSISTENT DOMINANCE BY A SMALL ELITE, CHRONIC FINANCIAL crises, and widespread insolvency—any industry characterized in this way might be thought to be failing rather badly. But, as we have seen, soccer is growing both in terms of its global following and its capacity to generate revenue. Even during troubled economic times that followed the 2008 global banking crisis, soccer clubs continued to sustain rapid revenue growth. In the six years from 2007, the combined economies of the twenty-eight member states of the European Union failed to grow. Gross domestic product (GDP) in 2013 was still 1 percent below the 2007 level. Yet UEFA figures show that between 2007 and 2012 the revenues of top division clubs in Europe grew by 28 percent. Soccer's position as the major global sport is not only unchallenged, its dominance is growing as new markets in North America and China are absorbed. In August 2014, the University of Michigan sold out the 110,000 capacity of its football stadium to stage a preseason exhibition between Manchester United and Real Madrid (typical ticket prices were $150).

For years the critics have been arguing that something must be done—about excessive dominance, about excessive commercialization, about rising costs, and above all about ceaseless insolvency. Finally, in 2009, UEFA proposed a new set of regulations called Financial Fair Play (FFP). These rules, both in the eyes of advocates and critics, have the potential to dramatically re-align the field of play.

In 1999, UEFA decided to embark on a system of licensing for clubs entering UEFA competitions.[1] According to UEFA, initially the purpose was to explore the possibility of creating a salary cap, but it was soon decided that this could not be done without first creating a legal framework. The rules of the licensing system are laid down by UEFA, and the award of the licenses is overseen by the national associations, so as to bring "member associations closer to their clubs." Initially, the licensing system laid down rules relating to sporting development (youth training), infrastructure (stadiums), personnel and administration (key posts to be filled), legal (documentation), and financial issues. The financial requirements were that clubs had to provide periodic audited financial statements and that they should have no "overdue payables" to other clubs or players. These requirements were applied from the 2004/05 season. They were extended in the 2008/09 season to prohibit overdue payments to tax authorities and require the provision of budget forecasts. In 2009, UEFA announced the introduction of Financial Fair Play.

According to FFP, any club that wishes to take part in UEFA's two main annual competitions, the Champions League and Europa League, must obtain a license from its national association certifying that it meets certain criteria. The key criteria are:

- No overdue payables. This means that a club must be fully up to date with payments to creditors.
- Break-even. This means that a club must be able to demonstrate that "relevant" income balances with "relevant" expenditure. For these purposes, the balance of income and expenditure are calculated over a three-year period, and the balance is subject to an acceptable deviation of €5 million ($8 million). Moreover, there is a transitional period to 2018 during which larger deviations are permitted.

The break-even constraint is complex because allowable income and expenditures are defined in great detail. They do not coincide with simple accounting definitions, and a club could in theory declare an accounting profit while failing to meet break-even, or declare an accounting loss but meet break even. Soccer income is broadly defined as income from ticket sales, merchandising, broadcasting rights, and sponsorship. Soccer expenditure is broadly defined as wage and transfer spending on players.

The stated objectives of the FFP regulations are "to achieve financial fair play in UEFA club competitions and in particular:

(a) to improve the economic and financial capability of the clubs, increasing their transparency and credibility;

(b) to place the necessary importance on the protection of creditors and to ensure that clubs settle their liabilities with players, social/ tax authorities and other clubs punctually;

(c) to introduce more discipline and rationality in club football finances;

(d) to encourage clubs to operate on the basis of their own revenues;

(e) to encourage responsible spending for the long-term benefit of football;

(f) to protect the long-term viability and sustainability of European club football."[2]

These objectives seem primarily to focus on efficiency concepts rather than fairness. For example, there need be nothing fair about "improving the economic and financial capability of clubs"; it's not even clear what the word "capability" means in this context. Likewise, part (c)'s "discipline and rationality" can be achieved without any appeal to fairness. Part (b) seems closest to the sense of fairness, in that it requires clubs to fulfill obligations into which they enter. However even in this case the rule is not self-evidently fair. For example, creditors may have been guilty of imposing unreasonable conditions in the first place (a problem not unknown in the world of soccer), and hence requiring teams to meet these obligations may simply enforce an unfair deal.

BOX 10.1: FINANCIAL FAIR PLAY IN OPERATION

Financial Fair Play was a long time in the making. The rules were agreed in 2010, and they required the accumulation of three years

CONTINUES

of historical accounting data on the clubs in order to determine compliance with the break-even rule. Decisions about whether clubs were in breach of FFP rules were not taken until early 2014, and penalties were not announced until May 16. In the years leading up to this, UEFA had announced the results of a hypothetical exercise to see how many clubs would have been in breach of the regulations if the rule had applied in that year. For the year 2012/13, 63 percent of clubs eligible for UEFA competition breached at least one FFP indicator. Eighty-three clubs would have been in breach of the break-even rule.

However, when UEFA announced the results in 2014, only nine clubs were sanctioned—three from Turkey, three from Russia, one from Bulgaria, Manchester City, and PSG. The largest penalties were for the latter two, and involved three elements:

- A fine of up to €60 million ($75 million)
- Restrictions on buying in the transfer market
- A reduction in the permitted squad size for the Champions League from 25 to 21 players

Cynics argued that these penalties were relatively limited and that a lot of clubs that were in breach must have been let off. Many fans of rival teams wanted Manchester City to be more severely punished. This might not be entirely fair. While the fine is easily afforded by Sheikh Mansour, the club still has to remain within FFP limits and so cannot bring in money from outside to cover it. It may be that UEFA wanted to begin with relatively mild punishments in order to ensure compliance and will get tougher as the system becomes better accepted. They may also want to wait until the court cases are disposed of.

The extent of any impact of FFP, and whether that impact is positive or negative, will only become apparent over the next few years.

It is clear that many, if not most, European soccer clubs have financial problems. According to the *UEFA Club Licensing Benchmarking Report* covering the financial year 2011, 63 percent of top division clubs in Europe reported an operating loss, 55 percent reported a net loss, 38 percent reported negative net equity, and in 16 percent of cases auditors raised "going concern" doubts. While UEFA views these figures with concern, its powers are limited. There are around 700 top division clubs in Europe, and many thousands that operate below this level, but only 235 clubs play in UEFA competitions and are therefore affected by FFP rules. Moreover, the FFP rules exempt clubs with revenues or expenses below €5 million ($8 million), which constitutes roughly half of all top division clubs and 41 percent of all clubs qualifying for UEFA competition—only 77 European clubs have revenues in excess of €50 million ($80 million).

How is efficiency affected by FFP, which aims to cut economic losses and strengthen balance sheets? In a market economy, prices are usually considered to act as signals that suggest courses of action to economic actors. When firms make losses, the value of what they produce is lower than the value of the inputs required. This suggests that there is over-production and that resources might be more profitably applied to some other economic activity. Shifting resources can be achieved voluntarily by the choices of the firm's managers—or it can be achieved through bank-ruptcy, which forces the firm to cease production altogether. From the perspective of economic efficiency, the losses of European soccer clubs appear to signal that there is "too much soccer."

This argument, though not expressed in quite these terms, has been commonly expressed in the literature. Sports leagues are often character-ized as a type of rat race. This notion draws on the contest literature in which firms dissipate rents through competition to win a prize.[3] Logi-cally, if there exists a fixed prize (e.g., a championship title) that can only be won by expending more effort than your rivals, then only effort *relative to your rivals'* matters, not the total amount of effort supplied. From the point of view of the competitors, an agreement by all to halve their effort leaves relative positions unchanged, while economizing on resources for all. A general theoretical argument for overinvestment in sports leagues is advanced by economists such as Helmut Dietl and Egon Franck.[4] This argument is adopted by those in favor of regulation.[5]

Suppose then that clubs scale back their expenditures, either because of UEFA's no-overdue-payables rule or the break-even rule. Most of a club's spending goes on players, and so a general fall in spending will tend to put downward pressure on player wages. Thomas Peeters and I estimated that the implementation of FFP would lead to a reduction in wage spending of between 15 and 20 percent in the biggest European leagues.[6] Because players at the highest level are already paid well in excess of their best alternative employment outside of soccer, this would not cause a reduction in the supply of players. Likewise, because owners are currently willing to absorb losses, increasing profitability thanks to wage reductions will not decrease the supply of clubs. So if there is oversupply of soccer at the moment, FFP will not change this.

However, not all clubs are currently loss-makers. FFP might cause some clubs to scale back their operations while causing others to expand. The expansion effect will arise if player salaries fall on average and therefore clubs that currently enjoy a surplus will be willing to improve team quality to the extent that it will raise revenues. This rebalancing will tend to favor clubs that are able to generate higher revenues from a given number of wins. These are likely to be clubs with more populous markets (in big cities) and richer fans. The latter effect is particularly notable given the gap in incomes between northwest Europe (Germany, Great Britain, Scandinavia, and the Benelux countries) and southern and eastern Europe (Spain, Italy, Greece, Poland, Hungary, Romania, and so on). Historically, the teams of Italy and Spain have tended to dominate European competition; in recent years, the English Premier League has become more competitive thanks to the high value of its broadcast rights and high ticket prices; in the future, one might expect German clubs, relative underperformers compared to clubs from these other countries, to improve thanks to FFP.

On the face of it, there is nothing efficient about this kind of rebalancing. The losses that clubs currently incur are voluntary, in the sense that the owners appear willing to pay for them by injecting new capital into the business. And when existing owners are no longer able to do so, new owners always seem to appear to replace them. There are hardly any professional soccer clubs that have been disbanded in recent years, and certainly none of any significant size, despite the persistence of loss making. If clubs are predominantly win maximizers, and potential investors are attracted by trophy assets, this is a perfectly rational and sustainable process. Given that the success of a club generates consumption benefits (glory) for the owner, it is not surprising that the owner is willing to pump money in (i.e., accept losses on ordinary business activities) rather than attempting to take money out (dividends on profits).[7]

At this point, the distinction between FFP's overdue payables rule and the break-even rule is important. The overdue payables rule is intended to ensure that creditors are repaid on time, and so prevent them from becoming involuntary investors in a club. This is in line with standard business practice, and indeed for most countries this is a legal requirement to continue trading. Creditors can have the business wound up if their repayments are overdue. The social significance of soccer clubs to local communities often means that creditors are unwilling to enforce their rights, and so FFP can be seen as redressing the balance in what is currently an unfair bargain.

The break-even rule, however, limits the ways in which owners can invest in their teams—even when they have the resources to do so. To be clear, some forms of investment are not restricted under FFP (e.g., development of training facilities and stadium enhancements), but the most secure route to improved success, namely buying top players in the transfer market,[8] is severely restricted. There is no doubt that most people view FFP in these terms. It is a mechanism to prevent extremely wealthy people (the so-called "sugar daddies") from using their money to win championships by hiring the best players.

BOX 10.2: IS IT REALLY FINANCIAL *FAIR* PLAY?

Names matter. Once upon a time every nation had a Ministry of War, and now it is called the Ministry of Defense. Businesses like to apply words such as "natural" and "organic" to their products, political parties adopt the word "democratic," whatever their intentions, and of course soccer clubs are variously United, Athletic, or Sporting. The decision by UEFA to call its financial regulations "Financial Fair Play" was a masterstroke. Who could argue against fair play being applied in financial matters, as in all aspects of the game? Unfortunately, names can be misleading. The United Nations seems anything but United, Northern Rock,

CONTINUES

a British bank, proved to be anything but solid when it collapsed in 2007 (following the first bank run in Britain in 150 years), while the content of TV shows such as *America's Got Talent* seems to flatly contradict their title.

So it is not unreasonable to ask whether FFP is really fair, and, indeed, whether it is really about fairness at all. Closer inspection of the stated objectives suggests that it is more about efficiency than fairness.

Fair Play is a concept given to the world by the English language, like the words "football" and "soccer." The English words "Fair Play" have been adopted in almost every other language (judging by my search on Google translate); and the German anglophile Rudolf Kircher, who wrote a book on the subject in 1928, roundly declared, "the words are untranslatable." He argued that the concept is something that you learn as a child "that it is wrong to take advantage of the weak, and unmanly to ill-treat a beaten adversary." The use of the term does not originate in sport but is first found in Shakespeare, when a character in *King John* says: "According to the fair play of the world, Let me have audience." When the witches in *Macbeth* say: "fair is foul and foul is fair"—words that might be spoken by a soccer coach determined to win at any cost—the word you should understand is "play." The earliest use of the word in a sporting context that I have been able to find relates to cricket, in a memoir of the Hambledon Cricket Club written by John Nyren in 1832, which includes the rules of the game, one of which states: "the umpires are the sole judges of fair and unfair play." Not that this prevented one hard-done-by cricketer from complaining that his defeat was attributable to the latter.

If we continue to focus on the issue of efficiency, it is not obvious why sugar daddies are inefficient. Clearly they bring more money into the game, allowing it to expand. When they hire talent they typically pay large transfer fees to rival teams, and therefore the benefits of their investment are, at least to some extent, shared. Their interest in soccer reflects the growing social significance of the game, which has grown at a remarkable rate in recent decades. Indeed, this is where the rat-race arguments referred to above tend to fail. It is assumed that excessive competition is of no value, whereas in reality fans are attracted by the quality of a competition as well as by its pure rivalry. In practice, a high level of investment in players has raised interest in the game. It has provoked a global search for talent, which in turn generally encourages increased participation in the sport and increased supply of facilities such as training grounds or stadiums. The shrinking fraction of the population that dislikes soccer bemoans the way the game has become all pervasive in modern society; it seems hard to argue that the "rat race" has done anything but enhance the game's popularity.

A related argument concerns the "soft budget constraint." Some economists have argued that the deficits of European soccer clubs are comparable to the financing arrangements that existed for enterprises in the Soviet planning system. In the Soviet case, the state was unwilling to close enterprises that made losses, and as a result managers lacked incentives to improve efficiency. This caused the undersupply and poor quality that was characteristic of the Soviet system. Researchers such as Wladimir Andreff, Rasmus Storm, and Klaus Nielsen, and especially Egon Franck, have argued that the same argument applies to soccer.[9] To the extent that those who run soccer clubs do not believe that they need to repay creditors, this argument may have some validity. However, a crucial difference between the Soviet case and the present issue is that European soccer is a highly competitive business, while the Soviet system encouraged state monopolies. Competition drives clubs to seek efficiencies in ways that Soviet state enterprises would never have considered. Indeed, the desire to attract a sugar daddy is in itself a motivation to improve efficiency. Sugar daddies are assumed to be motivated by success, and, after all, billionaires have choices.

Some argue that the sugar daddies' investments are not "sustainable." It is neither clear that this is the case (the supply of sugar daddies appears to be growing, not declining), nor that it would be a problem if it were not. Soccer can grow and it can contract, and neither trend is in itself efficient or inefficient. But if you really are worried about contraction, then you should surely worry that European club soccer will be adversely affected by limiting the capacity of wealthy individuals to invest in European clubs. To the extent that these people are unable to fulfill their ambitions by investing in Europe, they may look elsewhere. Hitherto,

European leagues have dominated the globe, but that need not necessarily continue forever. Soccer is followed fanatically in many developing regions of the world: Latin America, the Gulf, and the Far East. Although not traditionally associated with either, it is also growing in popularity in India and China. Frustrated billionaires in these regions might one day just decide to bring all the talent into their countries, just as European clubs currently attract most of the top talent from the rest of the world.

One problem for those who wish to argue that financial regulation of European soccer is necessary in order to promote efficiency is the requirement to demonstrate that there is currently some kind of market failure. Of course, in any market it is possible to postulate that there could exist some market failure, just as one can always argue that if we do nothing today then tomorrow the sky may fall. However, all the evidence at the moment points to the robust good health of soccer in general and European soccer in particular. The present arrangements have generated growing audiences both at the stadium and on screens (TV, computer, mobile phone, and other devices), exploding revenues and the continued survival of pretty much every club of almost any size that has ever existed. Even the worst economic crisis since 1945 knocked out barely a handful of minnows across the whole of Europe. Notwithstanding the parade of clubs entering insolvency, there is no evidence that the soccer system as a whole is in danger of collapse. I have been at pains to point out that financial distress has always afflicted *some* clubs since professional soccer began, while at the same time the system *as a whole* has flourished. Absent intervention, there is no sign that this would change.

Soccer developed first in Europe, and most of the history of the sport is a European history. This gives European soccer a first-mover advantage, which has been a significant source of its strength as markets have globalized in recent years. However, misdirected regulations that undermine efficiency also have the potential to drive resources away from Europe. There is no such thing as an *impregnable* dominant position.

From the start, the public statements of UEFA officials, notably by its president Michel Platini, made it clear that sugar daddies were the real target of FFP regulations.[10] It would be disingenuous to suggest that this was motivated primarily by efficiency concerns. It is obvious that many fans (and probably Platini himself) think it unfair that a team should be able to win simply because its (foreign) owner is wealthy. The investment by sugar daddies has been called "financial doping," by analogy with the use of performance-enhancing drugs (PEDs) in sports.

This argument is somewhat meretricious—an attempt to impute guilt by association. The original motivation for banning PEDs is that they are harmful to the athlete. For example, the preamble to the 1989 European Anti-doping Convention explains that European governments decided to intervene because they were "concerned by the growing use of doping agents and methods by sportsmen and sportswomen throughout sport and the consequences thereof for the health of participants and the future of sport."[11] Financial injections by wealthy owners cannot be shown to damage the health of the recipient soccer clubs, and indeed rather the opposite seems to be the case.

The proponents of FFP argue that allowing unlimited financial support by owners effectively displaces competition from the game itself into competition to find a wealthy owner, in the same way that PEDs are said to displace competition from the track to the laboratory. By that argument, however, all economic and financial competition is a form of doping. When Real Madrid, Bayern Munich, or Manchester United obtains a new sponsor it is a means to compete more effectively on the field, just as much as a cash injection by Roman Abramovich or Sheikh Mansour. For many fans, the difference is that in some sense the established clubs "earned it," thanks to the reputations they created with past successes, while Chelsea and Manchester City did not. To me, at least, this seems like an argument for perpetual dominance, a form of sporting class system where the aristocrats can never be challenged.

In any case, there is one sense in which FFP is like the regulation of PEDs, and that is the problem of where to draw the line. Anti-doping regulations draw arbitrary lines about what is and what is not permitted (is a cup of coffee a PED? Cough medicine?), and likewise FFP draws arbitrary lines about what are and are not legitimate cash injections. Under FFP rules, an investment by a Russian (e.g., in Chelsea or in AS Monaco) may not count toward meeting the break-even requirement, while a large sponsorship from the Russian energy company Gazprom

(Schalke 04) does count toward break-even. In reality, the two cases look rather similar, but the FFP rules treat these two investments differently.

The case for break even is usually presented in terms of the need to rely on a club's "own revenues"—see objective (d) above. Own revenues are usually defined as gate money, sponsorship, merchandising, and TV revenue, but their exact definition is clearly problematic. This is of course a problem with any regulatory regime and not in itself an argument against regulation. For example, it is sensible for governments to regulate levels of reserve capital to be held by banks to insure against systemic risk, even though defining exactly what is allowable for measurement purposes will always be problematic.

However, the meaning of "own" in "own revenues" seems especially difficult. In reality, soccer clubs do not start out with any resources of their own. They raise resources from investors initially and then seek to sustain themselves with any income sources they can generate. In the past, teams have run lotteries, organized social clubs, gone into manufacturing businesses, and much else besides. Indeed, many of Europe's biggest clubs today are multisport enterprises with opportunities for cross subsidy. There is an ancient saying: *pecunia non olet*—"money doesn't smell." Once one starts to define "good money" and "bad money" it is possible to introduce unimagined sources of unfairness, and regulations multiply. Typically, those who are able to navigate such a complex system are the wealthy—which most people would consider a form of unfairness. As has frequently been observed, the enforcement of the rules is sure to keep lawyers and accountants fully employed.

But the real problem with deploying the fairness argument is that the existing distribution of revenues in European soccer does not seem fair to most people, and the rules of FFP seem likely to ossify that distribution. Inequality has always been a characteristic of European soccer, which is both a cause and a consequence of dominance. American leagues make restrictive agreements in order to equalize resources because, they claim, fans prefer a more balanced competition. The evidence does not lend strong support to this view, and the highly unequal distribution of resources in European soccer has not stopped it from being very successful.

However, most fans of small teams hope that a wealthy person will one day turn up and bring glory to their club. FFP snuffs out that hope.

If this were being done with a view to equalizing resources across clubs then the fairness argument would have some weight. As it is, it just seems like a measure designed to maintain the existing pattern of dominance.[12] Worse still, UEFA's own competition, the Champions League, is helping to enhance dominance. As was shown earlier, most of the Champions League money goes to a select group of dominant clubs. Without a sugar daddy, how could any team in the future hope to rival them?

FFP is problematic both in terms of its stated objectives, which seem mostly to revolve around enhancing efficiency, and in terms of a reasonable standard of fairness. In May 2013, the lawyer Jean-Louis Dupont[13] filed a complaint with the European Commission on behalf of a player agent, Daniel Striani, challenging the legality of the break-even rule under EU law. Dupont argued in his complaint that:

> The "break-even" rule (which, according to article 101 of the Treaty on the functioning of the EU, is an "agreement between undertakings") generates the following restrictions of competition:
>   Restriction of investments;
>   Fossilization of the existing market structure (i.e., the current top clubs are likely to maintain their leadership and even increase it);
>   Reduction of the number of transfers, of the transfer amounts, and of the number of players under contracts per club;
>   Deflatory effect on the level of players' salaries; and
>   Consequently, a deflatory effect on the revenues of players' agents.[14]

In Dupont's view, the break-even rule constitutes a restraint on competition, which infringes on the free movement of capital, workers, and services. He further argues that the rule is not only unjustifiable, but also "in practice illegal, because the rule is not proportionate (since it can be replaced by another measure, equally efficient but less damaging as far as EU freedoms are concerned)." [15]

It is hard to predict whether this challenge will be successful.[16] Article 101 is essentially a law that prohibits cartels (agreements among firms, in this case soccer clubs). Its first section states that any agreements among firms that have as "their object or effect the prevention, restriction or distortion of competition" are prohibited. UEFA will presumably stand by its stated objectives and claim that none of these are *intended* to reduce competition.

Against this, Dupont would probably argue that the *effect* of the agreement is the reduction of competition among teams playing in soccer championships (domestic and UEFA), and the reduction of competition in the market for players. In the "championship" market, UEFA may try to argue that the rules are intended to enhance competition by enabling teams without sugar daddies to be more competitive. On the player market, UEFA may claim that even if reduced competition is a side effect it is not the main aim of the regulation. However, it will be hard for UEFA to maintain that competition has not been restrained in the sense that some competitors are no longer free to make choices that they would otherwise make.

BOX 10.3: EUROPEAN COMPETITION LAW: ARTICLE 101 OF THE EUROPEAN TREATY

1. The following shall be prohibited as incompatible with the internal market: all agreements between undertakings, decisions by associations of undertakings and concerted practices which may affect trade between Member States and which have as their object or effect the prevention, restriction or distortion of competition within the internal market, and in particular those which:

   (a) directly or indirectly fix purchase or selling prices or any other trading conditions;
   (b) limit or control production, markets, technical development, or investment;
   (c) share markets or sources of supply;
   (d) apply dissimilar conditions to equivalent transactions with other trading parties, thereby placing them at a competitive disadvantage;

(e) make the conclusion of contracts subject to acceptance by the other parties of supplementary obligations, which, by their nature or according to commercial usage, have no connection with the subject of such contracts.

2. Any agreements or decisions prohibited pursuant to this Article shall be automatically void.

3. The provisions of paragraph 1 may, however, be declared inapplicable in the case of:

— any agreement or category of agreements between undertakings,
— any decision or category of decisions by associations of undertakings,
— any concerted practice or category of concerted practices,

which contributes to improving the production or distribution of goods or to promoting technical or economic progress, while allowing consumers a fair share of the resulting benefit, and which does not:

(a) impose on the undertakings concerned restrictions which are not indispensable to the attainment of these objectives;
(b) afford such undertakings the possibility of eliminating competition in respect of a substantial part of the products in question.

The decision in the case, therefore, is likely to rest on the interpretation of the third section of the article. This involves balancing several potential effects. The prohibition in Article 101 does not apply if the restriction contributes to improving the product or promoting economic progress so long as consumers share the benefits. In the early stages of FFP, UEFA seemed inclined to argue that the regulations would enhance competitive balance and hence the quality of European soccer. However, more recently, it seems to have shied away from this argument, which does indeed sound rather implausible. The argument that the rules will "ossify" the system, by limiting opportunities for smaller clubs to rise up and compete with the established big clubs, seems more plausible. One might certainly argue that the rules on payment of creditors represent "economic progress"—but it is the break-even rule that is being challenged, not the overdue-payables rule. It appears that UEFA will rely on a rather general argument effect that FFP will eliminate the rat race or the soft-budget constraint, even though it is not clear that these issues have posed a serious problem for the development of European soccer.

UEFA may also face difficulties persuading a court that the break-even rule is really indispensable to its objectives. Alternative forms of regulation to ensure financial stability might easily be feasible. For example, UEFA could require owners to provide formal guarantees or post bonds to cover losses made by the club. Moreover the concept of "own revenues" for clubs that are owned by wealthy people may prove hard to sustain in law. Even if fans see themselves as holding a stake in their club, legally it may be the property of the owner and his to do with as he pleases.

Finally, it is hard to see how UEFA can contradict the argument that the break-even requirement will eliminate competition in the player market to the benefit of the clubs at the expense of the players, and with no obvious benefit to the fans.[17]

Nonetheless, UEFA may still win. I have argued that the regulations are flawed, but the courts do not like to get involved in telling private associations how to run their businesses. In 1995, the European Court of Justice forced a complete overhaul of the player transfer system because it was so flagrantly breaching the liberties guaranteed to workers inside the European Union. In the present case, the court would have to decide that FFP is similarly in conflict with fundamentals of the law. The judges might take the view that the regulations are merely foolish, not illegal.

George Orwell once wrote: "A man may take to drink because he feels himself to be a failure, and then fail all the more completely because he drinks. It is rather the same thing that is happening to the English language. It becomes ugly and inaccurate because our thoughts are foolish, but the slovenliness of our language makes it easier for us to have foolish thoughts." [18]

The real problem with Financial Fair Play is that it does not offer "Fair Play" at all. It is an abuse of language. Rather, it imposes some very specific restrictions on competition. On the one hand UEFA claims, through its official documentation, that these rules will enhance efficiency in ways that are far from clear. At the same time, the leaders of UEFA allowed it to be understood that the so-called sugar daddies are their target, in a bid to satisfy disgruntled fans. It's hardly surprising these rules have provoked a competition law challenge in the European Union.

CONCLUSION

IN THIS BOOK I HAVE SET OUT HOW PROFESSIONAL SOCCER OPERATES—in particular, the relationship between what happens on the field and what happens on the balance sheet. I believe that both aspects of the game form part of a common system, and that the operation of this system is not in any way mysterious but actually quite transparent. I hope that now you can see this too. The story of dominance and distress is characteristic of soccer leagues almost everywhere around the world. Dominance is the product of the promotion-and-relegation system, which ensures that there is an open, competitive market. It may seem counterintuitive at first, but open competition with unlimited freedom of entry has created a system in which only a few clubs win consistently. The market works relatively efficiently, in the sense that money buys success, and improving teams generate increasing revenues because they attract new fans. Dominant teams can maintain their dominance by investing their winnings in ever-better squads, creating a barrier to entry for the smaller teams that must either risk insolvency or find a sugar daddy in order to compete. Given the system, the outcome is, I believe, fated. The names of the clubs could be different, but the consequences of open competition seem inevitable in a largely unregulated market.

Soccer has been an almost unregulated market for more than a century. So there is very little that prevents a club getting any player it wants, as long as it's willing to pay enough money. Sometimes there are legal barriers, but even these often seem, miraculously, to disappear. Clubs can spend what they want, and also *not spend* as they please (with tragic consequences in the case of past stadium disasters). Against this background, professional soccer has grown at a phenomenal pace in financial terms. Twenty years ago, it could be described as a small business; and while even now only a handful of clubs fit into the category of medium-sized businesses, some clubs will become truly big businesses if current growth rates continue.

What accounts for this rate of growth? Part of the answer is that we live in an era when professional sports in general have grown—rising income, increased leisure, globalization, and the development of broadcast technology have all fed the demand for sports. More speculatively, the appeal of sports stars may have grown in proportion to our disillusionment with other public figures. To be sure, star athletes generate their share of scandals—they are hardly ethically pure. At the same time, the quality of their *athletic* performance is beyond doubt, unlike, say, the performance of bankers, CEOs, or politicians. They are genuine competitors—we see them compete; there is rarely any dispute about what they did when they won it on the field.

Whatever the causes, soccer has been especially well placed to profit from the growing interest in sports and the growing willingness of people to spend money on it. Within fifty years of the foundation of the Football Association in 1863, the game had already spread to most regions on the planet, and within one hundred years there was a well-established network of clubs and leagues. The game never really had a rival for global sporting attention, so once the world started to spend money soccer just absorbed the funds that were thrown at it. All this happened without planning, without regulation, and with a minimum of organization. In some ways the development of global soccer seems to be one of the purest manifestations of the power of the market that there has ever been.

This can all be summarized in four points:

- soccer is characterized by the dominance of a few clubs
- the remaining clubs survive on the edge of financial distress

- the regulation of soccer has been what is euphemistically called "light touch"
- soccer has grown dramatically in recent years

Some might disagree with the theoretical model that I have used to explain these facts, with the structure of cause and effect that I argue ties them together. This is a subject for genuine debate.

Perhaps of more interest to most soccer fans is another question: what, if anything, should be done about the current state of affairs? At this point we have to go beyond the facts and theories about those facts, and ask if we actually like things the way that they are. And if we do not, we must talk about what *ought* to be done—what policies should guide the development of soccer in the future?

So are things as they ought to be? The answer most commonly given is that they are not. Fans are particularly upset by financial distress, and dominance is not very popular except for the fans of the very biggest clubs. All of this has led many people to observe that light-touch regulation has failed and that we now need more thoroughgoing intervention. If the playing field is not level at present, the argument goes, it must be made to be level. And just as the banking system cannot be left to its own devices after the financial catastrophe of 2008, so the persistent insolvency of soccer clubs justifies a tighter regulatory regime.

I have argued here that it is a mistake to confuse the individual crises of specific clubs with systemic crisis. No matter how many clubs are on the brink, the system is in good health because of the intensely competitive nature of the game. The comparison with banking is misleading. You don't treat the common cold in the same way that you treat a heart attack. The common cold can in theory lead to deteriorating health and complications that end in death. But for the vast majority of people who catch a cold, it doesn't. The fact that clubs almost never die no matter how small, but are perpetually resuscitated to fight another day, suggests that we should be less concerned *in general* about financial distress in this particular economic activity (unlike in banking or, say, steelmaking or car assembly).

I do think that it would be a good idea to alleviate financial distress in soccer—but not at any cost. I think that the side effects of the proposed cures are too severe to make the treatment worthwhile. We could go down the American route and create closed leagues without the threat of relegation or the excitement of promotion. Owners would rush to embrace this solution because it would make their businesses more profitable. It would also make them more willing to adopt redistributive measures that might limit dominance. But I do not believe that this is in the best interests of the fans. Perhaps surprisingly, there is no convincing evidence that dominance in soccer has undermined interest in the game. And soccer has thrived in a world where it has failed to produce profits for its owners; I do not think it will suffer if this continues to be the case.

UEFA claims that Financial Fair Play is a more practical way to get rid of financial distress. I think UEFA is sincere in this belief, but I think it is mistaken. My view is that the regulations, if fully implemented, will only enhance the dominance of the big clubs without addressing the financial problems of the small teams, the vast majority of whom will not be directly affected by UEFA regulations. They will also discourage investment in European soccer—and while other regions of the world may benefit, it is odd to think that the European governing body is adopting regulations that disadvantage European soccer. If the regulations are fully enforced then they will harm the clubs they regulate. If the regulations are not enforced then the regulator's credibility will be undermined.

Some people want to go even further: they want the government to regulate soccer. My view is that government regulation of the entertainment business is inappropriate. The only market failure that we have identified in the soccer world is the "too big to fail" problem and this is typically exacerbated by government intervention. What often happens is that local government steps in to save a failing club. It would be better if governments agreed to stay out of professional sports and concern themselves more broadly with promoting amateur sport for the benefits that physical activity is proven to bring. And for the most part governments in Europe and the United States have adopted this position.

So am I really suggesting that there is nothing to be done, that "all is for the best in the best of all possible worlds"? Not entirely. I think rules that penalize teams in sporting terms if they fail to pay their debts are entirely justified and should be enforced. This kind of regulation would mainly fall on the smaller clubs, and is therefore politically unpopular, but it's one way to change the attitudes of those who run the clubs. It would do much to improve their reputation.

I also think that the supporter trust movement deserves support. Increasingly, clubs are required to engage in some kind of dialogue with fans, and mandating interaction via a supporter trust would be a step forward. I still think that the wealthy people who pump money into clubs for the glory of it are necessary to keep it afloat. As the recent Notts County debacle suggested, supporters' trusts cannot necessarily be trusted to do the right thing. But a partnership between owners and fans makes sense, and I think regulations to promote it are desirable. Owners and fans are largely on the same side so they should work together.

But, beyond that, I do not think there is much call for intervention, especially given the robust good health of the game today. I am sometimes accused of being unashamedly pro-capitalist. That would not be a crime in my view, but I think it misses the point. I value competition precisely because of the discipline it places on the owners. I fear that regulatory systems are likely to relax competition and enable owners to take money out of the game. After all, businesses are very good at dealing with government and regulators, and they are by no means averse to working in regulated environments that limit competition. I support the freedom of capitalists to lose a fortune investing in a soccer club.

We should be planning for the consequences of continued success rather than preparing for the apocalypse. Recognizing that soccer's growth has been remarkable over the last two decades and that the forces that propelled it thus far are likely to propel it further in the next two decades, we should be planning for the problems of success. Here is one of those problems. Soccer has in many ways become the most attractive athletic activity on the planet, and too many young kids (mainly boys) dream of making it as professional players. Soccer players have a long and respectable tradition of doing work in the community (as do athletes in other sports), but they need to address their own status as role models far more systematically. For children, participation in soccer should predominantly function as a pastime, not a pipe dream of future glory. Education departments across the world need to work with soccer clubs to push home the message that playing soccer is not a substitute for schoolwork.

Ultimately, the biggest issue concerning the future of the game is the restructuring of competition. We have seen the Champions League evolve over the last two decades in ways that suited the dominant teams under the threat that they would otherwise break away and form a rival competition. This remains a real threat as long as the big teams do not play each other very often. In the ten seasons from 2004/05 to 2013/14 eight clubs won the Champions League—AC Milan, Barcelona, Bayern Munich, Chelsea, Inter Milan, Liverpool, Manchester United, and Real Madrid. In those ten seasons these eight dominant clubs played each other in the Champions League only 97 times (and seventeen of the games were between teams from the same national league, duplicating domestic match-ups that were already being played). This meant that on average a top team played only once or twice a season against *any* of the other seven clubs. In some cases these clubs have not played a competitive game in more than a decade—for example Chelsea vs. Real Madrid or Bayern Munich vs. Liverpool. Yet the global audience for these games would be vast. If these eight clubs were to establish a league in which they played each other twice a year, creating 112 games each season, the value of the broadcast rights would be stratospheric. The dominant clubs have been eyeing the possibility of a league of their own for more than twenty years, and this example shows that the current system is not delivering the best quality of soccer possible.

I think the transition to a system that enabled the big clubs to play each other more often would involve breaking up some traditions. I expect many changes in the next few years. This might also mean allowing clubs to compete more often on a regional basis rather than being confined to their national borders. For example, it seems clear that the standard of competition at the highest level would improve if the clubs of the old Soviet bloc were allowed to form an international league of their own; clubs from other regions in Europe have similar aspirations. The men's leagues in Belgium and the Netherlands should be allowed to merge, just as the women's leagues have. It might also be possible to do more to promote competition between the clubs of Argentina and Brazil and European clubs. Time-zone differences should not pose an insurmountable problem, and competition across continents at the club level could prove attractive—as long as the teams travel to play each other home and away.

I think some reform and dislocation is preferable to a breakaway league that might not only end promotion and relegation but also limit the supply of the top players to the national teams for competitions such as the World Cup.

I think there is a real danger that promotion and relegation will cease to exist. Given the fact that it is so popular with fans and politicians, it might not end soon, and it might never be formally abolished, but there may be ways in which smaller clubs are effectively barred from the highest level of competition. I think that would destroy one of the best aspects of soccer's traditions: that almost every community can sustain a professional soccer team that participates in the same competitive system as the dominant clubs. These small clubs, the Scunthorpe Uniteds and Unterhachings, are tiny when placed alongside the dominant teams, but in aggregate they amount to a great deal. The loyalty of their fans is as much about community as it is about winning in a world where community seems more and more to be a thing of the past. Without the system of promotion and relegation, and the hope that the system creates, many of these clubs would fold.

The system of promotion and relegation does little to promote equality, but equality is a fool's errand in a competition with thousands of participants. Promotion and relegation is the cause of dominance and distress, and all the stress and anxiety that is borne by soccer fans across the world. But it is also the source of never-ending hope. I think the reason that every fan and every club benefits from this system is that there is always hope, no matter how small, no matter how fanciful, that one day you, too, could rise to rank alongside the high and mighty.

NOTES

CHAPTER 1: DOMINANCE AND DISTRESS

1. The method for calculating this probability is developed in Buzzacchi, Luigi, Stefan Szymanski, and Tommaso M. Valletti. "Equality of Opportunity and Equality of Outcome: Open Leagues, Closed Leagues and Competitive Balance." *Journal of Industry, Competition and Trade* 3.3 (2003): 167–186.

2. UEFA is the governing body of European soccer. Unlike the major leagues in the United States, all leagues in the soccer world are affiliated to a national association, which is in charge of maintaining the rules and regulations of the game at all levels, both professional and amateur. Leagues in soccer, therefore, have far less autonomy than American major leagues. National associations are federated into continental associations, and Europe is the federation of fifty-four "European" federations—although its members include countries such as Azerbaijan, Kazakhstan, and Israel, not conventionally identified as European. There are six continental federations: UEFA (Europe), AFC (Asia), CAF (Africa), CONMEBOL (South America), CONCACAF (North and Central American, and the Caribbean), and OFC (Oceania). FIFA is the world governing body; its role is to ensure common standards across the world and run the World Cup (among other things).

3. Roberto Carlos, another member of the *galácticos*, pre-dated Pérez.

4. Athletic Bilbao, the Basque club with the commitment to fielding only Basque players, is also financially sound, but has not posed a serious competitive threat for many decades.

5. The story is recounted in *Manchester United: The Betrayal of a Legend*, by Michael Crick and David Smith. Published in 1989, it stands as one of the best accounts of how soccer clubs worked before the days of huge media contracts.

6. The strange story of this penalty shootout appeared in chapter 8 of *Soccernomics*.

7. Of course, the German national team is one of the great powers of world soccer, with four World Cup victories and three European Championships. But judged by success in international club competition, Germany lags well behind Spain, England, and Italy, measured by championships and games won. In recent years, however, the Bundesliga is showing some signs that it is aiming to achieve a level of pre-eminence to match the national team.

8. Ten within a twenty-five mile radius: Accrington, Blackburn, Bolton, Burnley, Bury, Manchester City, Oldham, Rochdale, Stockport, Wigan, and a further seventeen between twenty-five and fifty miles: Barnsley, Blackpool, Bradford, Chesterfield, Crewe, Doncaster, Everton, Huddersfield, Leeds, Liverpool, Mansfield, Preston, Rotherham, Sheffield United, Sheffield Wednesday, Stoke, and Tranmere. Derby County is just outside the fifty-mile radius.

9. See *The Italian Club Licensing Manual* published by the FIGC, downloaded at www.dirittocalcistico.it/otherside/data/general_stagione/file/34/FIGCliceufa12ingl.pdf on 11/4/2014.

10. See G. Ascari and P. Gagnepain. "Spanish Football." *Journal of Sports Economics*, 7, 1, 76-89. There was an earlier restructuring plan in 1985 that failed. Athletic Bilbao, Barcelona, CA Osasuna, and Real Madrid were allowed to remain as member associations on the grounds that at the time of the first reform they still had positive net assets.

11. Barajas and Rodriguez, p. 74. The clubs were Las Palmas, Sporting de Gijón, Málaga, Alavés, Celta de Vigo, Real Sociedad, Polideportivo Ejido, Albacete, Recreativo de Huelva, Murcia, Xérez, Granada 74, Alicante, Zaragoza, Levante, Córdoba, Rayo Vallecano, Real Betis, Mallorca, Racing de Santander, Valladolid, and Hércules.

12. Accrington Stanley resigned from the Football League in 1962 because the directors believed the club was no longer able to meet its financial obligations. Having left the League the club continued to play at a

lower level until 1966 when it did finally go into liquidation. The club was revived in 1968, and currently plays in the fourth tier in England.

13. In some cases clubs merged to form clubs that survive to the present day (e.g., Rotherham Town and Aberdare) while others were revived, albeit with a gap (Durham City folded in 1938 and was refounded in 1950; Merthyr Town folded in 1934 and was refounded in 2010).

CHAPTER 2: PLAYERS

1. Player transfers in the soccer world operate differently from player trades in the North American major league sports. The key difference is that when another club wants to hire a player currently under contract, it has to compensate the current employer by payment of a transfer fee, which results in the player's old contract being terminated and a new one written. In economic terms, the transfer fee might be thought of as compensation for breach of contract. Of course, under the new contract, the player makes more money (otherwise he could refuse to move). In the major leagues, the player typically retains his existing contract and often the team that releases the player continues to pay some of the wage.

2. Another important difference from the major league model is that there is no player draft. The draft regulates the movement of players from colleges and high schools into professional sport, while in the soccer world there are almost unlimited ways for players to become professionals. Each club is free to search for talent as they please. Major League Baseball operates in this manner when it comes to recruiting talent from outside of North America.

3. Anderson, Christopher, and David Sally. *The Numbers Game: Why Everything You Know About Football Is Wrong* (2013). Penguin Books.

4. "Does performance consistency pay off financially for players? Evidence from the Bundesliga." *Journal of Sports Economics*, 2014.

5. The following paper shows that the betting odds for English soccer are at least as accurate as any statistical model: Forrest, David, John Goddard, and Robert Simmons. "Odds-setters as forecasters: The case of English football." *International Journal of Forecasting* 21.3 (2005): 551–564.

6. Actually, one theory is that bookmakers make their money off of mugs who don't really understand probability (most people) while they

lose money to a small number of professionals who do. I've met plenty of people who claim to be the smart bettors, but I've never been given access to their bank balances to conduct a proper audit.

7. This is done to deal with player salary inflation, which makes it difficult to compare wages across seasons. One solution is to express wage spending as a percentage of the average in a given season—what matters is how much you are spending *relative to your rivals at a given point in time*.

8. There are exceptions—players may be pleased about their average statistics when their career is over, and an agent negotiating a salary will be sure to emphasize averages if they look good. A failing manager or club owner may point to average performance in the past to justify their position. And, of course, there are people like me who study the averages to understand what is going on.

CHAPTER 3: STADIUMS

1. It's actually a misquotation—the line in the film is: "If you build it, he will come."

2. The reference is: Traité d'économie politique (1803), Livre I, chapitre XV, Des debouches. Interestingly, in January 2014, the French President François Hollande quoted Say's Law when arguing that France needed to do more to enhance its productive capacity.

3. Clapp, C. M., and J. K. Hakes (2005). "How long a honeymoon? The effect of new stadiums on attendance in Major League Baseball." *Journal of Sports Economics*, 6(3), 237–263.

4. Forrest, David, Robert Simmons, and Patrick Feehan. 2002. A spatial cross-sectional analysis of the elasticity of demand for soccer. *Scottish Journal of Political Economy* 49:336–355.

5. Polokwane Stadium in South Africa was built for the World Cup and has a capacity of 42,000, while the city's population is only 130,000.

6. US college sports are something of an exception. Ann Arbor, home to the University of Michigan where I work, has a population of 116,000 and a stadium with a capacity of 110,000—the third largest stadium in the world. This is mostly because alumni are willing to come back to Ann Arbor from all over the country to watch the Wolverines play football.

7. These regions have been the top five for the entire period. They currently account for one third of the population of England and Wales.

8. At the time of writing, several of these clubs are planning to increase the capacity of their stadiums. West Ham will move into London's Olympic Stadium 2016/17, and Tottenham, Chelsea, Liverpool, and Everton are all planning significant enlargements or entirely new stadiums; work has already begun at Manchester City and Liverpool.

9. These figures are based on about 90 percent of accounting records over this period. In only 29 percent of the accounts did the club spend less than two thirds of revenue on wages, and in only 6 percent of records did they spend less than 50 percent.

10. There is one possible source of value in an economic sense, and that is the "option value" of the stadium. In the event that somehow the club revived, created a strong team, which went on to become dominant and generate large profits, then some value can be attributed to it. However, as we will see, in soccer this is a very remote possibility.

11. See Baade and Matheson (2013) in White and Kotval, *Financing Economic Development in the 21st Century* (2ed).

12. See for example Devin G. Pope and Jaren C. Pope, 2009. "The Impact of College Sports Success on the Quantity and Quality of Student Applications," *Southern Economic Journal*, vol. 75(3), pages 750–780.

13. Taylor, Sir Peter. *The Hillsborough stadium disaster: 15 April 1989: inquiry by the Rt Hon Lord Justice Taylor: final report: presented to Parliament by the Secretary of State for the Home Department by command of Her Majesty January 1990.* HM Stationery Office, 1990.

14. My colleague at the University of Michigan, Mark Rosentraub, has been closely involved in a number of projects in the United States that seek to combine sports facilities with a larger program of urban redevelopment. See M. Rosentraub (2014) *Reversing Urban Decline: Why and How Sports, Entertainment and Culture Turn Cities into Major League Winners* (2ed), Florida: CRC Press.

CHAPTER 4: REVENUE

1. In fact, the distribution formula over the last decade has worked to create more equality. There are actually two formulae—one for domestic

income from TV, and another for overseas TV income. The domestic formula is complicated—50 percent is shared equally, 25 percent is distributed on the basis of league position, and 25 percent on the number of appearances on British television (since not all the games are shown in the UK). This formula favors the bigger clubs. By contrast, 100 percent of overseas TV income is shared equally. When the formulae were agreed upon in 1992, overseas TV income was not expected to be significant—maybe 5 percent of the total TV income. However, the Premier League has enjoyed a remarkable growth in international appeal, so that by the mid-2000s almost 50 percent of TV income came from this source. This has, among other things, been a force in the direction of greater equality of resources.

2. See Dobson, Stephen, and John Goddard. *The economics of football*. Cambridge University Press, 2011, p. 163.

3. See Chester N. (1968) *Report of the Committee on Football*. HMSO.

4. A small number of teams actually increased attendance, usually because they were promoted back up in the season after relegation. Seventy-seven percent of teams relegated from the second to the third tier experience an attendance decline, averaging 13 percent. In *Soccernomics*, Simon Kuper and I examined in detail the issue of fan loyalty; see chapter 13: "Are Soccer Fans Polygamists?"

5. Deloitte *Annual Review of Football Finance 2014*, figures relate to 2012/13 season.

6. See, for example, Dunning, E., P. Murphy, and J. Williams (1988). *The Roots of Football Hooliganism: a Historical and Sociological Study*. London: Routledge and Kegan Paul; Marsh, P., E. Rosser, and R. Harré. (1978). *The Rules of Disorder*. London: Routledge & Kegan Paul; and Taylor, I. (1971). "Football mad: a speculative sociology of football hooliganism," in E Dunning (ed.) *The Sociology of Sport: A Selection of Readings*. London: Frank Cass.

7. Deloitte *Annual Review of Football Finance*, various years.

8. Average match-day income per fan is a good way to look at changes in pricing over time, but does not necessarily reflect the prices paid by the typical fan. This is because prices tend to be skewed, with a small number paying very high prices (e.g., in executive boxes) while most fans pay much less. A good indicator of what fans pay would be the median price, which

would be calculated by ranking prices paid from lowest to highest and then identifying the price that was exactly in the middle. Unfortunately, data on median prices is not available. But it would not be unrealistic to guess that median prices are anything between two thirds to half of the average match-day income per fan.

9. Figures for the US majors taken from Rodney Fort's *Sports Business Data* archive. The 2014 figure for European soccer is from Deloitte's *Annual Review of Football Finance*, and the figure for Europe in 1990 is based on £128 million revenue of the top division in England. In 2014, the EPL revenue was 15 percent of the total European figure; if this percentage had applied in 1990 then total European soccer revenue would have been $1.5 billion.

10. While the upward trend in attendance that has accompanied increased broadcasting exposure of league soccer is striking, clubs also fear that (1) broadcast of their own game will deter their fans from attending, and (2) broadcasting of rival teams' games will divert fans away from attending—especially if the televised game is between big teams (e.g., the Champions League). On the first point there is mixed evidence. Jaume Garcia and Plácido Rodriguez found that attendance in Spain by those not holding season tickets was adversely affected when a game was shown on live TV (Garcia, J., and P. Rodriguez [2002]. "The determinants of football match attendance revisited: Empirical evidence from the Spanish Football League." *Journal of Sports Economics* 3, 18–38). However, research by myself in collaboration with David Forrest and Rob Simmons found that there was little evidence of an adverse effect in the English Premier League or the Football League Championship (Forrest, D., R. Simmons, and S. Szymanski [2004]. "Broadcasting, attendance and the inefficiency of cartels." *Review of Industrial Organization* 24, 243–265). On the second point, David Forrest and Rob Simmons find that attendance at lower division games, if played at the same time as a midweek Champions League game, can fall by as much as 20 percent (Forrest, D., and R. Simmons [2006]. "New issues in attendance demand: The case of the English Football League," *Journal of Sports Economics* 7, 3, 247–266). In order to protect attendance from such threats, each national association has the right to create its own black-out window (usually a Saturday or Sunday afternoon) during which no soccer can be scheduled on TV.

11. As well as nineteen home games in the Premier League, United played another nine competitive games in the FA Cup, League Cup, and Champions League, whereas QPR played only four games in the FA Cup and League Cup combined, and no European games.

12. It seems that when the division was agreed in 1992/93, the big clubs never imagined that the sales of rights overseas could become so important, and so they didn't think it worth haggling for a larger share.

13. It could be argued that the greatest inequality in the Champions League is among the smallest nations. There are 30 nations that account together for 10 percent of the population within UEFA, and they won just over 8 percent of the places in the Champions League group stages (this amounts to two or three places per season). However, these slots were shared among just eight of the smaller nations. Twenty-two smaller nations did not manage to get a single team to this stage of the competition over an entire decade.

14. PwC (2011). "Changing the Game: Outlook for the Global Sports Market to 2015." Downloaded from www.pwc.com/en_gx/gx/hospitality -leisure/pdf/changing-the-game-outlook-for-the-global-sports-market -to-2015.pdf.

15. Although some teams do have sponsors' logos on practice jerseys, and in 2014 the NBA commissioner stated that NBA jerseys would carry ads within five years.

16. Even if clubs such as Real Madrid, Barcelona, and Arsenal have had logos on their jerseys for much longer.

CHAPTER 5: DEBT

1. The parallel is most forcefully drawn in Nietzsche's *The Genealogy of Morals*, in which he uses the link between the two to explore the foundations of Christian morality.

2. This is not be confused with "third party ownership," a business model in which an investor takes a stake in a player's career by writing a contract that promises to pay the investor a share in all future transfer fees paid for the player. While this form of financing has become popular in some countries it has been outlawed in the Premier League for some time, and FIFA announced in 2014 that it would ban third-party ownership worldwide.

3. Burns, Tom. "Structured Finance and Football Clubs: an Interim Assessment of the use of Securitisation," *Entertainment and Sports Law Journal,* ISSN 1748-944X, December 2006.

4. Securitization does make some sense as a way of raising money for stadium investment, as the case of Arsenal illustrates (see "The financing of Arsenal's new stadium"), because in this case the asset can be expected to generate revenue over many years—unlike player contracts that typically last only three years and then need replacing.

5. UEFA Club Licensing Report (2008), p. 75.

6. Barajas, Ángel, and Plácido Rodríguez. "Spanish football clubs' finances: crisis and player salaries." *International Journal of Sport Finance* 5.1 (2010): 52–66.

7. According to the 2008 UEFA Club Licensing Report, December 31 is the most common financial year-end, used by 64 percent of top-division clubs, followed by June 30 used by 26 percent of clubs. Most countries have a season that runs from the fall to the spring, but often in colder climates the season runs during the summer. UEFA found that in only 56 percent of cases was the sporting and financial season aligned. However, almost 90 percent of the largest clubs in Europe were aligned.

CHAPTER 6: OWNERSHIP

1. Holt, R. *Sport and the British*, p. 167.

2. It is true that some clubs have developed long-term relationships with clubs in other countries that have promoted their image to a wider audience, and even launched clubs using their own name (e.g., Ajax Cape Town plays in the South African Premier League and is a wholly owned subsidiary of the Dutch club Ajax), but such arrangements are relatively rare and in any case do not generate much by way of support for the parent club.

3. See, for example, Goldblatt, David. *The ball is round: A global history of soccer*. Penguin, 2008.

4. Birley, Derek. *Land of sport and glory: sport and British society, 1887–1910*. Manchester University Press, 1995, p. 40.

5. Vamplew, Wray. *Pay up and play the game: Professional sport in Britain, 1875–1914*. Cambridge University Press, 2004, chapter 10.

6. Conn, David. *The football business: Fair game in the '90s?* Mainstream Publishing Co (Edinburgh) Ltd, 1997, p. 158.

7. UEFA 2008 Club Licensing Benchmarking Report, p. 25. Only 15 percent of clubs had dispersed ownership, meaning that no single shareholder controlled more than 5 percent of the equity.

8. Sloane, Peter J. "The economics of professional football: The football as a utility maximiser." *Scottish Journal of Political Economy* 18.2 (1971): 121–146.

9. Késenne, S. "League management in professional team sports with win maximizing clubs." *European Journal for Sports Management* 2.2 (1996).

10. Birley, Derek, ibid, p. 39.

11. Hirsch, Fred. *Social Limits to Growth.* Harvard University Press, Cambridge, MA (1976).

12. For example, Dietl, H., E. Franck, and M. Lang. "Over-investment in European football leagues." No. 38. University of Zürich Department of Management working paper, 2005.

13. Demsetz, Harold, and Kenneth Lehn. "The structure of corporate ownership: Causes and consequences." *The Journal of Political Economy* (1985): 1155–1177.

14. Aglietta, Michel, Wladimir Andreff, and Bastien Drut. "Floating European football clubs in the stock market." No. 2010-24. University of Paris West-Nanterre la Défense, *Economix*, 2010.

15. UEFA *Club Licensing Benchmarking Report* 2011.

16. La Porta, Rafael, Florencio Lopez-de-Silanes, Andrei Shleifer, and Robert W. Vishny. "Legal determinants of external finance." *Journal of Finance*, Vol. 52, no. 3 (1997).

17. L'Elefant Blau in *The Business of Football: A Game of Two Halves?* edited by Sean Hamil, Jonathan Michie, and Christine Oughton. Mainstream Pub. (1999).

CHAPTER 7: STRATEGY

1. This is a puzzle because though the extent of dominance has increased a little in English soccer, dominance was an established pattern fifty years ago. Today, the clubs dominate largely with their checkbook,

yet the data suggests that would have been much more difficult back then. Moreover, we know that in those days clubs were much more profitable. It may be that social networks were much more important then. This is analogous to the diplomatic concepts of "hard" and "soft" power. The United States has hard power in terms of military hardware, but to achieve its foreign policy goals it needs to use soft power, meaning personal ties and persuasion. Perhaps in the 1960s and 1970s the big clubs relied more on the soft power that went with their status as dominant teams than the hard power of money. Perhaps back in the day, like the old British class system, everyone knew their place.

2. Chapman's Huddersfield team also won a third consecutive title the year after he left the club to join Arsenal, and his Arsenal team also won two titles in the seasons following his early death in 1934, so he might reasonably be credited with seven League titles rather than four.

3. "Luck versus Skill in the Cross-Section of Mutual Fund Returns." Fama, Eugene F., and Kenneth R. French, *Journal of Finance*, Vol. 65, No. 5 (October 2010): 1915–1947.

4. Kaplan, Steven N., and Bernadette A. Minton. "How has CEO turnover changed?" *International Review of Finance* 12.1 (2012): 57–87.

5. Sir Clive Woodward, who had successfully coached the English national rugby team to victory in the 2003 World Cup, took up a role as performance director and then director of football in 2005/06 at Southampton Football Club, a senior role working alongside the manager. The experiment was not viewed as a success.

6. Gould, Stephen Jay, and David Halberstam. *Triumph and tragedy in mudville: a lifelong passion for baseball*. WW Norton & Company, 2004.

7. Mauboussin, Michael J. *The Success Equation: Untangling Skill and Luck in Business, Sports, and investing*. Harvard Business Press, 2012.

8. Szymanski, S., and T. Kuypers. *Winners and Losers: the Business Strategy of Football*. London: Viking, pp. 31–33, 1999. In this book, we looked at the financial performance of the club during Ferguson's early years. Manchester United's profitability was rising, but many of the players hired by the previous manager had been let go, and Ferguson was not allowed to spend heavily on replacements until 1989. He won his first trophy in 1990.

CHAPTER 8: INSOLVENCY

1. When the Premier League started in 1992 it had twenty-two teams but it was reduced to twenty in the 1995/95 season.

2. See Szymanski (2012). "Insolvency in English professional football: Irrational Exuberance or Negative Shocks?"

3. www.companieshouse.gov.uk/about/busRegArchive/Companies RegisterActivities2013-2014.pdf

4. Enterprise Act 2002. Corporate Insolvency Provisions: Evaluation Report January 2008, p. 17: "Between 1998 and 2006, total corporate insolvency levels were relatively stable, fluctuating between around 15,500 and 19,000 cases per year."

5. Both French and both more than four decades ago: FC Nancy was disbanded in 1965 and CO Roubaix-Tourcoing in 1970.

6. One club, Hearts, did go into administration the season following Rangers' exit, but the club had longstanding problems.

7. John Harding (2009). *Behind the Glory: 100 Years of the PFA*. Derby: Breedon Books, p. 141

8. Chester Report (1968), pp. 50–51

CHAPTER 9: AMERICA

1. The revenues of the top European clubs are usually known; the revenues of American teams are often impossible to obtain directly, but by estimating ticket sales from attendance numbers, broadcast income from the value of deals announced, and other sources using educated guesses, a reasonably plausible figure can be arrived at.

2. Fort, Rodney, and James Quirk. "Cross-subsidization, incentives, and outcomes in professional team sports leagues." *Journal of Economic Literature* (1995): 1265–1299.

3. This is a classic example of the well-known "prisoner's dilemma," which has been much analyzed in the economic context, among others. There are now many popular books that explain the prisoner's dilemma and related concepts from game theory—an excellent example is Dixit, Avinash, and Barry J. Nalebuff. *The art of strategy*. New York: WW. Norton (2008).

4. Smith, Adam. *Wealth of Nations*. University of Chicago Bookstore, 2005, Book I, chapter 10.

5. Reviewed in Szymanski, Stefan. "The economic design of sporting contests." *Journal of Economic Literature* (2003): 1137–1187. In Ross, Stephen, and Stefan Szymanski. *Fans of the World, Unite!: A (capitalist) Manifesto for Sports Consumers*. Stanford University Press, 2008, we explore the interaction of the legal and economic issues in American sports. See also Szymanski, Stefan. *Playbooks and checkbooks: An introduction to the economics of modern sports*. Princeton University Press, 2009.

6. However, it should also be noted that in recent decades the focus in the United States has shifted away from unilateral rules imposed by the leagues to collective bargaining with player unions, which have consented to restrictive agreements such as salary caps and draft rules in exchange for concessions from employers on minimum wages, pension, insurance coverage, and so on.

7. Although, at the time of writing, Lerner had announced his intention to sell Aston Villa.

CHAPTER 10: REGULATION

1. UEFA (2008) "Here To Stay—Club Licensing." *Club Licensing 2004–2008*, p. 8.

2. Union of European Football Associations (UEFA). (2012). *UEFA Club Licensing and Financial Fair Play Regulations, Edition 2012*.

3. This literature originates with a paper by Gordon Tullock (Tullock, G. (1980). "Efficient rent seeking." In: J.M. Buchanan, R.D. Tollison, and G. Tullock (Eds.), *Toward a theory of the rent-seeking society*. College Station, Texas: Texas A&M University Press). This paper reviews the relevance of the theory to sports: Szymanski, Stefan (2003), "The Economic Design of Sporting Contests," *Journal of Economic Literature* 51, 1137–1187.

4. For example, Dietl, H. M., M. Lang, and A. Rathke. (2009). "The Effect of Salary Caps in Professional Team Sports on Social Welfare." *The B.E. Journal of Economic Analysis and Policy* 9(1), 1935-1682, and Franck, E., and M. Lang. (2012). "What is Wrong with Sugar Daddies in Football? A Theoretical Analysis of the Influence of Money Injections

on Risk-Taking." University of Zürich, Center for Research in Sports Administration, Working paper 46.

5. Müller, J. C., J. Lammert, and G. Hovemann. (2012). "The Financial Fair Play Regulations of UEFA: An Adequate Concept to Ensure the Long-Term Viability and Sustainability of European Club Football?" *International Journal of Sport Finance* 7(2), 117–140. Müller was head of the licensing system of the Bundesliga and worked closely with UEFA in drawing up the FFP regulations.

6. Peeters, T., and S. Szymanski. (2014). "Financial Fair Play in European Football." *Economic Policy*, Vol. 29, Issue 78, pp. 343-390. We did this by simulating league competition, with and without FFP, based on accounting data for four of the five largest soccer nations in Europe (England, France, Italy, and Spain). Given that FFP was modeled on the German club-licensing system, and given the aspiration of transparency, it is ironic that we could not simulate the Bundesliga because financial disaggregated results for all clubs are not available.

7. This seems to create cognitive dissonance for many soccer fans who appear to think that "losses are bad" and "profits are good" but prefer an owner such as Chelsea's Roman Abramovich who puts money into his club (Chelsea) rather than owners such as the Glazer family that take money out (Manchester United). Moreover, this view seems to characterize not just fans at the respective clubs, but fans at rival clubs too.

8. On this relationship see, for example, Szymanski, S., and R. Smith. (1997). "The English Football Industry: profit, performance and industrial structure." *International Review of Applied Economics* 11(1), 135–153; Stephen Hall, Stefan Szymanski, and Andrew S. Zimbalist (2002). "Testing Causality Between Team Performance and Payroll: The Cases of Major League Baseball and English Soccer." *Journal of Sports Economics* 3: 149–168, as well as Peeters and Szymanski (2014).

9. Andreff, W. (2011). "Some comparative economics of the organization of sports: competition and regulation in North American vs. European professional team sports leagues," *The European Journal of Comparative Economics* 8, 3–27; Storm, R.K., and K. Nielsen. (2012). "Soft budget constraints in professional football," *European Sport Management Quarterly* 12, 183–201, and Franck, E. (2013). "Financial Fair

Play in European club Football—What is it all about?" No. 328, *UZH Business Paper Working Series*, University of Zürich.

10. See, for example, *The Daily Telegraph*, August 28, 2009: "Platini dismissed the idea that billionaire benefactors like Sheikh Mansour were good for football because they challenge the elite. He gestured to Infantino. 'We think that the opposite will happen,' said Infantino, 'because if you have a rich sugar daddy coming in and throwing money around, this is unhealthy in the medium-term and unsustainable in the long-term. For the club to be healthy it has to live on its own means and generate income and this is not impossible. Otherwise it is an artificial bubble.'" See also *The Guardian*, August 28, 2009: "If you have a sugar daddy it is unhealthy," UEFA's deputy general secretary, Gianni Infantino, said. "The club has to stay on its own legs and generate its own revenue."

11. www.coe.int/t/dg4/sport/Source/CONV_2009_135_EN.pdf.

12. It also seems perverse that the owners against whom Platini railed, people like Abramovich and Sheikh Mansour, will benefit from the ossification because they have already made their investments.

13. Dupont is the lawyer who successfully led the legal challenge to the European player transfer rules resulting in the Bosman judgment of 1995.

14. Dupont, J.-L. (2013). Press Release May 6, 2013, p. 1.

15. Ibid, p. 2.

16. Although the outcome may be known by the time this book is published.

17. For a more detailed discussion of FFP and competition law see Budzinski, Oliver, and Szymanski, Stefan, 2014. "Are restrictions of competition by sports associations horizontal or vertical in nature?" Ilmenau Economics Discussion Papers, Ilmenau University of Technology, Institute of Economics 86, Ilmenau University of Technology, Institute of Economics.

18. George Orwell. "Politics and the English Language." *Horizon*, April 1946. First published: Horizon—GB, London, April 1946. Available at http://www.orwell.ru/library/essays/politics/english/e_polit.

INDEX

STEFAN SZYMANSKI is the Stephen J. Galetti Professor of Sport Management at the University of Michigan's School of Kinesiology. He has written many books including the bestselling *Soccernomics* (coauthored with Simon Kuper) and *Winners and Losers: The Business Strategy of Football*. Tim Harford has called him "one of the world's leading sports economists." He lives in Ann Arbor, Michigan.

NATION
BOOKS

The Nation Institute

Founded in 2000, **Nation Books** has become a leading voice in American independent publishing. The inspiration for the imprint came from the *Nation* magazine, the oldest independent and continuously published weekly magazine of politics and culture in the United States.

The imprint's mission is to produce authoritative books that break new ground and shed light on current social and political issues. We publish established authors who are leaders in their area of expertise, and endeavor to cultivate a new generation of emerging and talented writers. With each of our books we aim to positively affect cultural and political discourse.

Nation Books is a project of The Nation Institute, a nonprofit media center dedicated to strengthening the independent press and advancing social justice and civil rights. The Nation Institute is home to a dynamic range of programs: the award-winning Investigative Fund, which supports ground-breaking investigative journalism; the widely read and syndicated website TomDispatch; the Victor S. Navasky Internship Program in conjunction with the *Nation* magazine; and Journalism Fellowships that support up to 25 high-profile reporters every year.

For more information on Nation Books, The Nation Institute, and the *Nation* magazine, please visit:

www.nationbooks.org

www.nationinstitute.org

www.thenation.com

www.facebook.com/nationbooks.ny

Twitter: @nationbooks